*. 1/5

BrBc

An Illustrated Guide to
British Jugs

An Illustrated Guide to
British Jugs

From Medieval Times
To The Twentieth Century

R. K. Henrywood

SWAN·HILL
PRESS

Copyright © 1997 R. K. Henrywood

First published in the UK in 1997
by Swan Hill Press, an imprint of Airlife Publishing Ltd

British Library Cataloguing in Publication Data
  A catalogue record for this book
  is available from the Britsh Library

ISBN 1 85310 747 6

Typeset by Phoenix Typesetting,
Ilkley, West Yorkshire.
Printed in Singapore by
Kyodo Printing Co (S'pore) Pte Ltd.

Swan Hill Press
an imprint of Airlife Publishing Ltd
101 Longden Road, Shrewsbury, SY3 9EB, England.

Contents

Acknowledgements

Writing a general book of this nature is a fascinating experience. Although only one author's name appears on the cover, it is by no means a solo effort and many delightful individuals have contributed their knowledge, experience and support. They have given their help unstintingly and my photographic excursions, in particular, have been tolerated with considerable good humour and fortitude. The storehouse of precious pots in private collections never ceases to amaze me, and as a result of the great kindness shown by many collectors, we can all share their treasures. I am delighted to record a considerable debt of gratitude to Victoria Bergesen, Alan Blakeman, Ramsay and Sylvia Bowes, Bill and Marguerite Coles, Bill and Janet Coysh, David and Gwen Drakard, Audrey Dudson, Mairead Dunlevy, Geoffrey A. Godden, Anne Graham, Jack Hacking, Pat and Geoff Halfpenny, John and Griselda Lewis, Ron Lintott, Terry Lockett, Jim and Sheila McAuliffe, Lyn Miller, Barbara Mitchell, Jack Palfery, Colin and Patricia Parkes, Robert and Carol Pugh, Bill and Beryl Rees, John Sandon, Ray Shilton, Derek Styles, Margo and Ken Swift, Marion Thomas, George Worlock and Micky van Zwanenberg. Many others have contributed indirectly through their correspondence over the years, and while they are far too numerous to list individually, their help and readiness to share information have also proved invaluable and have been much appreciated.

I am also grateful for assistance and information received from the National Museum of Ireland at Dublin, the National Museum of Wales at Cardiff, the Wedgwood Museum at Barlaston, and particularly the City Museum & Art Gallery at Stoke-on-Trent.

Any book of this nature would suffer in stature without recourse to the store of knowledge built up by auction houses throughout the country. They have seen and recorded many thousands of interesting pieces, and I have been extremely fortunate to receive help with illustrations from many of them. Each photograph supplied by them has been credited individually, but I must record my grateful thanks to them all: BBR Auctions of Elsecar near Barnsley; Boardman Fine Art Auctioneers, Haverhill; Bonhams, Chelsea; Bonhams, Knightsbridge; Christie's, London; Christie's Scotland Ltd, Glasgow; Christie's South Kensington Ltd; Dreweatt Neate, Newbury; Francis Fine Art Auctioneers, Horsham; Greenslade Hunt, Taunton; Andrew Hartley Fine Arts, Ilkley; Lawrence Fine Art Auctioneers, Crewkerne; Locke & England (Black Horse Agencies), Leamington Spa; Neales, Nottingham; Phillips North West, Chester; Phillips, Leeds; Phillips, London; Phillips, Sevenoaks; Pretty & Ellis, Amersham; Sotheby's, London; Sotheby's, Sussex; Charles A. Whitaker Auction Co., Philadelphia; Peter Wilson Fine Art Auctioneers, Nantwich; Wintertons, Lichfield; and Woolley & Wallis, Salisbury.

Finally, my wife Melanie and young son Ross Hamilton have both played their part, although I suspect a book on trains might have been more appreciated by one of them. This effort is dedicated to them.

Introduction

I cannot recall the first jug that really claimed my attention, although strangely enough I do remember the first I ever purchased. It was while I was studying at Imperial College and was a mid-nineteenth-century copper lustre jug which I now know was of little real distinction. I bought it at the Fulham end of the King's Road, not specifically because it was a jug, but since it matched a few other pieces of lustre I had acquired. These were my first forays into collecting, and other things followed quite rapidly, mostly bought at the junky antique shops which then existed in Fulham, Clapham Junction and Wandsworth.

The interest in lustre didn't last for too long, and my squirrel instincts soon developed through a collection of Goss and other crested china, the appeal of which proved a little longer lasting. I then settled more seriously on the blue and white printed pottery which was to become an abiding passion for some years.

As time went on, my enthusiasm for blue and white became rather tempered by its popularity and high prices, and jugs started to make an impression on me. At first I developed a taste for relief-moulded jugs which offered a similar degree of interest to the blue and white, but at that time could be bought quite cheaply. Sadly, that was not to remain the case for much longer, and my own book on them, to my chagrin, contributed to size-able inflation in that area. I frequently console myself with the thought that it would have happened anyway, since most other collectables have undergone similar price rises. The great benefit to come out of that book was the contact with a large number of fellow collectors, several of whom have become firm friends.

It was perhaps inevitable that time should see my horizons widen to cover jugs with sprigged decoration, and as my collection grew, it became apparent that there was relatively little literature on the subject. It is partly as a result of that observation that the present book has arisen, giving me a fortunate opportunity to revisit both blue and white and relief-moulded jugs, to assemble an introduction to the lesser known sprigged wares, and both to learn about and to share my thoughts on all the other interesting jugs I have envied in my years of loitering around junk shops, antiques markets, boot fairs and the like.

In concept the jug is, of course, very simple: a vessel to contain liquid, with a handle for lifting and a spout for pouring. However, as with many simple things, human ingenuity has led to considerable variety, with jugs differing greatly in size, shape and particularly decoration. While the decoration contributes to any jug's attraction, it is the basic shape which should first catch the eye. Some shapes are both functional and appealing, some fail badly in one or other of these. Some handles feel comfortable and work well, others seem to alienate the user. Some spouts pour particularly effectively, others drip to an infuriating degree.

As with any significant survey, I ought to define my self-imposed brief. First and foremost, I have restricted myself to what I can best describe as serving jugs – those which are of a sufficient size to serve, store or carry a significant amount of liquid. The main result is to exclude small milk jugs or creamers. My justification for this may be a little weak, but such jugs would normally have been made as part of tea or dessert sets, and hence are more properly related to the wares with which they were supplied. Larger serving jugs, on the other hand, were made and sold individually, or at most in matching sets of three, four or occasionally five.

It is interesting to note that nowadays these larger jugs have become uncommon. Most of the liquids we use are supplied in glass or plastic bottles, tins or cardboard containers. As a result the need for jugs for transport and storage has all but disappeared. Our lifestyles have also changed in such a way that we seem to have little need for the larger jugs for serving purposes. I put this down to the sad and lingering demise of good old British custard, but whatever the socio-economic reasons, any visit to a decent china shop will show that the market for these jugs has diminished. Most that are sold are made primarily for decoration, and indeed a large number of collectable old jugs may still be found hidden away at the back of cupboards, sought out only when a vessel is needed for a welcome, but possibly infrequent, bunch of flowers.

In view of the vast number of different jugs that have been made through the centuries, it has been necessary to classify them in some way. It would be quite possible to do this on the basis of size, shape, age, the body from which they are made, or even the maker, but none of these approaches seems ideal. In this book I have chosen to consider jugs in terms of the techniques used for their decoration: thus jugs which appear similar and would logically be placed together within a collection, will be considered together here. In order to bring a little further order to the chaos, I have allowed myself three exceptions. Jugs made of porcelain and fine china are sufficiently distinct to justify a separate chapter and, at the other end of the spectrum, jugs made of brown stoneware are also treated separately. The third exception covers novelties such as puzzle jugs and Toby jugs, never really intended for everyday use.

Commemorative jugs could easily have justified a separate chapter. However, the subject of this book is the jug itself rather than discussion of historical events, so examples have been included within relevant chapters for the decorative technique used. There are, of course, books devoted to commemorative wares to which the reader may care to refer for historical detail.

This leaves two other chapters which call for comment. Despite every effort, a few jugs just do not fit into convenient categories and these have been covered in a miscellaneous chapter. Likewise, my own interests, and until recently those of many other collectors, have not progressed into the twentieth century, so these later wares have been grouped in a final chapter, which may be considered something of an epilogue. Interest in them has been developing greatly in the last two or three years and as such they are receiving much more attention in the literature, and sometimes quite dramatically at auction. This is a rapidly expanding field of study and I hope that my very brief comments may help to stimulate the reader's appetite.

I have endeavoured to select a very wide range of jugs for illustration, and the captions have been designed to supply useful detail. I hope they are self-explanatory, but specific comments concerning lids, marks and sizes may be appropriate.

A significant minority of jugs were supplied with a lid, sometimes made of the same body as the jug itself, but often of some type of metal. Some are silver and appropriately hallmarked, although most of these will either be relatively early or, inevitably, of higher than average quality. In the nineteenth century many jugs were fitted with Britannia metal lids, riveted to the jug through small holes in the rim. These lids are frequently marked with their makers' names, so this information is included in each caption where relevant. Some lids are silver-plated, but they are much less common. The presence of a strainer spout almost invariably means that the jug was originally supplied with a matching ceramic lid, so this fact has also been noted where appropriate.

As most collectors will know, a large number of jugs are unmarked, and while I have tried to include as many marked specimens as possible, a significant number remain anonymous. This was normal practice in the earlier years, and even well into the nineteenth century. It has been suggested that impressed marks are less common on jugs than other wares due to the relatively flimsy nature of the vessel while the clay was still plastic. This may be a moot point, but it could certainly explain why the impressed marks that are found are often very near to or even on the footrim. This problem would in any case have disappeared with the wider use of printed marks, which are applied after the first firing.

It is safe to assume that each jug illustrated is unmarked unless otherwise stated. Any marks that do exist are described as completely and accurately as possible, with the single exception of odd letters, numbers and symbols, most of which will be potters' marks which add little to our knowledge except at a very detailed level, certainly well outside the scope of this book. Towards the end of the nineteenth century printed marks became quite detailed, so descriptions of them may have been condensed somewhat, I hope without any significant loss of clarity.

The third point concerns the size of each jug. Many were made in several different sizes, so the size of an individual example may not be important. However, I have chosen to quote the height of each jug as accurately as possible, to the nearest millimetre. This has always been measured to the highest point, be it rim, spout, handle or lid. As a related aside, jugs and other hollow wares were made in sizes which were often described by a system known as the potter's count. Thus a jug of size 12 was intended to hold one pint, size 6 would hold two pints, and size 24 would hold half a pint. This strange system explains many numbers to be found impressed on jugs, particularly from the nineteenth century. In view of the possibility that these size numbers may be of interest, where they exist they are included in the caption following the height. As a general rule the number will be impressed, but its presence is felt to be of more interest than its method of application.

With regard to both marks and dimensions, quite a few illustrations have very kindly been supplied by auctioneers. Where such a credit appears at the end of the caption, it is fair to assume that I have not personally handled the jug, and in such cases I have relied on the appropriate catalogue descriptions. As a result, information as to height, marks and other details must be considered approximate.

While I have made every effort to cover the field dispassionately, it is inevitable that any general survey will reflect the tastes and interests of the author. I have allowed myself the luxury of longer than average chapters on sprig-moulding and relief-moulding, and elsewhere there may be some omissions, possibly a little unintentional bias, but I hope few real errors. It is now up to you, the reader, to assess the result, and I hope it will prove either useful or interesting, or even both.

But now to end this introduction, it is perhaps most important to reflect on the pleasure we can all derive from these treasures of the past, be they large or small, old or young, plain or ornate. I certainly enjoy my collecting and I hope that others can share my enthusiasm through this book. If anyone of like mind would care to impart their thoughts, letters via the publisher will always find an avid reader.

R. K. Henrywood

1.
Early Jugs

Ceramic vessels for holding liquids have been made for literally thousands of years, but exactly when the addition of a handle turned a simple jar or vase into a flagon or jug will probably never be known. Jugs as we know them today were certainly in existence by medieval times and examples from Nottingham, Stamford and elsewhere dating from the eleventh century through to the fifteenth are quite recognizable as such (Colour Plates 1–2). Their shapes would still serve well today. Slightly later London examples from the fifteenth and sixteenth centuries, although clearly improved with higher quality lead glazes, do not differ greatly (Plate 1).

One of the first really significant developments was the introduction of stoneware as opposed to the lower-fired and less robust earthenware. One example excavated in Somerset and dating from the late sixteenth century serves to emphasize the improvement (Plate 2). The quality of the mottled brown glaze is apparent even from a photograph, and related wares of increasing sophistication became staple products in many areas through to the present day (see Chapter 12).

Developments in the manufacture of pottery were

PLATE 1: *Three typical 'Tudor Green' earthenware jugs from the 15th or 16th centuries excavated in the City of London. Note the green or copper-coloured lead glazes around the upper bodies. Heights 20 cm, 17 cm, and 16 cm.* (Courtesy: Sotheby's, London)

PLATE 2: *Late 16th-century stoneware jug with mottled brown glaze, excavated near Norton St Philip, Somerset. Height 21.5 cm.* (Courtesy: Dreweatt Neate, Newbury)

concentrated on improvements to the body itself, to the covering glaze, and in the decorative techniques used. The early earthenwares were of poor quality and it is not surprising that potters should have attempted to improve them by covering the inferior body. Developments here took two main courses, one using a coating of finer quality clays mixed with water to a creamy consistency, known as slip, and the other using an opaque white glaze containing tin. Neither was to prove entirely satisfactory, although the slip decorating technique lasted longer and is still used by some art potters today.

Tin-glazed earthenwares, known generically as delft-wares after the Dutch town with which the technique is associated, were made in several areas, including London (both Lambeth and Southwark), Liverpool, and Bristol. Dated wares have survived from around 1630, although the technique was in its heyday throughout the second half of the seventeenth century and well into the eighteenth. It was never ideal for utilitarian wares which suffered chipping around the edges and cracking of the poor quality body. Several typical London jugs are shown here, including a plain white example dating from about 1650 (Plate 3), a small jug decorated with figures in blue and manganese (Plate 4), a fine armorial jug dated 1691 (Plate 5), and a similar impressive harvest jug dated 1699 (Colour Plate 3). The difficulties facing collectors in identifying these early wares are demonstrated by a jug dated 1696, once attributed to Lambeth but actually either German or Dutch (Plate 6).

The technique lasted well into the eighteenth century, particularly in Bristol and Liverpool. These two centres

PLATE 4: *Lambeth delftware jug painted in blue and manganese with a chinoiserie scene, c.1690. Height 14.2 cm.* (Courtesy: Sotheby's, London)

PLATE 5: *London delftware jug painted in blue with a coat of arms, the initials 'SLM' and date 1691. Height 22 cm.* (Courtesy: Christie's, London)

are represented by a fine jug dated 1730 (Plate 7) and a very typical puzzle jug which could well have been made as late as 1760 (Plate 8). Further delftware puzzle jugs are shown in Chapter 13 (Plates 604–7, Colour Plates 28–9). Given their basic shortcomings, it was inevitable that tin-glazed wares would be superseded by finer bodied earthenwares, but their total demise did not occur until about 1780.

The alternative technique entailed covering the coarse earthenware bodies with finer liquid clays. These slip-wares take two forms: one in which the slip is trailed decoratively over the surface and the other in which the whole body is immersed in slip through which decora-

PLATE 3: *Mid-17th-century white tin-glazed jug, probably made in London. Height 20 cm.* (Courtesy: Sotheby's, London)

PLATE 6: *German or Dutch delftware jug painted in bright blue and manganese. Note the cartouche with initials 'IB' and the date 1696. Height 17.8 cm.* (Courtesy: Christie's, London)

PLATE 8: *Liverpool delftware puzzle jug of conventional type with a common verse, c.1760. Height 17 cm.* (Courtesy: Christie's, London)

PLATE 7: *Three views of a Bristol delftware jug painted in blue, inscribed and dated 1730. Height 23.5 cm.* (Courtesy: Christie's, London)

tion is subsequently carved. A very fine jug of the first type made by George Richardson and dated 1651 is representative of wares made at Wrotham in Kent (Plate 9). Another example made in 1700 in Staffordshire is clearly more useful (Plate 10), while this is not true of a puzzle jug dated 1709 (Plate 600). A final jug of this type, dated 1704 and bearing the unidentified initials 'DS', is representative of the more decorative examples (Colour Plate 4).

Wares which have been dipped in liquid slip are usually somewhat later, dating from around 1700 onwards. One example, possibly made in Barnstaple towards the end of the eighteenth century, is very typical of harvest-type jugs, usually of West Country origin (Plate 11). A later puzzle jug, dated 1830 and made at the Ewenny Pottery in Wales, is of the same type (Colour Plate 30). Two similar but later jugs are also shown, the first dated 1851, made by Edwin Fishley at Fremington in Devon (Plate 12). The other would be of similar date and has also been attributed to the pottery at Fremington (Plate 13). Similar hand-produced and personally designed jugs are still being made to order in Bideford today.

PLATE 10: *Staffordshire slipware jug covered in cream and trailed in dark brown, with initials 'SB' and the date 1700 on either side. Height 31 cm.* (Courtesy: Sotheby's, London)

PLATE 9: *Rare Wrotham slipware jug by George Richardson, signed with his initials and dated 1651. Height 25.4 cm.* (Courtesy: Christie's, London)

PLATE 11: *Late 18th-century jug, probably made at Barnstaple, incised and decorated in cream slip with a design featuring a galleon and the four suits of cards. Height 22 cm.* (Courtesy: Christie's, London)

PLATE 12: *Harvest-type jug in red earthenware covered with yellow slip, incised with verses and inscribed 'J & G. Dennis, Monkleigh, January 1st 1851'. The design features blacksmith's tools and is signed 'Edwin Fishley, Fremington'. Height 23.6 cm.* (Courtesy: City Museum & Art Gallery, Stoke-on-Trent)

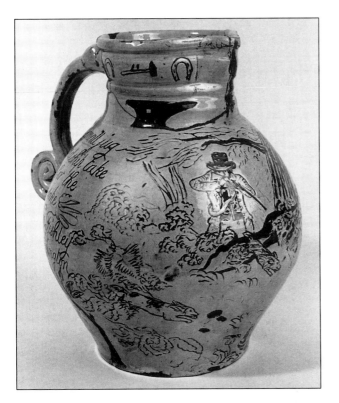

PLATE 14: *Black-glazed redware jug of Jackfield-type but probably made in Staffordshire. The decoration is cold enamelled in red, green, yellow, white and pink, and gilded with the name 'JAMES SKIDMORE'. Height 18.7 cm.*

PLATE 13: *Another mid-19th-century Fremington harvest jug, this one decorated with flowers and a long verse. Height 23 cm.* (Courtesy: Sotheby's, Sussex)

There is one other early type of covering which is quite distinctive. Red-bodied wares coated with a shiny black glaze are generically called Jackfield wares, after the Shropshire town where some were made, although similar pieces were also produced in Staffordshire. Two typical examples are shown, the first attractively painted in colours and inscribed in gilt lettering (Plate 14). This form of painting used cold enamels which wear very easily, and the second example shows signs of similar decoration, including a date in the 1760s (Plate 15). Three more jugs, also probably from Staffordshire, show typical shapes in production in the third quarter of the eighteenth century (Plate 16).

As already mentioned, these early wares were superseded during the eighteenth century by the introduction of higher quality clays in Staffordshire, but the basic shape of two of the Jackfield-type jugs survived. The first example is made of solid agate, achieved by wedging together clays of different colours (Plate 17). The second is made of a creamware-type body sponged with coloured glazes which have run together (Plate 18). This second jug also has moulded figures applied to the body, an early example of the use of sprig-moulding (see Chapter 6).

PLATE 15: *Another Jackfield-type jug showing traces of gilding with a cartouche initialled 'T & B' and an indistinct date in the 1760s. Height 23 cm. (Courtesy: Lawrence Fine Art, Crewkerne)*

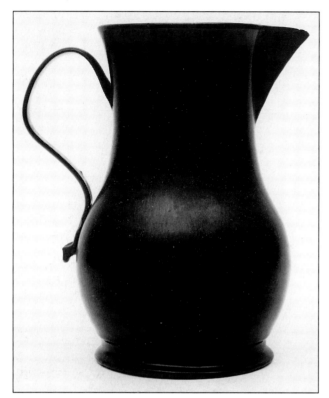

PLATE 17: *Mid-18th-century Staffordshire solid agate jug, made with striated grey and brown clays. Height 13.5 cm. (Courtesy: Sotheby's, Sussex)*

PLATE 16: *Three further Staffordshire black-glazed jugs showing typical shapes. The example on the right is sprigged with a design of fruiting vines. Heights 12.5 cm, 18 cm, and 14 cm. (Courtesy: Lawrence Fine Art, Crewkerne)*

PLATE 18: *Staffordshire creamware jug and cover sponged with coloured glazes in green, yellow, and manganese. Note the relief-moulding of Orientals amongst foliage. Height 16.5 cm. (Courtesy: Christie's, South Kensington)*

A fine and unusual solid agate puzzle jug is shown in Chapter 13 (Plate 601). Another solid agate jug is decorated to great effect with inlaid cream slip and an applied creamware panel (Plate 19). Once again the shape is not unlike that of the simpler Jackfield examples, and yet another jug of the same basic shape is also shown (Plate 20). This one is made of redware, but with creamware used for the spout, handle and two inlaid bands around the body.

PLATE 19: *Agate-ware jug with striated red and brown body inlaid with a cream slip chain and applied with a creamware panel inscribed 'ALE'. Height 21.8 cm.* (Courtesy: City Museum & Art Gallery, Stoke-on-Trent)

PLATE 20: *Jug with glazed redware body, inlaid with two creamware bands and fitted with creamware spout and handle. Height 17.8 cm.* (Courtesy: City Museum & Art Gallery, Stoke-on-Trent)

The wider development of creamware is covered elsewhere in chapters about hand-painted decoration and early transfer printing, but although it came to dominate the market in the second half of the eighteenth century, other bodies were developed in parallel. Fine redwares were used for utilitarian objects, particularly jugs and teapots, and one such jug is illustrated (Colour Plate 5). In some ways this is similar to the jugs just discussed, with additional creamware decoration sprigged on to the body and slip-lined around the rim. Some of these red bodies are earthenwares, while others are more highly fired stonewares. This example could be described as Astbury-type, while the stonewares are clearly developments of the earlier bodies developed by, amongst others, the Elers brothers.

The mention of stoneware recalls the fact that other wares were in production throughout this period, particularly brown salt-glazed stonewares. These were understandably widely valued for their toughness, and the potters naturally sought a body which retained this durability while offering greater potential for decoration. To a large extent they achieved this with white salt-glazed stoneware, which was produced widely in the middle of the eighteenth century. A particularly fine but completely plain example is shown (Plate 21), together with another which has a drab-coloured body decorated with white sprigged scrolls (Plate 22). Both these jugs are surprisingly sophisticated. Another example has scratch-blue decoration (Plate 23), which can also be seen on a fine puzzle jug in Chapter 13 (Plate 602). A final example features attractive enamelled decoration, once again demonstrating remarkable quality for the

PLATE 21: *Simple and elegant jug of very fine quality in white salt-glazed stoneware. Height 16.4 cm.* (Courtesy: City Museum & Art Gallery, Stoke-on-Trent)

PLATE 22: *Another salt-glazed stoneware jug, this one having a drab body with white slip interior, fitted with white handle and spout. Note the finely sprigged decoration. Height 13.8 cm.* (Courtesy: City Museum & Art Gallery, Stoke-on-Trent)

PLATE 23: *Typical mid-18th-century white salt-glazed stoneware jug with scratch blue decoration. The sprigged oval medallion is moulded with a crown and 'GR' cypher. Height 21.4 cm.* (Courtesy: Sotheby's, Sussex)

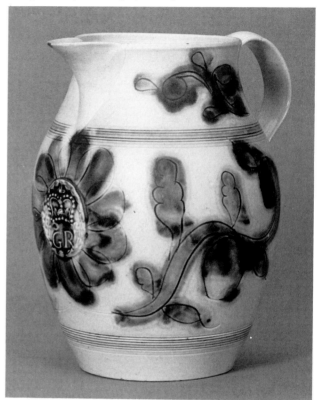

period (Plate 24). Fully moulded jugs were also made, but these brought out the body's main disadvantage, a relative coarseness which did not generally lend itself to fine detail. It was this aspect which probably led to its demise and the corresponding dominance of creamware, pearlware and the later fine-bodied earthenwares and stonewares.

Right:

PLATE 24: *Mid-18th-century white salt-glazed stoneware jug of less common form, enamelled in pink, red, yellow, green and black. The pecking parrot design is reminiscent of a print engraved by Robert Hancock for use on Worcester porcelain. Height 12.4 cm.* (Courtesy: City Museum & Art Gallery, Stoke-on-Trent)

2.
Hand-painting

Painting was amongst the earliest of decorative techniques and some medieval jugs show crude signs of hand-applied colouring. Many seventeenth-and early eighteenth-century jugs bear more sophisticated painted decoration, particularly the blue and white tin-glazed wares (Plates 4–8). Multi-coloured painting using unfired oil colours is found on some black-glazed wares of the Jackfield type in the mid-eighteenth century (Plate 14) and polychrome enamelling, some of a very high standard, appears on white salt-glazed stonewares of similar date. One good example has already been discussed (Plate 24) and another is of extremely fine quality (Plate 25).

This type of painting was clearly inspired by imported Chinese porcelains and hand-painted decoration, both in blue and polychrome, was extensively used by the porcelain factories which emerged in England from the mid-1740s. Porcelain and fine china are covered

PLATE 26: *Yorkshire creamware jug enamelled in dark iron-red and black and dated 1772. The decoration features groups of farm and gardening implements and the intertwined strap handle is touched with blue, yellow and green enamels. Height 18.2 cm.* (Courtesy: Sotheby's, Sussex)

PLATE 25: *Another white salt-glazed stoneware jug enamelled in colours. A fine quality example painted in the chinoiserie style, c.1755–60. Height 13.8 cm.* (Courtesy: City Museum & Art Gallery, Stoke-on-Trent)

in the next chapter, where many superbly painted jugs are illustrated. However, hand-painting was not restricted to these more expensive bodies: it was widely used on finer earthenwares, initially creamware but later pearlware, and eventually the standard white earthenwares and stonewares which were the backbone of pottery manufacture through the nineteenth century.

An exact definition of these bodies need not concern us here, but creamware was in production by the 1750s and pearlware emerged during the 1770s. Their development closely coincided with that of transfer-printing, and in the second half of the century printing and hand-painting were employed in parallel. At this period few wares bore makers' marks and a glance at the Northern Ceramic Society's exhibition catalogue *Creamware & Pearlware* will show that many pieces can only be described with phrases such as 'possibly Liverpool', 'possibly Staffordshire or Lancashire' or even less emphatically 'Yorkshire, Staffordshire or Derbyshire'.

PLATE 27: *Another Yorkshire creamware jug, attributed to Leeds, inscribed and dated 1774. Once again the decoration is painted in iron-red and black. Height 18.5 cm.* (Courtesy: Christie's, London)

PLATE 28: *Leeds creamware jug painted in iron red, dated 1777, and an unattributed pearlware jug with a painted scene of two sportsmen with dogs beneath a blue and red border, c.1790. The earlier jug has gardener's implements on the reverse; the later one a coat of arms with the motto 'Certanti Dabitor' beneath the spout and a printed and coloured hunting scene on the back. Heights 20 cm and 24.5 cm.* (Courtesy: Christie's, London)

Since attribution is so fraught with difficulty, it is easier to consider these wares chronologically. Fortunately many of the hand-painted jugs, by their very nature, were presentation pieces and hence are inscribed and dated. These enable us to put together an overall picture of developments in both shape and decorative style.

While some dated creamwares survive from the later 1760s, the earliest shown here is inscribed 1772 (Plate 26). This jug features farm implements – possibly the owner was a farmer – and the design is enamelled predominantly in dark red and black. These colours are often associated with Yorkshire and two similar jugs, one said to be decorated by J. Robinson of Leeds and the other dated 1769, are shown by Donald Towner in *Creamware*. Two further jugs in similar colours are shown here, both attributed to Leeds. One has a mask spout and is dated 1774 (Plate 27), while the other is dated 1777 (Plate 28). The latter is shown alongside an unattributed pearlware jug, probably made a decade or so later, again with a mask spout but decorated with a coat of arms and a finely painted hunting scene. Interestingly enough, another hunting scene on the reverse is printed and coloured rather than hand-painted.

The decoration on these red and black enamelled jugs is relatively simple, but some jugs with scenic painting like the last example are also attributed to Leeds. Two are illustrated alongside another later pearlware jug (Plate 29). One, painted with an equestrian figure, is dated 1776, while its companion with the coaching scene would have been made slightly later, about 1780. The pearlware jug on the left, of the same basic bulbous shape but with a much more pronounced foot, is dated 1800.

These early jugs usually have a bulbous or ovoid body supported on a flared foot or are of a simple barrel shape; relatively late examples of both types dated 1796 and

PLATE 29: *Pearlware jug inscribed 'David Hoult, Middlewich, Cheshire, 1800'; a rare Leeds creamware coaching jug, c.1780; and another Leeds creamware jug, dated 1776, painted with an equestrian figure. Heights 22.9 cm, 20.9 cm, and 24.8 cm.* (Courtesy: Christie's, London)

1797, are shown here. The first (Plate 30) bears a fine coat of arms which has been hand-enamelled, although the wreath beneath the spout and a sailing ship on the reverse have both been printed and coloured. This combination of hand-painting and printing was not unusual at this period. The other jug again features a sailing ship, with a mock coat of arms on the reverse, but the designs appear against an uncommon mottled green ground (Plate 31).

The last decade of the eighteenth century saw many changes, notable amongst which was the emergence of a distinct neck. This feature can be seen in the next three illustrations showing pearlware jugs with floral decoration and inscriptions dated between 1791 and 1798 (Plates 32–4). None of them can be attributed with any confidence, although there is a Newthorpe in Yorkshire, about ten miles to the west of Leeds. The last is very attractively painted and although the design is relatively simple, it exhibits the high quality to be found on quite a few presentation jugs.

During the early nineteenth century the fashion for hand-painted jugs diminished, reflecting the high cost of skilled workmanship and the natural tendency for potters to concentrate on more easily produced printed wares. However, some excellent jugs were still made. Four good examples are shown here, the first dating from 1803 (Plate 35). This continues the earlier tradition of a simple inscription with just a name and date, although the jug itself is engine-turned and the body is heavily enamelled with a border-type design.

The next jug is in a different class, tentatively attributed to the Don Pottery and made for a butcher in 1813 (Plate 36). It is superbly painted with a scene featuring farm animals and a coat of arms bearing tools of the owner's trade. A very different style of painting, with

PLATE 30: *Creamware jug hand-painted with a fine coat of arms, monogrammed and dated 1796 within a black-printed and enamelled floral wreath. The rim is lined in green and there is a three-masted man-of-war printed on the reverse. Height 21.4 cm.* (Courtesy: City Museum & Art Gallery, Stoke-on-Trent)

colourful flowers typical of William Fifield's work at the Bristol Pottery, can be seen on a fine puzzle jug dated 1819 (Plate 608).

PLATE 31: *Another creamware jug featuring a man-of-war, in this case inscribed in gilt and dated 1797 on a mottled moss-green ground. The reverse has a mock coat of arms including farming implements. Height 20 cm. (Courtesy: Christie's, London)*

Above:
PLATE 33: *Good quality pearlware jug dated 1797, enamelled in blue, mauve, iron-red, green and grey. The verse reads 'In friends we meet, in friends we part, another jug with all my heart', particularly appropriate within this book. Height 19.1 cm. (Courtesy: City Museum & Art Gallery, Stoke-on-Trent)*

PLATE 32: *Two late 18th-century pearlware jugs, inscribed and dated 1791 and 1792. The left-hand example is enamelled in colours with flowersprays, the other has agricultural implements on the reverse. Heights 18.5 cm and 18 cm. (Courtesy: Dreweatt Neate, Newbury)*

PLATE 34: *Another pearlware jug of high quality, dated 1798 and enamelled in iron-red, black, green, puce, grey and yellow. Height 18 cm.* (Courtesy: Jack Hacking)

PLATE 35: *Pearlware jug inscribed and dated 1803 and heavily enamelled in orange, maroon, black, yellow, green and ochre. Note the engine-turning around the base. Height 17.8 cm.* (Courtesy: City Museum & Art Gallery, Stoke-on-Trent)

PLATE 36: *An impressive and well-enamelled earthenware jug, possibly made at the Don Pottery, the reverse featuring an oval medallion inscribed 'Thomas Jones / Butcher / 1813'. Note the butcher holding his cleaver and the shield bearing the tools of his trade. Height 19.4 cm.* (Courtesy: Sotheby's, Sussex)

Various forms of lustre decoration were introduced in the early nineteenth century and were soon used on presentation jugs. One example dated 1819 with a well-painted coat of arms between broad bands of copper lustre also has a pink lustre landscape on the reverse (Plate 37). Hand-painted presentation jugs steadily became less common as the century progressed, but various potteries in the north-east of England which specialized in pink and purple lustre developed a strong market for jugs with personalized inscriptions. Most of these have printed rather than painted decoration, and a range of examples can be seen in Chapter 10.

While the last dated jug shown here is of an unusual cylindrical shape, it is notable mainly for its subject (Plate 38). The few printed patterns depicting early locomotives are eagerly sought by railway enthusiasts, so it is not surprising that such a rare and documentary jug should be highly valued. It would be fascinating to seek out the story behind such a fine piece.

The above jugs are all clearly dated, but many others were made to order with inscriptions but no dates. Bearing in mind the shapes and styles already shown, they are relatively easily dated. Examples are considered here in two groups, the first comprising jugs of the early bulbous shape, dating between about 1780 and 1805. These include a fine creamware jug painted with a waggoning scene, possibly made in Staffordshire about 1785 but decorated elsewhere (Plate 39); a rare marked Wedgwood jug painted with the arms of the Honourable East India Company (Plate 40); a pearlware jug painted in the manner of Absolon of Yarmouth with a windmill and the named owners out riding (Plate 41); and another creamware jug with a simple verse, possibly made in Staffordshire but decorated by Robert Allen at Lowestoft shortly after 1800 (Plate 42).

PLATE 37: *Staffordshire jug inscribed and dated 1819 and painted with a coat of arms on a blue ground. Note the prominent copper lustre bands. The reverse shows a church within a landscape, all painted in pink lustre. Height 27.6 cm.* (Courtesy: Sotheby's, Sussex)

PLATE 39: *Creamware jug, probably potted in Staffordshire c.1780–90. The decoration in red, yellow, black and grey enamels, and the inscription for Sarah Mountain of Monmouth, may well have been added locally. Height 22.4 cm.*

PLATE 40: *An impress-marked Wedgwood jug, painted with the arms of the Honourable East India Company in blue and red. The bouquets of flowers to the sides are enamelled in colours, one featuring a monogram in blue. Height 21.5 cm.* (Courtesy: Lawrence Fine Art, Crewkerne)

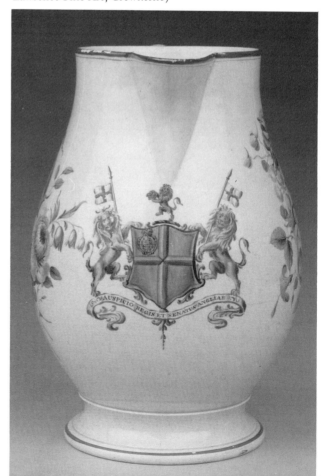

PLATE 38: *Rare documentary jug decorated with a steam train and carriage, possibly made in South Yorkshire. The inscription reads 'Joseph and Stella Addy 1843'. Height 24 cm.* (Courtesy: Phillips, Leeds)

PLATE 41: *Two views of a pearlware jug with blue and ochre line rim, painted in colours in the manner of Absolon of Yarmouth. The windmill scene is inscribed 'Success to the Toll Dish'; the couple out riding are titled 'Mr. & Mrs. Binsteed taking the Air'. Height 18.5 cm.* (Courtesy: Christie's, London)

PLATE 42: *Creamware jug decorated with a verse and enamelled in red, green, purple, brown and ochre. This jug has previously been attributed to Shorthose and is thought to have been painted by Robert Allen at Lowestoft, shortly after the Lowestoft porcelain factory closed about 1800. Height 17.2 cm.*

A final jug in this group deserves special mention since it was made for display at 'Francis Brown's Staffordshire Warehouse' (Plate 43). It was not uncommon for retailers to commission such pieces. Several others appear in existing literature or museum collections, but relatively few remain in private hands. The auction catalogue dates this impressive example to about 1830, but on the basis of shape alone this would appear to be too late. The decoration includes some pink lustre, so it cannot be eighteenth century, but an early nineteenth-century date, possibly about 1805, appears likely. Unfortunately the inscription gives no clue to the location of Mr Brown's establishment, but the firm might be traceable from directories or other local sources.

The second group of inscribed jugs are all of early nineteenth-century date and include two decorated with military figures (Plates 44–5); three with waggoning or coaching subjects, including one by New Hall (Plate 46); a pearlware harvest jug with an appropriately painted scenic border (Plate 47); and a marked Davenport jug in that company's distinctive orange chalcedony body with a monochrome rural scene personalized with a monogram (Plate 48). A final jug to complete this group is of significantly later date, possibly the 1840s, and is enamelled with an enigmatic inscription 'Little Matthew has got up', the meaning of which could enliven many dinner conversations (Plate 49).

The remaining jugs are still all decorated by hand but with everyday patterns produced in reasonable quantities. Although transfer-printing was widely adopted, some simple painted designs remained in production, but quality deteriorated steadily through the nineteenth century. The first two jugs are both

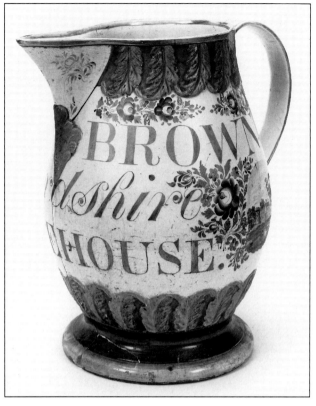

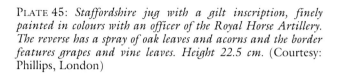

PLATE 45: *Staffordshire jug with a gilt inscription, finely painted in colours with an officer of the Royal Horse Artillery. The reverse has a spray of oak leaves and acorns and the border features grapes and vine leaves. Height 22.5 cm. (Courtesy: Phillips, London)*

PLATE 43: *Impressive large pearlware jug made for display at 'FRANCIS BROWN'S Staffordshire WAREHOUSE', probably c.1805. Decorated in red, turquoise and grey-brown enamels, and also pink lustre. Note the leaf-moulding around the rim and foot, and also the printed and coloured country house scene. Height 44.5 cm. (Courtesy: Sotheby's, London)*

PLATE 44: *Two views of an early 19th-century pearlware jug depicting a soldier from the 2nd Regiment of Manchester and Salford Volunteers. Note the uncommon fluted body and the gilt monogram on the front. Height 15 cm. (Courtesy: Phillips North West, Chester)*

PLATE 46: *Two pearlware jugs featuring finely enamelled waggoning and coaching scenes, flanking a Newhall coaching jug. The Newhall example shows a coach from the Crown Inn, Stone, on the route between Liverpool and London; the other coach is the Lord Wellington, serving York, Newcastle, and Edinburgh. Heights 22.9 cm, 18.4 cm, and 19.7 cm (approx).* (Courtesy: Christie's, London)

Right:
PLATE 47: *Pearlware harvest jug painted with a lengthy verse extolling the farmer's life, c.1800. Note the farming implements thrust through the wheatsheaf and the continuous harvesting scene around the neck. The reverse has a spray of wild flowers. Height 16.2 cm.* (Courtesy: Sotheby's, London)

PLATE 48: *Dutch-shape jug potted by Davenport in their distinctive orange chalcedony body with white slip interior. The scene is hand-painted in black and augmented with gilt lining, border and monogram. Impressed mark 'Davenport' curving above an anchor. Height 14.4 cm.* (Courtesy: Jack Hacking)

PLATE 49: *Large Staffordshire pottery jug, probably made in the 1840s, the glaze suffering from extensive crazing. The sprays of roses are accompanied by an enigmatic motto which reads 'Little Matthew has got up'. Height 35 cm.* (Courtesy: Sotheby's, Sussex)

PLATE 50: *Leeds creamware jug with typical entwined handle, c.1780, enamelled in colours with a rose, flowers and leaves. Height 13 cm.* (Courtesy: Dreweatt Neate, Newbury)

PLATE 51: *Late 18th-century creamware jug, the body covered with mustard-yellow slip attractively painted in black and iron-red with husk festoons hung from roses. Height 15 cm.* (Courtesy: Sotheby's, London)

painted with floral designs, a wide range of which are found on early creamwares and pearlwares. These are both creamware; one with a coloured flower spray, probably made at Leeds around 1780 (Plate 50); the other more unusual with the body covered in yellow slip before being decorated in red and black (Plate 51).

The next five jugs all date from the first quarter of the nineteenth century. The first two are of pearlware enamelled in colours with chinoiserie scenes (Plates 52–3), the second of which has been tentatively attributed to Swansea, although with little apparent justification. The next jug is typical of the period around 1810 and, as with some others, it is surprisingly difficult to tell whether the design is painted freehand or coloured over an outline print (Plate 54). The fourth jug is of chalk-body earthenware enamelled with a rural scene (Plate 55), rather reminiscent of painted and bat-printed designs found on china at this period. Some similar jugs have traditionally been attributed to Brampton (or Torksey) in Lincolnshire, although there is still some debate as to whether earthenware was made there. The final jug from this group illustrates a combination of decorative techniques, with a moulded body, an overall yellow glaze and attractively enamelled floral bands (Plate 56).

One manufacturer who used painted patterns rather later than most was William Ridgway. In the 1830s he made a range of stonewares, usually in a distinctive pastel blue colour (Colour Plate 17) but also in drab and green, all with numbered enamelled patterns. A jug decorated with pattern number 795 is quite typical (Plate 57). This basic shape, registered in 1835, is more commonly found relief-moulded with Tam o' Shanter scenes.

PLATE 52: *Unattributed pearlware jug painted with a chinoiserie group in a bright* famille rose *palette, c.1800. There is a landscape on the reverse. Height 20.5 cm.* (Courtesy: Christie's, London)

Left:

PLATE 53: *Early 19th-century jug, tentatively attributed to Swansea. The chinoiserie scenes are enamelled in grey, red, carmine, turquoise, yellow, blue and black, with red and yellow bands around the rim and neck. Height 15.9 cm.*

PLATE 56: *Yellow-glazed earthenware jug of moulded form attractively enamelled with running borders in shades of red and blue. Height 13 cm.*

PLATE 54: *Pearlware jug, possibly outline-printed, enamelled in colours with an exotic bird perched amongst branches. There is a painted monogram and also a vignette of cherubs on the front. Height 22.5 cm. (Courtesy: Sotheby's, Sussex)*

PLATE 55: *Jug in chalk-body earthenware painted with a rural scene, of a type traditionally attributed to Torksey. It is enamelled in grey, brown, greens and blue, with added gilding. Height 16.2 cm. (Courtesy: Jack Hacking)*

PLATE 57: *Typical William Ridgway & Co. blue stoneware jug enamelled in colours and gilded with pattern number 795. This shape is commonly found with a relief-moulded Tam o'Shanter scene. Impressed mark 'Published by / W. RIDGWAY & Co / HANLEY, / October 1 1835'. Height 17.9 cm (size 12).*

Right:
PLATE 58: *Octagonal ironstone jug attributed to Hackwood, finely enamelled and gilt with birds and butterflies in red, maroon, blue, green and yellow. Note the moulded panels, one depicting Britannia. Blue-printed mark in the form of an urn with 'IRON STONE / CHINA' on a drape. Height 18.9 cm.*

The next two jugs are superficially similar, both being of the well-known octagonal shape with alternately moulded and painted panels. There the similarity ends, since one is ironstone china finely painted with birds and butterflies (Plate 58) while the other is simple earthenware crudely painted with flowers (Plate 59). The first bears a printed mark which is associated with Hackwood and dates from about 1835; the second would have been made a little later, probably at Bristol but possibly at Swansea, and can be seen as the start of a gradual decline in standards, clearly visible in the remaining jugs.

Another rather angular shape, registered in 1845 by Bayley & Ball of Longton, is shown with a crudely applied flow-blue chinoiserie design highlighted with overglaze enamels and pink lustre (Plate 60). Another version was made with surface moulding in low relief. Pink lustre was also commonly used at this period for painting rather naïve rural scenes of cottages and churches (see Chapter 10), but a similar design on a jug attributed to Swansea is enamelled in green and maroon (Plate 61). Another Welsh jug, this time attributed to the South Wales Pottery at Llanelly, is also crudely painted with a floral band around the hexagonal body (Plate 62). It is not difficult to discern the development of the so-called 'Gaudy Welsh' style, popular in the later nineteenth century (Plate 63), although it must be emphasized that similar wares were made in Staffordshire, and probably elsewhere.

These crudely painted jugs, albeit exhibiting some degree of naïve charm, represent a low point in hand-painting. Quality was eventually revived in the 1920s and 1930s with a new fashion for bright, colourful and frequently very striking designs (see Chapter 15), but it seems unnecessary to leave this chapter on such a low note. Three final examples may serve to lighten the gloom. The first is a simple, utilitarian jug of plain tankard shape (Plate 64). This shape was commonly used by the Dudson firm for fine-bodied stonewares with sprigged ornament, but this earthenware version bears a workmanlike if rather uninspired floral pattern. The second jug shows considerable artistic merit, having been made at the Doulton art studio in the 1880s (Plate 65). The Doulton art wares are more famous in brown stoneware (see Chapter 12), but this is an example of their earthenware known as Lambeth faience. The final jug was made at the Cambrian Pottery in Swansea and superbly painted by Thomas Pardoe (Colour Plate 8). It is quite magnificent and seems appropriate as a lead into porcelain and fine china, much of which was decorated with similarly high quality painting.

PLATE 59: *Another octagonal jug of similar design, possibly made in Bristol or Swansea in the 1840s. Moulded in earthenware and crudely enamelled with flowers in red, blue, green, yellow and pink. The twig handle is enamelled green and the rim is lined with ochre. Height 14.3 cm.*

PLATE 60: *Earthenware jug of hexagonal form made by Bayley & Ball of Longton. The decoration is underglaze in flow-blue with overglaze green and red enamels and pink lustre. The basic shape was also made with a surface-moulded trellis design. Black-printed registration diamond for 15 November 1845. Height 13.8 cm. (Courtesy: City Museum & Art Gallery, Stoke-on-Trent)*

PLATE 62: *Angular earthenware jug with moulded mask spout attributed to the South Wales Pottery at Llanelly. The simple band of flowers is hand-painted in red, orange, green, blue and grey. Height 13.2 cm.*

PLATE 63: *Typical late 19th-century jug of poor quality decorated in 'gaudy-Welsh' style in underglaze blue with iron-red and green enamels, pink lustre and ochre rim. This style was by no means exclusive to Wales but was also widely used in Staffordshire. Height 21.2 cm. (Courtesy: City Museum & Art Gallery, Stoke-on-Trent)*

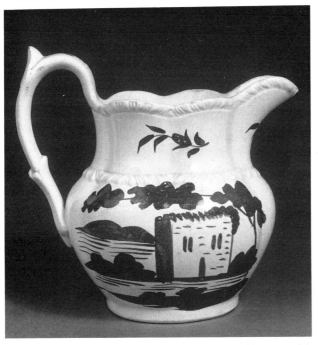

PLATE 61: *Jug of lobed form with gadroon moulding, crudely enamelled with naïve landscapes in green and maroon. Attributed to the Cambrian Pottery at Swansea. Height 15.8 cm.*

PLATE 64: *Tankard-shaped jug in white earthenware with gilt bands, hand-painted with flowers in pink, greens, brown, red, grey and blue. Attributed to Dudson. Grey-painted pattern number 703. Height 17.1 cm.*

PLATE 65: *Jug with plated lid, made at the Doulton Lambeth art studio in their faïence body, c.1880. This example is typically painted with pink and white apple blossom by Mary Capes. Impressed mark 'DOULTON' with painted artist's monogram. Height 24 cm.*

3.
Porcelain and Fine China

Throughout most of this volume jugs have been grouped by their decoration rather than the material from which they are made, but this appears inappropriate for the various types of porcelain and fine china. Serving jugs were made at most porcelain factories, but they were relatively expensive and are much less commonly found than the mass-produced earthenwares and stonewares. The sheer quality of some examples makes them stand apart from more utilitarian jugs, and while a few china jugs are included in other chapters where appropriate, the early porcelains and higher quality china jugs are dealt with separately here.

The earliest successful attempts to manufacture porcelain in England date from the 1740s, when various soft-paste bodies were developed at London factories including Limehouse and Chelsea (1745), Bow (1747) and Vauxhall (1751). Similar wares were made at factories outside London such as Derby (1748), Bristol (1749), Longton Hall in Staffordshire (1750), Worcester (1751), Liverpool (1754), Lowestoft (1757) and Caughley in Shropshire (1772). These soft-paste porcelains attempted to emulate wares imported in quantity from China, but the necessary ingredients were not known to the potters. True hard-paste porcelain, requiring china clay and china stone, was eventually developed by William Cookworthy at Plymouth in 1768. Production was transferred to Bristol in 1770 and the patent rights were later acquired by a new manufactory at New Hall in Staffordshire. Other unidentified factories produced various hybrid porcelains before the patent finally expired in 1796, but its importance was soon superseded by the development of bone china, which became virtually universal in the nineteenth century.

A more detailed evaluation of porcelain would be out of place here, and a range of excellent texts are available. Typical amongst them are Geoffrey Godden's *English China* and John and Margaret Cushion's more recent and excellent introduction *A Collector's History of British Porcelain*. There are also many books covering specific factories such as Worcester, Bow, Chelsea, Derby, New Hall, Spode, Coalport, Minton, Ridgway, Davenport and others. Many smaller concerns are covered in more general books such as Godden's *Staffordshire Porcelain* and *Encyclopaedia of British Porcelain Manufacturers*. It must, however, be noted that this field boasts many active and distinguished researchers, and with specialist

PLATE 66: *Jug painted underglaze in blue with a design of peonies, c.1746, assembled from factory wasters excavated on the site of the Pomona Pot Works at Newcastle-under-Lyme. Height 13.7 cm.* (Courtesy: City Museum & Art Gallery, Stoke-on-Trent)

papers being published regularly, attributions in earlier books may have been superseded.

While the names of most of the eighteenth-century factories mentioned will be familiar, some of the earliest attempts to make soft-paste porcelain outside London took place at the Pomona Potworks at Newcastle-under-Lyme in 1746. Since no perfect wares appear to have survived it has been suggested that wasters excavated at the factory site are the results only of unsuccessful experiments. However, reassembled wasters in the Newcastle and Stoke museums show a range of identifiable wares, and it is not impossible that matching items will be discovered. One reconstructed jug painted underglaze in blue with a peony design is shown here (Plate 66) and other similar jugs with a chinoiserie landscape are illustrated by John and Margaret Cushion and also by Arnold Mountford in Godden's *Staffordshire Porcelain*.

Simple underglaze blue decoration was used at all the early porcelain factories, initially hand-painted but soon making use of the newly developed printing techniques. A range of examples are shown here originating from Derby (Plate 67), Lowestoft (Plates 68–9), Worcester (Plates 70–3) and Caughley (Plate 74). The cabbage-leaf moulded jug with mask spout was a common design used by several factories, and attribution is often a problem. Another example is attributed to Caughley (Plate 75), although a similar design was also used at Worcester. One final example has been attributed to Liverpool (Plate 76), although the printed pattern has already been shown on a Worcester jug (Plate 72). This is a complex field which can be pursued in more detailed texts such as Godden's *Caughley and Worcester Porcelains 1775–1800* or Branyan, French and Sandon's definitive work *Worcester Blue & White Porcelain 1751–1790*.

PLATE 67: *Derby jug with a chinoiserie scene painted underglaze in blue, c.1760. Height 17 cm.* (Courtesy: Sotheby's, Sussex)

PLATE 69: *Another Lowestoft porcelain jug painted underglaze in blue. This example has a very crisp painted floral pattern and again there is a strainer spout, probably indicating a missing lid. Height 22.6 cm.* (Courtesy: City Museum & Art Gallery, Stoke-on-Trent)

PLATE 68: *Early Lowestoft strainer jug and cover painted in runny underglaze blue with chinoiserie scenes, c.1760. As with most covered jugs there is a strainer behind the spout. Height 22 cm.* (Courtesy: Sotheby's, London)

PLATE 70: *Worcester sparrow-beak jug with fluted body deco-rated in bright blue with flowers and leaves, and with a gilt cartouche on the front. Blue seal mark. Height 11.8 cm.* (Courtesy: Dreweatt Neate, Newbury)

PLATE 72: *Large Worcester cabbage-leaf jug painted in blue with the Cabbage-Leaf Jug Floral pattern, c.1755–60. Blue pseudo crossed swords mark. Height 27.5 cm.* (Courtesy: Phillips, London)

PLATE 73: *Another Worcester cabbage-leaf jug, this one with a mask spout, printed underglaze in blue with scattered floral sprigs, the Gilliflower Print pattern, c.1775–85. Blue-printed hatched crescent mark. Height 14.4 cm.*

PLATE 71: *Good quality Worcester jug with mask spout, printed overglaze in blue with the Plantation Print pattern, c.1765–70. Height 17.4 cm.*

33

PLATE 74: *The Caughley version of a cabbage-leaf mask jug printed in blue with the Fisherman pattern and with additional gold borders added in the Chamberlain workshop. Height 23.5 cm.* (Courtesy: Phillips, London)

PLATE 76: *A fifth cabbage-leaf moulded jug, c.1770. This example, painted in blue, has been attributed to Liverpool although the same pattern appears on Worcester wares (see Plate 72). Height 28 cm.* (Courtesy: Christie's, South Kensington)

PLATE 75: *Another cabbage-leaf moulded jug attributed to Caughley, printed underglaze in blue with sprays of flowers, c.1770. Height 23.4 cm.* (Courtesy: Christie's, South Kensington)

While simple blue and white decoration was extensively used, underglaze blue was often enhanced with overglaze colouring. Two well-documented jugs feature iron-red enamelling, one from Liverpool with a chinoiserie scene also picked out with gilding (Plate 77), and a second from Plymouth (Plate 78). The colour of the Plymouth example is the typical inky blue found on hard-paste porcelain. Both these jugs are discussed by Geoffrey Godden in *Eighteenth-Century English Porcelain, a Selection from the Godden Reference Collection.*

As already noted, the manufacture of hard-paste porcelain was transferred from Plymouth to Bristol in 1770, and it is interesting to compare the Plymouth jug with another from Bristol (Plate 79). Both the basic shape and the mask spout correspond closely, although the later jug is attractively enamelled in colours with flower sprays. Coloured enamels were, of course, very widely used to decorate porcelain, and three fine jugs dating from the 1760–5 period may serve to represent the earlier wares. The first, again with a mask spout, is from Worcester and features a puce urn within a floral frame (Plate 80). The remaining two are attractively painted with exotic birds in parkland scenes and were made at Derby (Plates 81–2).

PLATE 77: *Two views of a Liverpool porcelain jug hand-painted underglaze in blue and enamelled in iron-red with some ochre wash and gilding, c.1765. Height 22.6 cm.* (Courtesy: Geoffrey A. Godden/City Museum & Art Gallery, Stoke-on-Trent)

PLATE 78: *Plymouth hard-paste porcelain jug with mask spout painted underglaze in grey-blue and enamelled iron-red, c.1768–70. Height 16.8 cm.* (Courtesy: Geoffrey A. Godden/City Museum & Art Gallery, Stoke-on-Trent)

PLATE 79: *Bristol hard-paste porcelain jug painted in colours and gilded with a design of floral swags, c.1770–78. Note the similarity with the previous Plymouth jug. Height 19 cm.* (Courtesy: Phillips, London)

PLATE 80: *Worcester porcelain jug painted with a prominent puce urn with gilt scrolls, flowers and floral bouquets, c.1765. Crescent mark in blue. Height 19 cm. (Courtesy: Sotheby's, Sussex)*

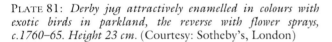

PLATE 81: *Derby jug attractively enamelled in colours with exotic birds in parkland, the reverse with flower sprays, c.1760–65. Height 23 cm. (Courtesy: Sotheby's, London)*

PLATE 82: *Another Derby jug featuring exotic birds, again with flower sprays on the reverse, c.1760–65. Height 17 cm. (Courtesy: Sotheby's, London)*

PLATE 83: *Two impressive Worcester cabbage-leaf moulded jugs, enamelled and gilt with exotic birds in parkland and winged insects on a rich blue-scale ground, c.1770. Both with underglaze blue pseudo-seal marks. Heights 29.5 cm and 23 cm. (Courtesy: Sotheby's, London)*

Exotic birds proved a popular subject, and it is not surprising that they were also used at Worcester. Two fine examples dating from about 1770 feature birds painted within gilt scroll cartouches, brightly enamelled and extensively gilt with a rich blue-scale ground (Plate 83). Three further Worcester jugs of the same popular moulded cabbage-leaf shape also illustrate polychrome enamelling, two with landscapes and one with chinoiserie reserves and a yellow ground (Colour Plate 6). The use of finely painted decoration on top of this uneven moulded body may seem rather incongruous, but it is not untypical of many eighteenth-century wares.

One common form of moulding which lent itself rather better to enamelled decoration was spiral fluting. It features prominently on the next jug, which is one of many whose makers remain unknown (Plate 84). This example is attractively enamelled in colours and the use of moulded leaves around the base is reminiscent of some of the earthenware jugs decorated with so-called Pratt colours (see Chapter 7). Indeed, from the photograph it may well be thought that this jug could be pearlware, but it is definitely porcelain. Floral sprays were always popular subjects on porcelain and china, and examples appear around a framed armorial crest on one Derby jug with an impressive mask spout representing Lord Rodney (Plate 85).

One of the most important porcelain factories of the later eighteenth century was New Hall, set up by a group of Staffordshire potters to exploit the remaining patent for hard-paste porcelain which they acquired from Richard Champion, previously at Bristol. The New Hall factory and its competitors have been the subject of much research and it is represented here by two very different jugs. The first is of a characteristic shape enamelled with a popular floral pattern numbered 241 (Plate 86). The subject of pattern numbers is complex since some designs were used at several different factories, each of which allocated its own number. This one is an excellent example since it was used at two important unidentified factories, known as Factory X and Factory Z, and also by the Mason firm. The second jug is of very different character, made of bone china rather than porcelain and painted with two ship portraits and a fine coat of arms (Plate 87). This jug would date from 1814 or so, and being specially made for export to America is by no means typical of the factory's output. A third New Hall jug hand-painted with a coaching scene is featured in Chapter 2 (Plate 46). For further information on New Hall the reader is referred to David Holgate's *New Hall*.

PLATE 84: *Unattributed porcelain jug with spiral fluted body, hand-painted with polychrome floral sprays and a black and yellow border. Note the moulded leaves enamelled green and yellow around the base. Height 16 cm.*

PLATE 85: *Derby jug with spout modelled as the head of Lord Rodney. The painted and gilt decoration features pink flowers and an armorial crest with the motto 'An Droit Devant'. Height 24 cm. (Courtesy: Lawrence Fine Art, Crewkerne)*

These jugs represent two distinct aspects of the market for porcelain and china which became clearly identifiable in the early nineteenth century. On the one hand jugs were made to special order, very finely enamelled, often inscribed, and frequently featuring scenic or still-life painting of the highest order. Examples shown here include several from various firms and partnerships operating at Worcester (Colour Plate 7, Plates 88–93), one from Derby (Plate 94), three by unknown makers (Plates 95–7) and four others which have been attributed with varying degrees of conviction to H. & R. Daniel (Plate 98), Spode (Colour Plate 9), Machin (Plate 99) and Coalport (Plate 100). The last of these, with its cricketing association, is particularly rare and desirable.

PLATE 86: *New Hall hard-paste porcelain jug of a typical shape enamelled with flowers in orange, red, greens, and black, c.1795–1800. Red-painted pattern number 'N241'. Height 15.4 cm.* (Courtesy: City Museum & Art Gallery, Stoke-on-Trent)

PLATE 88: *Worcester porcelain jug with fluted body enamelled with a blacksmith scene within a gilt frame. Height 18.1 cm.* (Courtesy: City Museum & Art Gallery, Stoke-on-Trent)

Bottom Left:
PLATE 87: *Documentary New Hall bone china jug painted in colours with an early American steamboat. The reverse is similarly painted with the American 74-gun* Independence, *built in 1814. On the front is a coat of arms with motto 'Fais-Bien Ne Crains Rien'. Retailer's mark painted in red script 'G. Dummer & Co., China Dealers, 112 Broadway, N. York'. Height 18.5 cm.* (Courtesy: Phillips, London)

PLATE 89: *Another Worcester porcelain jug, this example printed in black with a view of Worcester bridge, with added gilding including monogram initials 'JR'. Height 12.8 cm.* (Courtesy: City Museum & Art Gallery, Stoke-on-Trent)

PLATE 90: *Flight, Barr & Barr jug with a sage green marbled ground, finely painted and gilt with a panel of shells and seaweed. Impressed crown mark. Height 17.8 cm.* (Courtesy: Phillips, Sevenoaks)

PLATE 92: *Rare Chamberlain's Worcester lilac-ground jug painted in the manner of Humphrey Chamberlain with a huntsmen's celebration. Note the armorial crest and the finely gilt frame. Two further circular still-life panels feature a woodcock, kingfisher and snipe, and a brace of English partridges. Painted script mark. Height 25.5 cm.* (Courtesy: Christie's, Glasgow)

PLATE 93: *Flight, Barr & Barr jug painted with a titled view of 'Kirkstall Abbey, Yorkshire', c.1820. The ground features broad pink bands and fine quality gilding. Painted and impressed marks. Height 11.5 cm.* (Courtesy: Sotheby's, Sussex)

PLATE 91: *Another Worcester jug, this one by either Chamberlain or Grainger with a deep-blue ground, gilt with cailloute, the front panel finely painted with a hunting scene in the manner of John Wood. Height 18.7 cm.* (Courtesy: Phillips, London)

PLATE 94: *Derby jug with two circular panels painted with colourful birds by Richard Dobson, c.1813–20. The deep blue ground is richly gilt. Marked with crossed batons and 'D' in red. Height 17 cm.* (Courtesy: Phillips, London)

PLATE 96: *Another unattributed porcelain jug painted with a blackamoor in yellow turban above a gilt inscription. The sides are painted with two coats of arms, one inscribed 'The Hand that reveals, & the Heart that conceals' and the other 'Success to Trade'. Note the finely gilt neck with a coral-red ground. Height 21.5 cm.* (Courtesy: Christie's, London)

PLATE 95: *Unattributed Staffordshire porcelain jug painted with a scene of a young maid ignoring the blandishments of two suitors. The panel is titled 'Ni l'un ni l'autre'. Floral sprays adorn the sides beneath a brown and gilt rim. Height 15.5 cm.* (Courtesy: Sotheby's, Sussex)

Right:
PLATE 97: *Bone china jug of a well-known shape but by an unknown maker, c.1820–30. The dark blue ground is heavily gilt and the panel hand-painted in red, pink, black, brown, green, yellow, and mauve. The jug is designed for display this way round, the reverse being relatively plain. Height 18.8 cm.* (Courtesy: Jack Hacking)

PLATE 100: *Rare porcelain jug painted with a scene titled 'Cambridge Cricket Club' featuring early curved bats, c.1820. King's College Chapel can be seen in the background. The sides and border are colourfully painted with flowers. Height 24 cm.* (Courtesy: Bonhams, Chelsea)

PLATE 98: *Another jug of similar shape, this one painted with a rustic scene and attributed to Henry and Richard Daniel, c.1825–30. The ground is again dark blue while the spout and neck are flesh-coloured. As before, the reverse is relatively plain with foliate scrollwork. Height 24 cm.* (Courtesy: Sotheby's, London)

PLATE 99: *China jug painted with extensive rural landscapes and heavily gilt. A monogram 'SWB' appears under the spout and the jug is inscribed underneath in purple 'Mr Wright, May 11, 1815'. Although otherwise unmarked, it has tentatively been attributed to Machin. Height 16.3 cm.* (Courtesy: City Museum & Art Gallery, Stoke-on-Trent)

The second type, associated mostly with bone china, consists of jugs decorated with standard patterns which, although sometimes still made to order, were production lines. Stock patterns were made at all the main factories and examples shown here are from Worcester (Plate 101), Chamberlains of Worcester (Plates 102–3), Spode (Plates 104–6), Davenport (Plate 107) and Coalport (Plates 108 and 154). The type is also well represented by a fine pair of unattributed jugs profusely decorated with flowers (Plate 109).

All these jugs are typical of the first thirty years or so of the nineteenth century, but the next, although of the same shape as the last pair, is more unusual (Plate 110). It has a deep blue ground with a moulded grapevine border and bears an applied portrait medallion depicting King George IV. It is one of a pair, presumably made to mark his coronation, and hence dating from 1820. It has an incised mark for Evans & Son, but no manufacturer using this style is recorded.

The use of a coloured ground became popular later in the century, particularly with outline printed designs. Classical figure subjects were widely used on earthenwares, some of very poor quality, but are not so common on china. One typical design with figures on a matt green ground appears on a jug registered by George Grainger & Co. of Worcester in 1866 (Plate 111). Patterns of this type were also used on china by Samuel Alcock & Co., and a similar style with interlaced scrolls on an orange ground can be seen on one flask-like jug, clearly intended for decoration rather than use (Plate 112).

PLATE 103: *Another Chamberlain's Worcester jug, one of a pair painted with a colourful Japan pattern in red, blue, pink and gold, c.1810–15. Script mark in red 'Chamberlains Worcester No. 240'. Height 18 cm.* (Courtesy: Lawrence Fine Art, Crewkerne)

PLATE 101: *Flight, Barr & Barr gadrooned edge toilet jug and basin decorated with broad claret ground borders with finely gilt framing. The complete set also has a small bowl, a soap dish and cover, and a toothbrush stand and cover.* (Courtesy: Lawrence Fine Art, Crewkerne)

PLATE 104: *Three octagonal Spode felspar porcelain jugs, outline-printed in grey and enamelled in colours with variations of a very popular design of Chinese figures, c.1822. The two larger jugs have a grey-printed wreath mark containing 'Spode' and 'Felspar/Porcelain'. All three have pattern number '3644' painted in red. Heights 18.7, 13.4, and 4.5 cm.*

PLATE 105: *Another Spode octagonal jug richly decorated in Kakiemon style with coloured enamels and gilding, c.1810–20. Unmarked except for pattern number '868' painted in red. Height 16 cm.* (Courtesy: Jack Hacking)

PLATE 102: *Chamberlain's Worcester jug decorated with orange motifs and panels containing flowers and birds on a blue honeycomb ground. Script mark in red 'Chamberlain's Worcester'. Height 10.9 cm.* (Courtesy: Woolley & Wallis, Salisbury)

Right:

PLATE 108: *Early 19th-century Coalport jug, brightly decorated with flowers and leaves in Imari style. Height 16.5 cm. (Courtesy: Dreweatt Neate, Newbury)*

PLATE 106: *Spode felspar porcelain jug of antique shape outline-printed in grey and enamelled in colours, c.1823. Grey-printed wreath mark containing 'Spode' and 'Felspar/Porcelain', with pattern number '3863' painted in black. Height 13.4 cm.*

PLATE 109: *Attractive pair of unattributed antique shape jugs profusely painted with colourful garden flowers, c.1830. Height 24 cm. (Courtesy: Sotheby's, Sussex)*

PLATE 110: *One of a pair of deep blue ground porcelain jugs made to commemorate the coronation of George IV, c.1820. Note the applied grapevine border and the portrait medallion of the king in Roman dress. Unrecorded incised mark for Evans & Son. Height 23 cm. (Courtesy: Sotheby's, Sussex)*

PLATE 107: *Bone china jug attributed to Davenport, enamelled with a design of Chinese figures in iron-red, purple, pink, yellow, green and blue, and heavily gilt. Height 15.8 cm. (Courtesy: Jack Hacking)*

43

PLATE 111: *White china jug with matt green ground, registered by George Grainger & Co. of Worcester in 1866. The classical figures are outline-printed and enamelled in orange and black. Purple-painted mark 'G Grainger/Worcester' and printed registration diamond for 15 November 1866. Height 15.9 cm.* (Courtesy: City Museum & Art Gallery, Stoke-on-Trent)

PLATE 112: *China flask-like jug by Samuel Alcock & Co. with matt orange ground enamelled with maroon outline and coloured with ochre, blue and green, and gilding. Maroon-printed initial mark 'S.A. & Co.'. Height 18.0 cm.*

PLATE 113: *Presentation jug by Samuel Alcock & Co. of a shape registered in 1854. Attractively painted and gilded with colourful flower sprays, inscribed and dated 'John Bourne / Madeley 1860'. Green-printed registration diamond for 27 December 1854. Height 17.3 cm.* (Courtesy: Jack Hacking)

The same snake handle appears on another Alcock jug, which would be much more usable (Plate 113). It is colourfully painted with roses, convolvulus and other flowers, heavily gilt, and inscribed for presentation to John Bourne of Madeley. Although dated 1860, the basic shape was registered in December 1854 and is more usually found printed in black with Crimean War subjects, issued as the 'Royal Patriotic Jug' to raise funds for widows and orphans (Colour Plate 18). China was a popular choice for ornately hand-painted presentation jugs and another fine example dating from 1848, although unmarked, is attributed to William Adams & Sons of Stoke (Plate 114).

In the second half of the nineteenth century much poor quality china was churned out, particularly in Longton, and most of these wares are unmarked. Apart from the high-quality manufacturers, many smaller potters produced utilitarian jugs, often ornately moulded and decorated with undistinguished floral patterns. One typical jug, although clearly marked, remains something of an enigma (Plate 115). The maker's name is Bodley but the address is given as Hanley. There were two Bodley firms making china at this period but they potted at Burslem and Longport, and neither is recorded at Hanley. As with many smaller

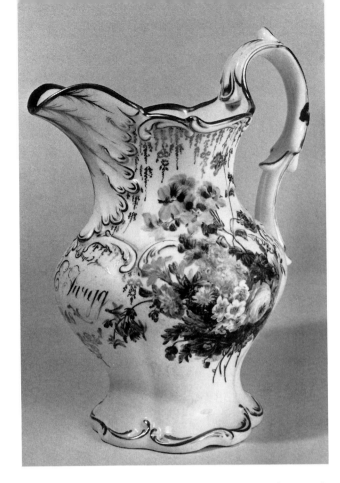

PLATE 114: *Ornately moulded china jug attributed to William Adams & Sons, profusely gilt and enamelled with flowers, and inscribed 'W.E. Twigg/1848'. An old paper label records that it was made for Mr Twigg, second son of Joseph Twigg of Burslem, who married Ann, elder daughter of William Adams of Fenton Hall, in 1817. Height 21.4 cm.* (Courtesy: City Museum & Art Gallery, Stoke-on-Trent)

PLATE 115: *Typical later 19th-century moulded china jug, the surface washed with blue, outline printed in grey and enamelled in colours. Grey-printed mark with 'BODLEY.HANLEY / ENGLAND' in circle around a monogram. Height 14 cm.* (Courtesy: City Museum & Art Gallery, Stoke-on-Trent)

firms, more detailed research is needed before such problems can be solved.

While lesser wares were made in quantity, some major factories continued to produce top-quality pieces, as the remaining four jugs show. They originate from the Royal Worcester factory and all feature an attractive and popular ivory ground. Three are tusk-shaped ice jugs dating from the late 1880s, decorated with various floral and bird subjects (Plate 116). The fourth is purely ornate with a prominent mask spout, decorated with flowers and a butterfly (Plate 117). Although a world apart from everyday utilitarian jugs, these are representative of the high quality achieved by British producers of porcelain and fine china for the top end of the market.

PLATE 116: *Three Royal Worcester Tusk ice jugs of shape number 1116. Each is decorated in colours and gilding on an old ivory ground. Marks with date codes for 1888 and 1889. Heights 25 cm.* (Courtesy: Phillips, London)

PLATE 117: *Another Royal Worcester jug with old ivory ground. This very ornate design featuring a female mask spout with plumed head-dress and decorated with flowers, leaves and a butterfly, can by no means be considered utilitarian. Printed and impressed marks. Height 26 cm.* (Courtesy: Dreweatt Neate, Newbury)

4.
Early Transfer-printing

A s wares became more sophisticated and demand increased, the eighteenth-century potters became more adept at production. Since hand-painting required expensive artistic skill, they sought more economic methods of decoration. Printing seemed an obvious option but, as with other advances, it proved far from straightforward. This is not the place for a detailed history, but successful transfer-printing seems to have been achieved on enamels by 1753. It was not long before the process was adapted for use on porcelain, certainly by 1756, and it soon became widespread. Several porcelain examples appear in the previous chapter, but it is earthenwares which most concern us here.

Several individuals experimented with printing on pottery, but commercial success is credited to John Sadler and Guy Green of Liverpool. In 1756 they prepared a petition for patenting their process, perfected on tin-glazed tiles, and although they did not proceed with the application, they soon adapted their technique for other wares. By 1761 they came to an arrangement with Josiah Wedgwood to decorate creamware, which was shipped to Liverpool, printed and then returned to Staffordshire for sale. The logistical problems must have been enormous, but the business surprisingly survived for three decades.

Although Sadler & Green had a good start, the technique soon spread to other pottery centres in Staffordshire, Yorkshire and Derbyshire. Prints were applied over the glaze, usually in black, and it was some time before successful underglaze printing was developed. The earlier on-glaze examples are discussed here, while later underglaze printed wares are covered in the next chapter.

Unlike hand-painting, which lent itself naturally to personalized inscriptions, printing was more automated and fewer wares are dated. However, jugs with added names, initials or monograms do exist, and a few also bear dates. Two are shown here, coincidentally both dated 1792, one with a plain black print of huntsmen (Plate 118), the other also black-printed but with added overglaze colours (Plate 119). The latter has been attributed to Liverpool, although a different version of the same subject shown by Cyril Williams-Wood in *English Transfer-printed Pottery and Porcelain* is signed by Joseph Johnson of Liverpool on a jug made by Wedgwood & Co., possibly at Ferrybridge.

PLATE 118: *Creamware jug dated 1792 printed in black with a fine scene of huntsmen with their guns and dog. The reverse has a farmyard scene. Height 21 cm.* (Courtesy: Phillips North West, Chester)

PLATE 119: *Liverpool creamware jug printed and enamelled in colours with Colonel Tarleton beneath a green-line rim. The reverse features the Watchtool Makers Arms and the front has initials 'EMH' with date 1792. Height 14.5 cm.* (Courtesy: Christie's, London)

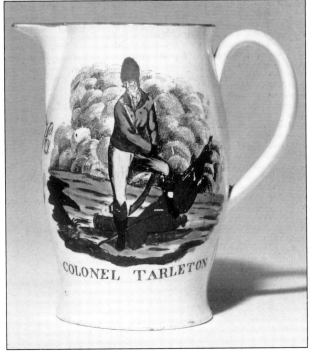

PLATE 120: *Creamware jug, possibly Liverpool, printed in black with a country house scene. The reverse has an amusing print depicting courtship one way and matrimony when inverted. Height 16.7 cm.*

PLATE 121: *Two black-printed Liverpool creamware jugs, one inscribed 'J. & L. Bradbury 1810' with a print commemorating the golden jubilee of George III in that year, the other with Nelson subjects including the Battle of the Nile of 1798. The jubilee print is signed with a capital 'D', believed to refer to the engraver T. Dixon. Heights 23 and 24 cm.* (Courtesy: Christie's, London)

Dated examples are inevitably of interest, but stylistic points can assist in dating other jugs, most of which are unmarked. In the eighteenth century and through to about 1810, jugs were commonly of a bulbous or ovoid shape. As a general rule, a distinct foot suggests an earlier date, usually before 1790 (Plate 120). Thereafter the shape tended to become more barrel-like, and despite some variations in the profile, sometimes more slender or flaring out at the rim and foot, this remained popular until it was superseded in the early years of the nineteenth century. Two extremes are represented by one slender jug commemorating the Battle of the Nile of 1798, alongside another more bulbous example dated 1810 (Plate 121).

Although relatively few of these jugs can be attributed with any degree of confidence, many are of interest for their subject matter. Some prints are purely decorative (Plate 122), others were clearly made to order (Plate 123), and many commemorate famous people or events. Much fascinating information can be found in David Drakard's *Printed English Pottery, History and Humour in the Reign of George III*, but a small selection of commemorative jugs shown here represent politics (Plate 124), royalty (Plate 125), satire (Plate 126) and naval and military heroes (Plate 127). The centre jug in this last illustration, commemorating the golden jubilee of George III, has previously appeared as a late example of this ovoid shape (Plate 121).

As already mentioned, by far the majority of these jugs are unmarked, but three fine exceptions are shown here. Two were made by Wedgwood at Etruria, one printed in black by Sadler & Green at Liverpool, probably dating from the early 1770s (Plate 128). The other, from the mid-1780s, is also black-printed but with oval scenes which are coloured over and an attractively enamelled border (Colour Plate 10). The third marked example was made by Ralph Wedgwood & Co. as a presentation piece, with the recipient's name above the arms of the Cordwainers' Company (Plate 129). Ralph Wedgwood had no direct connection with the main Wedgwood concern, but potted at Burslem in the early 1790s until he became bankrupt; he then worked at the Knottingley Pottery at Ferrybridge in Yorkshire for a short time. Wares with this mark could have been made at either place.

While few jugs bear makers' marks, a significant number feature signatures within or below the prints. These may refer to the engraver, the printer or, more rarely, the potter, and have been the subject of much research. Examples with the names Abbey, Baddeley, Brammer, Brindley, Fletcher, Radford and Robinson are shown here, and many more are discussed by Cyril Williams-Wood in *English Transfer-printed Pottery and Porcelain*. Signed prints are rarely found on underglaze printed wares, but engravers' names occasionally appear on some later lustre wares from the north-east of England (see Chapter 10). Several of these are discussed by Nick Dolan in 'Sunderland Pottery, Some New Views' in Volume 9 of the *Journal of the Northern Ceramic Society* (1992).

PLATE 122: *Typical creamware jug printed in black with a farmyard scene, c.1800. Initials 'JAS' are painted on the front and the other side has a framed verse beginning 'May the Mighty and Great . . .' Height 14.3 cm.* (Courtesy: Sotheby's, Sussex)

PLATE 124: *Electioneering jug printed in black with portraits of Henry Grattan and Lord Fitzgerald, both of whom were elected to represent the City of Dublin in the Irish elections of 1790. Height 21.5 cm.* (Courtesy: Christie's, London)

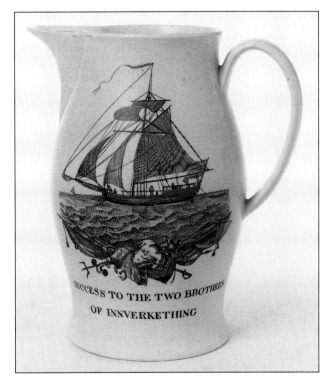

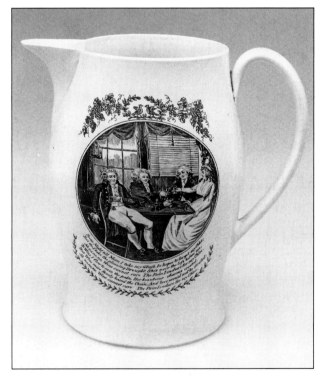

PLATE 123: *Yet another Liverpool creamware jug printed in black on one side with a sloop inscribed 'Success to the Two Brothers of Innverkething' [sic], the 'Two Brothers' being a common ship's name. The reverse has a different print showing shipwrights at work on a large vessel on the stocks. Height 21 cm.* (Courtesy: Phillips, London)

PLATE 125: *Large unattributed creamware jug printed in black with a drinking scene, possibly depicting the Prince Regent at the time of his abortive marriage to Mrs Fitzherbert in 1785. The reverse has 'Gretna Green or the Red Hot Marriage'.* (Courtesy: Black Horse Agencies – Locke & England, Leamington Spa)

PLATE 126: *Another typical creamware jug, printed in black with a satirical scene depicting Lumley Skeffington and Montagu Matthews, leaders of a fashion for highly polished boots. The reverse has 'An Old Performer playing on a new Instrument', a Napoleonic print dating from 1803–4. Height 22.7 cm.*

PLATE 128: *Wedgwood Queen's Ware jug printed in black by Sadler & Green, c. 1770–75. This print depicts 'An Opera Girl of Paris in the character of Flora' from a Robert Sayer engraving of 1771. The reverse has 'The Pretty Mantua Maker' from an engraving by Grignion after Brandoin. Impressed mark 'WEDGWOOD'. Height 19 cm. (Courtesy: Trustees of the Wedgwood Museum, Barlaston, Staffordshire)*

PLATE 127: *Three black-printed creamware jugs depicting Prince William with British men o'war on the reverse, Wedgwood & Co. c.1789; George III's golden jubilee with a printed and coloured man o'war on the reverse, Herculaneum Pottery 1809–10; and Lord Wellington with the Dixon coat of arms on the reverse, c.1810. Heights 21 cm, 23 cm, and 22.8 cm.* (Courtesy: Bonhams, Knightsbridge)

PLATE 129: *Wedgwood & Co. creamware jug black-printed with the arms of the Cordwainers Company and inscribed 'JOHN TAYLOR'. The front has a verse 'Thus Happy with my Friend and Bowl. . .' while the back has a panel representing Charity. Impressed maker's mark. Height 18 cm. (Courtesy: Phillips, London)*

To return to the signed jugs under consideration here, one of the most interesting bears imprints for John Robinson of Burslem and Richard Abbey (Plate 130). Both names appear beneath the print showing 'Hudibras and the Bear', while the reverse, the 'Youthful Lovers' is not signed. Robinson and Abbey both worked for Sadler & Green at Liverpool, but left to set up their own businesses, Robinson as a printer at Burslem. He must have employed Abbey, his former colleague, to engrave some printing plates.

While Liverpool claims distinction for the development of transfer-printing on pottery, it was eventually overtaken by Staffordshire. All but one of the signed prints featured here are of Staffordshire origin, including two jugs with the imprint of Thomas Baddeley, an engraver and printer at Hanley. Both date from the first decade of the nineteenth century, one printed with a prominent American eagle (Plate 131), the other with an extremely detailed print 'The End of the Upright Man is Peace' (Plate 132). Two others made around 1800 bear less common signatures. One, printed with 'The World in Planisphere' is signed by the engraver Thomas Radford of Shelton and Stoke (Plate 133). The other features 'Werter [sic] Going to Shoot Himself', signed by George Brammer, a little-known printer based at Shelton (Plate 134).

PLATE 130: *Two views of a creamware jug printed in black with 'Hudibras and the Bear' signed 'I Robinson Burslem' and 'R Abbey Sculp', the reverse with 'The Youthful Lovers', c.1790–1800. Height 21.3 cm. (Courtesy: City Museum & Art Gallery, Stoke-on-Trent)*

PLATE 131: *Staffordshire creamware jug printed in black with an American eagle signed 'T.BADDELEY / HANLEY / STAFF'SHIRE'. The reverse has an unsigned print of a man o'war. Height 13.7 cm.* (Courtesy: City Museum & Art Gallery, Stoke-on-Trent)

Above Right:
PLATE 132: *Another signed Baddeley print 'The End of the Upright Man is Peace', c.1800–10, based on an earlier engraving published by Carrington & Bowles in 1785. The reverse features allegorical classical figures with Masonic emblems. Height 28.9 cm.* (Courtesy: Sotheby's, London)

Below:
PLATE 133: *Two views of a creamware jug with rather bulbous body printed in black with 'The World in Planisphere' and 'His Excellency Geo. Washington'. The planisphere print is signed 'Engraved by Radford'. Height 23.7 cm.* (Courtesy: City Museum & Art Gallery, Stoke-on-Trent)

PLATE 134: *Staffordshire creamware jug with two black prints signed by G. Brammer of Shelton. This side depicts 'Werter Going to Shoot Himself', while the reverse has 'Charlotte Weeping over the Tomb of Werter'. Height 19.9 cm.*

PLATE 135: *Staffordshire creamware jug printed by Thomas Fletcher with 'The Last Drop', the reverse with a seated toper holding a jug of frothing ale. This print is signed 'T. Fletcher'. Height 17 cm.* (Courtesy: Sotheby's, Sussex)

If the number of signed prints illustrated here is any guide, one of the most publicity-conscious printers must have been Thomas Fletcher. Three examples all have different signatures; 'T. Fletcher' (Plate 135), 'T. Fletcher, Shelton' (Plate 136), and 'Thos. Fletcher & Co., Shelton' (Plate 137). The history of Fletcher and his partnerships is discussed by Eileen Hampson in the Northern Ceramic Society's exhibition catalogue *Creamware and Pearlware*. A fourth indistinctly signed example also appears to be from Fletcher's workshop (Plate 138). A fifth jug, both sides bearing the same print signed 'T. Fletcher, Shelton', is clearly later, printed in maroon rather than black, with added enamel decoration and gilding (Plate 139).

Other prints signed by the manufacturer Thomas Harley of Lane End and the independent Swansea engraver James Brindley are associated with Napoleonic subjects and are discussed below along with other jugs of the same genre.

With just one exception, the jugs above are all printed in black, although some are also enamelled or coloured over. One jug with a maroon print has just been discussed and another is shown here (Plate 140). Like one of the signed Fletcher jugs, it features a print titled 'Come Box the Compass', although this anonymous version is much more detailed, with information about the instrument's history. The rim is silver-lustred and the companion print commemorates Lord Nelson's death late in 1805, both useful pointers to dating.

PLATE 136: *Another black-printed Staffordshire creamware jug, c.1800–15. 'Come Box the Compass' is signed 'T. FLETCHER' and 'SHELTON' in the centre. Height 16.6 cm.* (Courtesy: City Museum & Art Gallery, Stoke-on-Trent)

PLATE 137: *Two views of another creamware jug printed by Fletcher, c.1810–15. The print titled 'Conjugal Felicity' is signed 'Thos. Fletcher & Co, Shelton'. Height 17.1 cm. (Courtesy: City Museum & Art Gallery, Stoke-on-Trent)*

PLATE 138: *Staffordshire creamware jug black-printed with 'Twenty Thousand I've Got – How Lucky's My Lot', c.1790–1810. This design is based on a Carrington Bowles engraving published in 1786 and is indistinctly signed, probably 'Thos. Fletcher, Shelton'. The reverse is printed with Masonic emblems. Height 19.5 cm. (Courtesy: Sotheby's, London)*

PLATE 139: *Very clearly signed print by 'T. FLETCHER SHELTON', c.1800–15. This pearlware jug is printed in maroon and features blue and maroon lining with added gilding. The same print is repeated on the reverse. Height 17.3 cm. (Courtesy: City Museum & Art Gallery, Stoke-on-Trent)*

PLATE 140: *Two views of an unattributed Staffordshire creamware jug, possibly from the mysterious W(***) factory, c.1805–10. The prints are in maroon, and silver lustre adorns both the rim and handle. Height 17.4 cm.* (Courtesy: City Museum & Art Gallery, Stoke-on-Trent)

PLATE 141: *Another Staffordshire creamware jug attributed to the W(***) factory, c.1805–15. The sepia print, depicting George IV as Prince Regent surrounded by Peace, Justice and emblems of freemasonry, is repeated on the reverse. Height 27 cm.* (Courtesy: Phillips, London)

The compass subject provides an interesting link to the next jug, which is printed in sepia with designs incorporating Masonic emblems (Plate 141). The main print, on both sides, is a portrait of the Prince of Wales, later George IV, surrounded by female figures including a blindfolded Justice. This appears alongside the compass print already mentioned on a large earthenware jug bearing the mystery impressed mark 'W(***)' illustrated in Godden's *Encyclopaedia of British Porcelain Manufacturers*. This mark is found on both porcelain and earthenwares and has aroused considerable interest. The favourite attribution is currently one of the Whitehead firms, although this may be amended in due course.

One jug already discussed (Plate 140) laments the death of Lord Nelson in 1805, an event which led to a flood of commemorative wares. At this period there was a marked shift away from the earlier bulbous shape and Nelson commemoratives can be found in both the old and new shapes (Plate 142). The newly fashionable Dutch shape started to predominate around this time (Plate 143), although it was not a recent development. Earlier dated pearlware jugs have already been illustrated (Plates 32–4), and another is shown here with 'The Prodigal Son in Misery' (Plate 144). This print is one of a pair known to have been used by William Greatbatch at Fenton around 1780, reputedly engraved by Thomas Radford. The jug, with its attractively enamelled border, is clearly too late to be attributed to Greatbatch and a date in the 1790s would appear appropriate. However, a Napoleonic print on the reverse shows that it could not have been made before 1803.

Left:
PLATE 142: *Two Nelson commemorative jugs, both c.1805–10. The left-hand example is black-printed creamware with a scene of the Battle of Trafalgar on the reverse, the other is of pearlware printed in puce. Heights 18.1 cm and 14 cm. (Courtesy: Dreweatt Neate, Newbury)*

PLATE 145: *Don Pottery 'Orange Jumper' jug, c.1807. It depicts Mellish, a local horse breaker, who was employed by Earl Fitzwilliam to campaign for his son, Lord Milton, in the 1807 Yorkshire election. The design is printed and coloured and the reverse has a humorous verse on a yellow scroll. Height 18 cm. (Courtesy: Phillips, London)*

PLATE 143: *Another Staffordshire pearlware jug printed in black with a portrait of Nelson, c.1805–10. In this case the reverse features a rhyme lamenting his loss. Height 12.5 cm. (Courtesy: Christie's, London)*

PLATE 146: *Orange Order jug in creamware, printed in black, heavily enamelled in colours and with pink lustre bands. The reverse has a mass of masonic emblems and two panels with a coded jumble of letters including the date 1811. Height 11.5 cm.*

Left:
PLATE 144: *Pearlware jug printed in black and enamelled in colours, the border hand-painted in blue, red and purple, with reddish-brown lining. The reverse has a Napoleonic print derived from 'John Bull giving Boney a pull', an engraving originally published in 1803. Height 14.9 cm.*

The early years of the nineteenth century saw great changes in fashion, and although underglaze blue printing became widespread, the overglaze technique remained in use. A wide range of subjects were depicted, although extra decoration, either enamel colouring or lustre rims, became more common. Four representative examples feature politics in 1807 (Plate 145), royalty and freemasonry in 1811 (Plate 146), a strange combination of sport and political crime in 1812 (Plate 147), and a novel form of transport based on the newly invented velocipede around 1820 (Plate 148). The last of these features a bright canary-yellow glaze which was fashionable at this period, often combined with other decorative techniques such as moulding and hand-painting (Plate 56).

Alongside Nelson, one of the most commemorated figures of the early nineteenth century was Napoleon Bonaparte. He made his first appearance on our pottery in 1802, but following the declaration of war in 1803 prints belittling or reviling him proliferated. The full story is told by David Drakard in *Printed English Pottery, History and Humour in the Reign of George III*, but a representative sample of the many prints is shown here.

Notable amongst these are several satires, copied by Thomas Harley of Lane End from engravings published during 1803 and 1804. Most are signed with Harley's name at the base of the design, usually printed in brown and crudely coloured. One typical subject is 'John Bull Shewing the Corsican Monkey!!' (Plate 149), another example of which can be seen together with 'Facing the Enemy' and 'Bonny in his New Clothes' (Plate 150). The latter is slightly later, referring to Bonaparte's self-proclaimed role as Emperor, and some examples are also signed by the designer Clive. Other Harley jugs include 'Bonaparte and the Quaker' and 'John Bull Giving Boney a Pull'.

PLATE 148: *Staffordshire canary-yellow glazed jug with silver lustre rim, printed and coloured with two early scenes of cyclists titled 'The Lady's Accelerator' and 'A Visit from Richmond to Carlton House', the home of the Prince Regent. The subjects were probably inspired by the velocipede, invented in 1818. Height 15.9 cm.* (Courtesy: Sotheby's, Sussex)

PLATE 149: *Pearlware jug by Thomas Harley, printed and coloured with 'John Bull Shewing the Corsican Monkey!!', c.1803–4. The reverse features a satirical declaration. The prints are signed 'Manufactured by T. Harley, Lane End'. Height 15.5 cm.* (Courtesy: Sotheby's, Sussex)

Left:
PLATE 147: *Pearlware jug with silver lustre bands and circular frames, printed in black with two apparently unrelated subjects, the boxers Molineaux and Cribb and portraits of John Bellingham. Tom Cribb knocked out the American boxer Molineaux in the first of two bouts in September 1812. Bellingham shot the Prime Minister Spencer Perceval on 11 May 1812 and was hanged a week later. Height 17 cm.* (Courtesy: Sotheby's, Sussex)

PLATE 150: *Three more Harley pearlware jugs, printed and coloured with 'John Bull Shewing the Corsican Monkey!!', 'Facing the Enemy', and 'Bonny in his New Clothes', c.1803–4. The prints on the first two are signed 'Manufactured by T. Harley, Lane End'. Heights 14.5 cm, 14 cm, and 19.5 cm. (Courtesy: Sotheby's, London)*

print is plain black, but others are coloured, including 'The Grand Triumphal Entry of the Chief Consul into London' on a low Dutch-shape jug in bone china (Plate 152).

A final print from the 1803–4 period depicts 'John Bull and his Companion Challenging Bonaparte and his Relation' on a pearlware jug with a yellow ground (Plate 153). At least two examples have survived, both with added inscriptions and printed on the reverse with 'One of the 71st taking a French Officer in Portugal'. This refers to the Peninsular War between 1808 and 1811. With their silver-lustre rims and yellow ground, these jugs probably date from around 1810.

Three more Napoleonic prints, all from the later period around 1812–14, conclude this selection. The first, on a hybrid hard-paste porcelain jug made at Coalport, depicts the 'Cossack Mode of Attack' (Plate 154). The reverse shows the 'Russian Boor' and both subjects are based on engravings published early in 1813. While the scenes are titled the jug itself is unmarked. The second, showing 'Boney's Return from Russia to Paris' (Plate 155), purports to depict Napoleon fleeing on horseback late in 1812, while the third, 'Bonaparte Dethron'd' (Plate 156), refers to the Allies' entry into Paris in 1814. This last jug is the signed example already referred to. Made at the Cambrian Pottery in Swansea, the print is signed by the independent local engraver James Brindley.

PLATE 151: *Unmarked Spode pearlware jug bat-printed in black with 'John Bull giving Boney a Pull', c.1803. Enamelled with a wide reddish-brown band and black lining. Height 14.3 cm.*

Another version of the latter 1803 subject appears on a bat-printed pearlware jug, recently identified as Spode (Plate 151). Although unmarked, it is one of a series of Napoleonic subjects used by the famous firm. Three more are illustrated in the form of pulls from original copper plates by David Drakard and Paul Holdway in their superb standard work *Spode Printed Ware*. This

PLATE 152: *Another unmarked Spode jug, this one in bone china, bat-printed in black and coloured over with 'The Grand Triumphal Entry of the Chief Consul into London', c.1803–4. Gilded rim and handle. Height 12.4 cm.*

PLATE 153: *Unattributed yellow-ground jug with silver lustre banding, inscribed 'John & Elizabeth Reeves', c.1810. Three circular reserves are printed with 'John Bull and his companion challenging Bonaparte and his relation', a verse and 'One of the 71st taking a French Officer in Portugal'. Height 20.3 cm. (Courtesy: Andrew Hartley Fine Arts, Ilkley)*

PLATE 154: *Hard-paste porcelain Coalport jug, bat-printed in brown and enamelled in colours, with gilt rim, c.1813–14. Unmarked but the scenes are titled in grey-blue, this side with 'Cossack Mode of Attack' and the reverse with 'Russian Boor'. Height 15.9 cm.*

PLATE 156: *Creamware jug attributed to Dillwyn's Cambrian Pottery at Swansea, printed in black and crudely coloured with humorous print titled 'Bonaparte Dethron'd April 1st 1814'. Unmarked but the print is signed 'J. Brindley'. Height 13.2 cm.*

While this chapter has been devoted mainly to over-glaze printing in black on creamware or whiter earthenware, other colours and bodies were used. The next jug is typical of the common Dutch shape but the body is partly enhanced by cream-coloured slip and the design is bat-printed in purple (Plate 157). The mask spout and other features suggest a date around 1820, by which time printing in underglaze blue was in full swing and the days of overglaze printing were virtually over. Two final examples, both unmarked but made by Spode, are again very different in style. One has black bat-prints on a drabware body, a subtle but attractive combination (Plate 158). The other has a black print within an oval white reserve on a redware body covered with a brown glaze (Plate 159). In *Spode Printed Ware* David Drakard and Paul Holdway describe this combination as revived Astbury ware and a similar version with black glaze as revived Jackfield ware. Examples frequently remain unrecognized.

Another group of jugs about which little has been published date from the first quarter of the nineteenth century. These are potted in brown earthenware and printed in yellow, although it is not always easy to tell whether the print is applied over or under the glaze. Both types seem to exist. Five typical examples include two with chinoiserie scenes (Plates 160–1), one with a reserve of Eastern figures (Plate 162), one with a sheet

Left:
PLATE 155: *Pearlware jug by an unknown maker decorated with silver lustre and printed and coloured on each side with 'Boney's Return from Russia to Paris', c.1812–13. Height 12 cm. (Courtesy: Sotheby's, Sussex)*

floral pattern (Plate 163) and another with a similar sheet design incorporating a medallion commemorating Lord Nelson (Plate 164). None of these is marked and all have a white slip interior.

It has been suggested that jugs like these are printed in white and then covered with a yellow glaze, but this is not the case. There is some confusion with later jugs which are superficially similar, produced by the Scott firm at Sunderland. These are made in a very different way, using a type of encaustic process, and are usually glazed yellow. The example shown here, however, has the pattern in white, clearly marked with the name 'Scott' near the base (Plate 165). Some of the design continues beneath the jug.

Before moving on to underglaze printed wares, it is worth noting that the style of some of these early jugs was reintroduced by Wedgwood in the middle of the twentieth century. One good example is a jug designed by Victor Skellern in 1959 to mark the 250th anniversary of the birth of Samuel Johnson (Plate 166). Printed in black with a famous quote, it is a fitting tribute, not only to Johnson but also indirectly to the potters of the late eighteenth and early nineteenth centuries who produced such a superb range of functional yet fascinating jugs.

PLATE 158: *Two views of an unmarked Spode drabware jug, bat-printed in black with sporting dogs, with gilt rim and handle, c.1807–15. Height 13 cm.*

PLATE 159: *Another unmarked Spode jug, of the so-called revived Astbury type with a fine redware body covered with brown glaze, c.1810–20. The interior and the oval panel are covered with white slip, the latter bat-printed in black with a classical humanity subject. Height 16.5 cm.*

PLATE 157: *Attractive but unattributed white earthenware jug, c.1815–25, with cream slip interior, spout, handle and base, the sides bat-printed in purple, and with added brown enamel and gilding including the monogram 'CHB'. Height 18.6 cm.* (Courtesy: Jack Hacking)

Right:
PLATE 160: *Unmarked and unattributed jug in brown earthenware with white slip interior, printed in yellow with a chinoiserie scene, c.1805–10. Jugs of this shape are sometimes associated with Thomas Harley of Lane End. Height 14.2 cm.*

PLATE 161: *Dutch-shape jug of similar type, also printed in yellow with a chinoiserie scene, c.1805–15. Height 11.7 cm.*

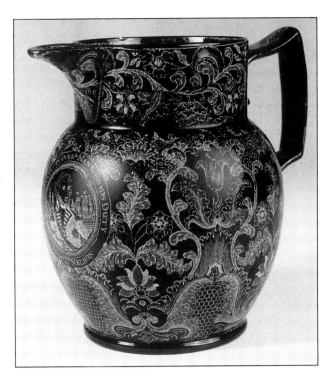

PLATE 162: *Another brown earthenware jug with white slip interior, printed in this case with an oval reserve of Eastern figures in a noticeably darker shade of yellow, c.1805–15. Height 13.4 cm.*

PLATE 164: *Commemorative jug of the same type as the previous four examples, c.1805–10. The sheet floral pattern is relieved by a portrait medallion of Admiral Lord Nelson with the famous quote 'England expects every man to do his duty'. Height 13.9 cm.*

PLATE 165: *Superficially similar jug of brown earthenware but decorated with an encaustic process, c.1840–50. In this case the floral pattern is white, but other examples are glazed in yellow. The maker's name 'Scott' appears in script beneath the design, which continues under the base. Height 11.9 cm.* (Courtesy: Jack Hacking)

Left:
PLATE 163: *Another typical and unmarked yellow printed jug, c.1805–15. Again the body is brown earthenware with a white slip interior, but the design is an attractive floral sheet pattern. Height 14.9 cm.*

PLATE 166: *Wedgwood black-printed Queen's Ware jug designed by Victor Skellern in 1959 to mark the 250th anniversary of the birth of Samuel Johnson. Circular printed mark 'WEDGWOOD OF ETRURIA & BARLASTON'. Height 19 cm.* (Courtesy: Trustees of the Wedgwood Museum, Barlaston, Staffordshire)

5.

Underglaze Transfer-printing

One problem of overglaze printing was that the design, despite being fired on to the glaze, was exposed to wear. Although adequate for decorative items, the technique proved unsuitable for heavily used dinner wares and, to a lesser extent, for utilitarian jugs. The obvious solution was to apply the print beneath the glaze. Although simple in concept, this proved technically difficult, involving improved engraving techniques and special inks capable of withstanding the heat of the glost oven. At first the only colour robust enough was blue, extracted from cobalt oxide. Underglaze printed wares were made almost exclusively in blue until about 1810, and other colours were not in widespread use much before 1830.

The first blue-printed earthenwares appeared around 1775, with designs that emulated imported Chinese porcelain of the period. Some of these early chinoiserie patterns are straight copies, although the engravers soon developed their own distinctive versions. Several typical jugs are shown (Plates 167–72). Some have tentatively been attributed to firms such as the Cambrian Pottery, Swansea (Plate 170), Shorthose (Plate 171) and the little known Greseley (Plate 172), but the subject of chinoiserie designs is a specialist field. The eighteenth-century wares are rarely marked, but from about 1800 marking gradually became more frequent, particularly by larger firms such as Spode (Plates 173–4).

To the inexperienced eye many of these designs would be described as Willow pattern although the true Willow, an entirely imaginary scene with a pagoda, three figures on a bridge, an island, a boat and two doves, evolved only gradually (Plate 169, right). By about 1820, when other chinoiseries had been superseded by more fashionable patterns, it became a standard design, subsequently produced by many firms in descending levels of quality throughout the nineteenth century. One good early example appears on a jug marked Herculaneum (Plate 175).

As the skill of the potters and engravers improved, fashions began to change and illustrated books proved a profitable design source. The earliest non-chinoiserie designs featured foreign places copied from travel books of the period. They include several views from India (Plate 176), mostly based on engravings by Thomas and William Daniell, and other areas like the Near East (Plate 177). Many patterns featured places which were part of

PLATE 167: *Typical early chinoiserie pattern printed underglaze in blue on a crisply moulded cabbage-leaf jug similar to 18th-century porcelains. Unmarked and unattributed, but possibly made by Joshua Heath, c.1785–90. Height 21.9 cm.*

the Grand Tour, particularly Italy (Plates 178–80). Views of America were also produced in quantity, usually in a much darker shade of blue, intended for the lucrative export market (Plate 181).

At this period, between 1815 and 1830, the use of printed marks became popular and a fair number of these patterns are titled. A typical but late example is a view of Mount Olympus, one of a series of scenes associated with Lord Byron issued by Copeland & Garrett (Plate 182). Identification of the many untitled views is a popular pastime for collectors, and two typical unidentified examples are continental in flavour (Plates 183–4).

PLATE 168: *Blue-printed earthenware jug of a standard shape with a typical but unrecorded chinoiserie scene. Note the blue lining on the handle. Height 12.1 cm.*

PLATE 170: *Cabbage-leaf moulded jug printed in blue with the Precarious Chinaman pattern, normally attributed to the Cambrian Pottery at Swansea, c.1790–1800. Height 14.5 cm.*

PLATE 169: *Two similar blue-printed jugs, c.1800–20, the right-hand example with the standard Willow pattern. In both cases the rims and handles are lined with ochre enamel. Height 11.8 cm each.*

Right:

PLATE 171: *Barrel-shaped jug with restored strainer spout, printed in blue with a Two Temples pattern sometimes called the Chinaman with Rocket. Tentatively attributed to Shorthose, c.1795–1810. Height 13.5 cm.*

PLATE 172: *Two views of a good quality but unmarked blue-printed jug with a Three Pennants pattern, c.1800. Height 16.9 cm.*

PLATE 173: *Covered barrel-shaped earthenware jug with a strainer spout, printed in blue with Spode's Queen Charlotte pattern, c.1805–15. Printed mark 'SPODE'. Height 16.5 cm.*

PLATE 174: *Another Spode earthenware jug, printed in paler blue on a gadrooned edge shape with the Broseley pattern, c.1815–25. Printed mark 'SPODE'. Height 12.7 cm.*

PLATE 175: *Tall blue-printed earthenware jug with the standard Willow pattern, c.1800–20. Impressed 'HERCULANEUM' in small capitals. Height 22.8 cm.*

PLATE 177: *Fine Dutch-shape earthenware jug printed with one of Spode's Caramanian patterns, c.1810–20. This view shows a 'Colossal Sarcophagus near Castle Rosso', taken from Mayer's* Views in the Ottoman Empire, *published in 1803. Printed mark 'SPODE'. Height 15.7 cm.*

PLATE 178: *Covered jug with strainer spout, blue-printed with a view of the Ponte Molle, near Rome, c.1815–25. The scene is based on a landscape by Claude Lorraine and has been reported on a plate with a rare mark for J. & W. Handley. Height 19 cm.*

PLATE 176: *Barrel-shaped jug with strainer spout, probably made at the Herculaneum Pottery, c.1810–20. The view is 'The Chalees Satoon in the Fort of Allahabad on the River Jumna', copied from Daniell's* Oriental Scenery, *published in 1795. Height 16.9 cm.*

PLATE 181: *Attractive blue-printed jug with a view of the Boston State House, c.1820. This relatively common American view was made by John Rogers & Son of Longport, but other versions are known. Height 20.3 cm.* (Courtesy: Christie's, South Kensington)

PLATE 179: *Toilet jug or ewer of a standard shape, printed in blue with Spode's prolific Tower pattern, c.1820–30. Printed mark 'SPODE'. Height 21.7 cm.*

PLATE 180: *Large Don Pottery earthenware jug, probably originally supplied with a matching footbath, printed in blue with the 'Residence of Solinenes, near Vesuvius', c.1815–30. Note the extra handle beneath the spout and also the flying putti in the border. Printed maker's marks. Height 29.9 cm.* (Courtesy: Christie's, South Kensington)

PLATE 182: *Good quality but rather late named view on an ornate ewer by Copeland & Garrett, c.1833–40. The scene is one of a series copied from engravings in Finden's* Landscape and Portrait Illustrations to the Life and Works of Lord Byron, *published 1832–4. Impressed and printed maker's marks, the latter with ribbon bearing title 'MOUNT OLYMPUS'. Height 26.3 cm.*

PLATE 183: *Vase-shaped earthenware jug printed in blue with a romantic scene of ruins, c.1815–25. Examples of this pattern sometimes bear a mark for James & Ralph Clews of Cobridge. Height 14.0 cm.*

It was not long before the potters introduced designs more appropriate to the home market. An early example is a commemorative jug depicting Nelson and his victory at Trafalgar in 1805 (Plate 185). Designs of this type are uncommon, but British scenes, particularly showing country houses, were made in large numbers in the 1820s. Again, many are titled, but marks are less common on jugs. Several identified scenes are shown here (Plates 186–8), along with two more from series, just a few of which have been identified (Plates 189–90).

Two titled views from a 'Northern Scenery' series made by John Meir & Son appear on jugs of very different shapes (Plates 191–2) and a cautionary note that attributions based purely on shape can be unsafe seems appropriate. It is also worth emphasizing that the copper plates used for printing were bought and sold as firms opened and closed, and while they are generally more reliable, attributions based on pattern alone can also be misleading.

While titled views are particularly collectable, many other designs were made, again usually copied from engravings in books, although relatively few have been identified. They include scenes with literary connotations (Plate 193), attractive genre scenes (Plates 194–6) and some featuring country pursuits such as hunting (Plate 197). No doubt more source prints for these patterns will be discovered and this could be a rewarding field for further study.

PLATE 184: *Another water jug or ewer of the standard shape, c.1820–30. The attractive harbour scene is printed in blue beneath a floral border of a common design, one version of which was used by John Rogers & Son. Height 22.2 cm.*

PLATE 186: *Unmarked earthenware jug printed in blue with a scene based on the famous Pulteney Bridge at Bath, c.1815–30. Wares with this pattern are usually attributed to Swansea. Height 15.4 cm.*

PLATE 185: *Three views of a fine early blue-printed jug commemorating Nelson's victory at Trafalgar, c.1805–10. Height 14 cm.* (Courtesy: Boardman Fine Art Auctioneers, Haverhill)

Above:

PLATE 187: *Two views of an unattributed earthenware jug, printed in blue with two country house scenes. The upper scene shows Stackpole Court in Pembrokeshire, based on an engraving in John Preston Neale's* Views of the Seats of Noblemen and Gentlemen, *published between 1818 and 1829. Printed leafy ribbon mark with title 'BRITISH SCENERY'. Height 11.9 cm.*

Below:

PLATE 189: *Another blue-printed jug attributed to Ridgway on the basis of a rare marked plate, c.1815–25. This is one of a series of views, many copied from engravings by William Angus in* Seats of the Nobility and Gentry in Great Britain and Wales, *published between 1787 and 1797. The spout has been repaired. Height 21.3 cm.*

PLATE 188: *Standard Dutch-shape jug printed in blue with a scene showing Osterley Park in Middlesex, c.1815–25. Although unmarked, this can safely be attributed to Ridgway on the basis of a few rare marked plates. Height 16.5 cm.*

PLATE 190: *Two views of a fine unattributed blue-printed earthenware jug, c.1815–25. The scene is one of the so-called Monks Rock Series, named after the first view to be identified. Neither the maker nor this view has been traced. Height 18 cm.*

Left:
PLATE 191: *Rather late Dutch-shape jug printed in blue by John Meir & Son with a view titled 'Kilchurn Castle, Loch Awe' from their 'Northern Scenery' series, c.1836–50. Printed Royal arms-type mark with titles and maker's initials. Height 9.5 cm.*

PLATE 194: *Simple blue-printed earthenware jug, possibly made at Swansea, c.1825–40. A version of this rural scene with a drover was also used by John & William Ridgway in their 'Rural Scenery' series. Height 15.4 cm.*

Above:

PLATE 192: *Another jug from John Meir & Son's 'Northern Scenery' series, again c. 1836–50. This view is titled 'Dunolly Castle, near Oban', but note the very different shape. Printed Royal arms type mark with titles and maker's initials. Height 13.2 cm.*

PLATE 195: *Blue-printed earthenware jug with an attractive but poorly printed genre scene titled 'Cottage Girl', made by Baker, Bevans & Irwin at the Glamorgan Pottery, Swansea, c.1813–20. Printed mark with title and maker's initials. Height 11.8 cm.*

Left:

PLATE 193: *Earthenware ewer of standard shape by an unknown maker, c.1820–30. The blue-printed scene, featuring a harpist and a castle, may have been inspired by one of Walter Scott's popular novels. Height 22.7 cm.*

PLATE 196: *Unattributed blue-printed earthenware ewer, still with its matching basin, c.1820–30. The attractive rural scene is titled 'Cow Boy'. Printed title mark. Basin diameter 33.0 cm.* (Courtesy: Dreweatt Neate, Newbury)

PLATE 197: *Earthenware jug by an unknown maker, printed in blue, c.1815–25. The hunting scene is rather similar to a common sprigged design. Height 19.6 cm.*

While scenic views have always been popular, many more general designs were made. These include a large number of floral or geometric patterns, some of very high quality (Plate 198), others of relatively little merit (Plates 199–200). Some are printed with very bold designs, occasionally taken from copper plates engraved for other larger items (Plate 201). Some designs are so-called sheet patterns, which were not engraved to fit any specific shape (Plate 202). These would require little transferring skill, and were presumably cheaper to produce. Some wares with simple outline prints were probably intended for colouring over with enamels, but for some reason were issued unfinished (Plate 203).

Other subjects include classical scenes (Plate 204), an obvious legacy from the eighteenth-century influence of Josiah Wedgwood; designs based on literature (Plate 205); and patterns still exhibiting Chinese influence (Plate 206). This last jug is of a common octagonal shape also found with sprigged decoration (see Chapter 6) but more common with brightly coloured Japan patterns (see Chapter 9).

PLATE 198: *Good quality Spode felspar china jug printed in blue with a Union Wreath pattern, c.1825–33. Note the gadrooning around the shoulder. Printed mark 'SPODE'. Height 12.6 cm (size 9).*

PLATE 200: *Another unattributed small blue-printed jug of rather poor quality, c.1840–50. Note the ornately moulded body and handle. Height 10.8 cm.*

PLATE 201: *Covered earthenware jug with a strainer behind the mask spout, printed in blue by Copeland & Garrett, c.1833–40. The design is one of Spode's Botanical patterns, and it seems unlikely that it was originally engraved to fit this shape. Impressed and printed maker's marks including the body name 'NEW BLANCHE'. Height 26.3 cm (size 12).*

PLATE 199: *Anonymous small earthenware jug with a distinctive flared rim, printed underglaze in blue, c.1830–45. This floral pattern featuring chrysanthemums is typical of many rather nondescript designs of the period. Height 14.9 cm.*

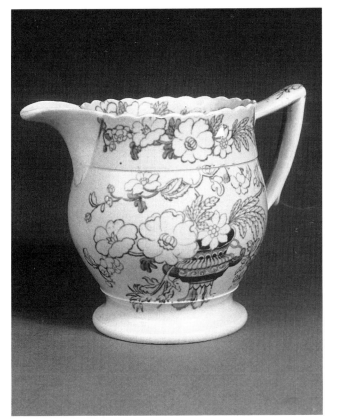

Top left:
PLATE 202: *Earthenware jug of a common octagonal shape, attributed to Swansea, c.1820–40. The blue-printed design is a typical sheet pattern, engraved to fit randomly on any shape. Height 14.2 cm.*

Above:
PLATE 204: *Tall earthenware wash ewer printed in blue with an Etruscan pattern, probably by Elkin, Knight & Bridgwood, c.1827–40. Height 26.4 cm (size 4).*

PLATE 203: *Crisply potted earthenware jug printed in blue, c.1820–30. The design is outline-printed, intended to be filled with coloured enamels. Although tentatively attributed to the Glamorgan Pottery at Swansea, similar wares were made at Sunderland. Height 12.0 cm.*

PLATE 205: *Two views of a simple earthenware jug by an unknown maker, printed in blue with a pattern titled 'Tam o'Shanter', c.1840. The designs are very similar to a relief-moulded jug published by William Ridgway & Co. in 1835. Printed title mark. Height 14.6 cm.*

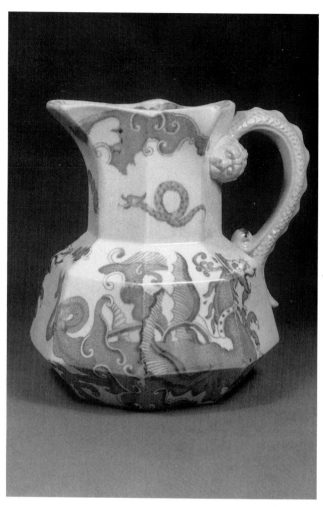

PLATE 206: *Typical Mason's ironstone china octagonal jug, this one printed in blue with a design of Chinese dragons, c.1820–25. Printed maker's crown and drape mark, also impressed 'MASON'S PATENT / IRONSTONE CHINA'. Height 18.5 cm.*

The predominance of country scenes diminished in the 1830s as floral and other designs became more popular, but their death knell was sounded by the Copyright Act of 1842. This effectively prohibited the potters from copying engravings in books, previously a lucrative design source. One result was the development of a rather flowery style of imaginary scenes, often grouped together under the loose heading of 'romantic' patterns. Normally printed in lighter blue, they follow a distinctive formula with hills in the background; a central river or lake with a building such as a castle, temple or pagoda on one bank; a tree overhanging from one side; and a feature such as a boat, vase, fountain or a group of people or animals in the foreground. Hundreds of these were made, often untitled (Plates 207–8), although many bear general titles such as 'Panorama' (Plate 209), or completely inappropriate placenames such as 'Andalusia', 'Corinth', 'Dacca', 'Rhine' or 'Athens' (Plate 210). Some were ornate and imaginative in the extreme (Plate 211).

PLATE 207: *Ornate earthenware jug by John Rogers & Son, printed in light blue with a romantic pattern, c.1835–42. Impressed mark 'ROGERS'. Height 19.1 cm.*

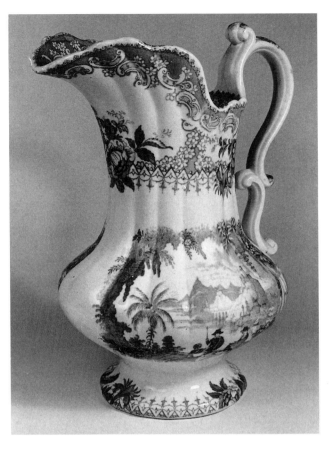

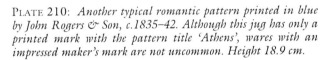

PLATE 209: *Tall wash jug with moulded body and ornate handle, printed in blue with the 'Panorama' pattern, c.1840–60. Unmarked, but the companion bowl has a printed vignette mark with title and factory name 'SOUTH/WALES POTTERY'. Height 29.8 cm.*

PLATE 210: *Another typical romantic pattern printed in blue by John Rogers & Son, c.1835–42. Although this jug has only a printed mark with the pattern title 'Athens', wares with an impressed maker's mark are not uncommon. Height 18.9 cm.*

PLATE 208: *Untitled romantic pattern in light blue on a simple earthenware jug by Davenport, c.1835–50. Printed mark 'DAVENPORT'. Height 15.5 cm.*

PLATE 211: *Utilitarian earthenware jug printed in blue by David Methven & Sons of the Kirkcaldy Pottery, Fife, c.1860–70. The highly imaginative pattern is titled 'Sultan' in a printed mark together with the maker's initials. Height 20.5 cm.*

PLATE 212: *Early 20th-century footed earthenware jug, printed in blue with rural scenes by James Kent at the Old Foley Pottery, Fenton. Printed globe and crown trademark with maker's name and address. Height 21.7 cm.*

Before leaving patterns printed in blue, it must be emphasized that, although superseded by about 1870, they never went entirely out of production. Some examples were made well into the present century (Plate 212). These late products rarely approach the quality of the classic wares from the 1820s, but some of them are workmanlike and successful in their own way.

While blue was the only colour technically suitable for underglaze printing at the end of the eighteenth century, other coloured inks were soon developed and wares can be found printed in mauve, grey, black and a few other colours from about 1810 or so. However, these early examples are uncommon and it was not until the mid-1820s that other coloured wares were produced in any quantity. The most common colours were black (Plates 213–15, Colour Plate 18), brown (Plates 216–18), green (Plates 219–21) and pink, although mulberry and various shades of red were also widely used (Plate 222). Yellow and grey (Plates 223–4) are amongst the less common colours.

As an aside, this last piece is an example of some very large jugs, some vast in size, often fitted with extra handles beneath the spout (Plates 180 and 219). They were normally intended for use in dairies or supplied along with matching footbaths (see for example Plate 493).

PLATE 213: *Earthenware jug of moulded form printed in black by Goodwin, Bridgwood & Harris of Lane End. The pattern commemorates the death of George IV in 1830. Printed lion mark with maker's initials. Height 13.7 cm.* (Courtesy: Sotheby's, Sussex)

PLATE 215: *Hexagonal jug by an unknown maker, printed in black with drinking scenes, c.1840–60. There is a verse with a clock on the front, and the words 'Labour in Vain' are printed on the base. Height 19.7 cm.* (Courtesy: Christie's, South Kensington)

PLATE 214: *Attractive unattributed earthenware jug printed in black with a rural scene titled 'Imperial', c.1830–40. Note the additional black lining on the rim, handle and foot. Printed title mark. Height 16.6 cm.*

PLATE 216: *Graduated set of three presentation jugs, printed in brown with landscapes by Baker, Bevans & Irwin of the Glamorgan Pottery, Swansea. The red-painted inscription reads 'Mr. Wm. Crang / Wheitefield / Barton / Challacombe / Bought at Swansea / By / Captn. Irwin / 1831'. Printed maker's marks. Height 15 to 21 cm.* (Courtesy: Dreweatt Neate, Newbury)

PLATE 217: *Another similar jug printed in brown by Baker, Bevans & Irwin. The maroon inscription reads 'Elizth. Jones/Born March 6th./1832'. Printed mark with 'Opaque China' and maker's initials. Height 13.4 cm.*

PLATE 218: *Two views of an unattributed tankard shape jug printed in brown with amusing cycling cartoons, c.1850–60. The 'Sailor's Velocipede' is an anchor whereas the 'Welchman' [sic] rides a goat with cheeses for wheels. Height 14.9 cm.*

COLOUR PLATE 1: *A group of five medieval jugs; Nottingham, 13th/early 14th century; Stamford, 15th century; Nottingham, 13th/early 14th century; Unattributed, 13th/14th century; Nottingham, 11th/12th century. Heights 36 cm, 28.8 cm, 39.3 cm, 20 cm, and 35.3 cm. (Courtesy: Sotheby's, London)*

COLOUR PLATE 2: *Two medieval baluster jugs from the 14th or 15th centuries. Heights 16 cm and 28 cm. (Courtesy: Sotheby's, London)*

COLOUR PLATE 3: *London delftware harvest jug painted in blue with the farmer's arms and related agricultural subjects. Note the initials with the date 1699 beneath the spout. Height 25.1 cm (approx).* (Courtesy: Sotheby's, London)

Opposite:
COLOUR PLATE 5: *Astbury-type Staffordshire jug, the reddish brown body sprigged in cream with the royal coat of arms and a band of running stags. Height 21 cm.* (Courtesy: Phillips, London)

COLOUR PLATE 4: *Fine Staffordshire slipware jug with a cream ground trailed in dark brown and dotted in cream. The decoration incorporates initials 'DS' and the date 1704. Height 23 cm.* (Courtesy: Sotheby's, London)

COLOUR PLATE 6: *Three Worcester cabbage-leaf moulded jugs, c.1760–5. The two smaller jugs feature puce flower sprays and landscapes enamelled in colours, the right-hand example probably painted by James Rogers. The larger jug has a yellow ground colourfully enamelled with flowers, and reserves with puce chinoiserie islands. Heights 19.5 cm, 29 cm, and 20 cm.* (Courtesy: Sotheby's, London)

COLOUR PLATE 7: *Flight & Barr jug painted by John Pennington in grisaille with a portrait of King George III, c.1790. This jug was reputedly produced to mark the King's visit to Worcester in 1788, when he ordered a set of china for the Queen. Gilded mark to base. Height 16.5 cm.* (Courtesy: Bonhams, Knightsbridge)

COLOUR PLATE 8: *Rare and impressive Cambrian Pottery jug, painted in the manner of George Stubbs by Thomas Pardoe, c.1800. Hand-painted mark 'CAMBRIAN' in gilt script. Height 26.8 cm. (Courtesy: Sotheby's, London)*

COLOUR PLATE 9: *Finely painted and gilt jug attributed to Spode, c.1815. Another panel on the reverse features a country shooting scene, and there are gilt initials 'JW' beneath the spout. Height 16 cm. (Courtesy: Sotheby's, London)*

COLOUR PLATE 10: *High quality Wedgwood Queen's Ware jug with a printed and enamelled design of music and dancing, c.1786. The reverse has a mounted cavalryman motif. Impressed 'WEDGWOOD'. Height 20.3 cm. (Courtesy: Trustees of the Wedgwood Museum, Barlaston, Staffordshire)*

COLOUR PLATE 11: *Barrel-shaped pearlware jug, made for the Pomfret family in 1806. The unusual design is hand-applied, probably using a sponge. Note all the family names in the roundel beneath the spout. Compare with another similar jug in Plate 654. Height 23.5 cm. (Courtesy: Dreweatt Neate, Newbury)*

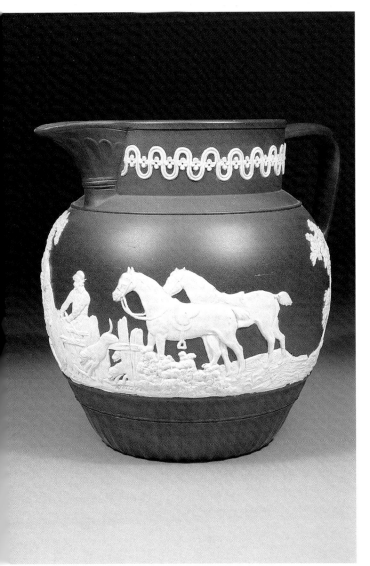

COLOUR PLATE 15: *Two similar Spode jugs, one in grey with blue sprigs, the other white with dark green sprigs, c.1810–25. A similar but poor quality example in drab stoneware can be seen in Plate 314. The smaller jug has impressed mark 'SPODE'. Heights 11.4 cm (size 36) and 17.8 cm.*

COLOUR PLATE 17: *Typical William Ridgway & Co. blue stoneware jug enamelled in colours, c.1835. This ornate Pompeii shape is relatively common. Moulded urn and anchor mark with maker's name, also gilt pattern number '190'. Height 15.2 cm (size 24).*

Left:
COLOUR PLATE 16: *Octagonal jug in unglazed redware, potted by Spode but decorated in the Copeland & Garrett period, c.1837. Impressed mark 'SPODE' with painted pattern number '5834'. A similar jug can be seen in Plate 679. Height 14 cm.*

Right:
PLATE 219: *Large earthenware dairy jug with additional handle beneath the spout, c. 1830. The unidentified floral design is printed in green. Height 38.8 cm.*

PLATE 220: *Spode earthenware jug of gadrooned antique shape, printed in green, c.1825. The pattern is number B143, a version of the firm's second Union Wreath design. Impressed and printed 'SPODE' marks. Height 26.7 cm.*

PLATE 221: *Another Spode antique shape jug printed in green, this time in felspar porcelain, c.1830. This pattern is known as English Sprays. Printed mark 'SPODE'. Height 14 cm.*

Left:
PLATE 222: *Moulded earthenware Reform jug, printed in puce, possibly by Baker, Bevans & Irwin of Swansea. The portraits show the promoters of reform and the reverse is inscribed 'Royal Assent to the Reform Bill, 7th June 1832'. Height 19.1 cm. (Courtesy: Christie's, South Kensington)*

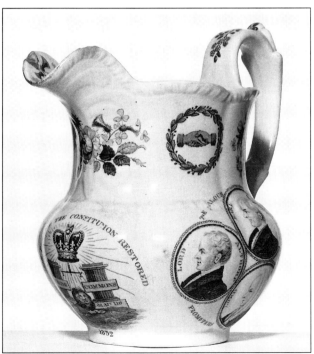

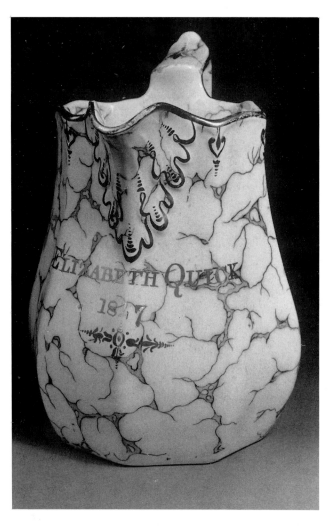

Opposite:
PLATE 225: *A group of six unattributed William IV commemorative jugs printed in various colours, c.1831-7. The four ornately moulded examples are very typical of the period. Heights between 12 cm and 21 cm.* (Courtesy: Bonhams, Knightsbridge)

The more widespread use of colours other than blue coincided with a period when commemorative jugs were popular. A group of such jugs, printed in a variety of colours, all relate to William IV (Plate 225). Note the ornate shapes, typical of the 1830s, marking a clear break away from the more traditional earlier shapes.

The novelty of printed designs inevitably faded with time, and it is not surprising that potters should have sought to introduce more attractive and saleable products. A few firms printed wares with the central design in one colour and the border in another, examples of which have been noted by Enoch Wood & Sons and Davenport. The expansion of this idea to genuine multi-colour printing was inevitable, and some attractive early wares were made, again by Davenport, in the 1830s. This author is not aware of any jugs amongst the surviving examples.

Davenport must be given credit for these early multi-colour printed wares, and they may well have pioneered the technique. However, it is widely associated with the firm of F. & R. Pratt & Co. of Fenton, who produced wares of great distinction. Unfortunately, examples have come to be known generically as Pratt wares, a confusion with the similarly named but moulded and underglaze-painted wares from earlier years (see Chapter 7). The new technique was applied particularly to pot lids, although some very attractive useful wares were made. Jugs are less common and often of relatively little merit. Two typical examples are shown here, the first of good quality, possibly made by T. J. & J. Mayer of Dale Hall (Plate 226), and the second by Morgan, Wood & Co. of Burslem (Plate 227). The dangers of attribution on the basis of pattern alone are amply demonstrated by this common design of shells, also shown on a wash jug and matching basin made by J. T. Close of Stoke (Plate 228). Without a magnifying glass, it can be surprisingly difficult to tell whether some designs are multi-colour printed, or printed in one colour and then carefully washed over (Plate 229).

PLATE 224: *Another grey-printed Swansea jug with the 'Lazuli' pattern. This large pail-like jug was almost certainly intended for use in a dairy. Printed title mark. Height 39.4 cm.*

Below:

PLATE 226: *Two views of a good quality jug with a maroon ground and gilt-framed reserves with multi-colour printed designs of cherubs, possibly made at the Dale Hall Pottery,* Longport. *Unmarked except for impressed date code for March 1873. Height 24.9 cm.* (Courtesy: City Museum & Art Gallery, Stoke-on-Trent)

83

PLATE 227: *Utilitarian earthenware jug with Britannia-metal cover, multi-colour printed by Morgan, Wood & Co. of Burslem, c.1860–70. This design of shells is relatively common. Printed bee mark with maker's initials. Height 24.3 cm.*

Another version of coloured printing associated with the Pratt firm features designs which appear very three-dimensional. They are usually found on terracotta bodies, often with classical scenes (Plate 230). Other subjects such as hunting, Eastern scenes and simple border designs were made, and several jugs are shown by Geoffrey Godden in *British Pottery, an Illustrated Guide.*

PLATE 228: *Ewer and basin with claret ground borders and gilt rims, multi-colour printed by J.T. Close of Stoke, c. 1865. Note the same design of shells as on the previous jug. Printed and impressed maker's marks. Height 23 cm.* (Courtesy: Phillips, London)

PLATE 229: *Rope-handled jug by G. F. Bowers of Tunstall, c.1854–5. This side shows the attack and capture of the Malakhoff by the French at Sebastopol, with the famous Light Cavalry charge at Balaclava on the reverse. Printed mark. Height 20 cm.* (Courtesy: Phillips, London)

Opposite:
PLATE 232: *Two views of a heavy earthenware tankard-shaped jug by Davenport, Banks & Co. of Etruria, c.1870. The portraits of 'Newton' and a lady are outline-printed in black with mauve enamelled grounds. The broad bands are enamelled in orange and the handle in black. Printed belt and castle trademark with maker's initials. Height 15.8 cm.*

Below:
PLATE 231: *Ochre-ground jug of a characteristic shape, attributed to G. L. Ashworth & Bros, c.1870. The classical figures are outline-printed in black and coloured over. This scene is titled 'Fight for the body of Patroclus'; the reverse has 'Diomed casting his spear against Mars'. Otherwise unmarked.*

PLATE 230: *Red terracotta jug strikingly printed in brown on yellow with a black ground, blue edges and gilding, c.1855–65. Although unmarked, this jug was almost certainly made by the Pratt firm at Fenton. Height 19.6 cm.* (Courtesy: City Museum & Art Gallery, Stoke-on-Trent)

Greek and other classical subjects made a considerable comeback in the second half of the nineteenth century. They were often outline-printed, with coloured grounds, one typical jug having two scenes featuring Diomed and Mars, and Patroclus (Plate 231). This example is unmarked, but others of the same series bear impressed marks for G. L. Ashworth & Brothers. A jug of similar type, decorated with broad orange bands and two portraits, one titled 'Newton', was made by Davenport, Banks & Co. of Etruria (Plate 232). Both these jugs are enhanced with some colouring, and they are closely related to wares decorated with outline prints which are then enamelled over (see Chapter 9).

The final jug is very typical of the late Victorian period, with an ornate but poorly moulded body, in this case printed with a simple border-like design in green (Plate 233). A large number of jugs like this were made, many with added colouring. Again these are discussed in Chapter 9.

Opposite:
PLATE 233: *Typical late Victorian jug printed in green with some gilding by the Ceramic Art Co. of Hanley. Printed vase mark with maker's name and address and design registration number 39268, dating from 1885. Height 17.1 cm.*

6.

Sprig-moulding

The use of sprig moulds to decorate pots dates back over many years. The process consists of making a small shallow mould, pressing wet clay into it, peeling out the resulting thin impression and attaching it to the surface of the pot using liquid clay or slip. The technique came to prominence with the advent of plaster of Paris in the mid-eighteenth century and sprigged decoration appears on several early jugs. They include examples with a Jackfield-type glaze (Plate 16, right), another streaked with tortoiseshell glaze (Plate 18) and a third in drab-coloured salt-glazed stoneware (Plate 22). Other examples are in fine redware (Plate 234, Colour Plate 5).

Although sprigging was used on earthenwares (Plate 235), it was more effective on stoneware-type bodies which required little or no surface glazing. These include the redwares mentioned above and related bodies developed by Wedgwood and his contemporaries such as black basalt (Plates 236–8), caneware (Plate 658) and jasper or jasper dip (Plate 239). For various reasons, particularly durability or cost, few of these proved ideal for mass-produced utilitarian wares. They were better suited to ornamental pieces and also more successful for tewares.

The search for improved bodies covered both earthenwares and stonewares, but one significant success is attributed to John Turner of Lane End. He used some fine white clay to great effect in a hard, dense stoneware which has come to be known as Turner's body. Many marked Turner jugs have survived, usually thrown in the traditional way on the potter's wheel, although some are oval and were made in a mould (Plate 240). The body is usually off-white with the necks ring-turned and covered with a dark brown glaze (Plates 241–2). Some are more creamy in colour (Plates 243–4), and one with an impressive serpent handle and spout is an unusual light oatmeal colour (Plate 245). Some feature a coloured background, usually brown or blue, to highlight the sprigs, but this is normally restricted to the neck (Plate 246).

PLATE 234: *Good-quality sprig decorated redware jug, probably made in Staffordshire, c.1755–65. Touches of gilding can be discerned on some of the sprigging. Height 10.9 cm.*

In view of Turner's success, other potters inevitably made similar wares. Some excellent examples come from the Adams factories, one shown here being almost indistinguishable from Turner versions except that the neck is much darker, almost black (Plate 247). Most are simply impressed with the surname, but some slightly later examples are marked 'B. ADAMS' for Benjamin Adams of Greengates (Plate 248).

Turner's body is slightly translucent and other potters' versions range from fine and highly translucent porcellanous or felspathic stonewares right through to dense, opaque bodies of varying quality. A rare marked example by Wedgwood & Co. is semi-translucent, probably felspathic (Plate 249).

Opposite:
PLATE 235: *Pearlware jug with mask spout, c.1780. The body is decorated with marbled slip and applied with a portrait medallion inscribed 'ADMIRAL RODNEY' suspended from green oak branches. Height 20 cm.* (Courtesy: Christie's, London)

PLATE 238: *Heavy black basalt jug by Adams, sprigged with cupid scenes. Impressed mark 'ADAMS / ESTBd 1657' with initials 'JC'. Wares of this type can be difficult to date although marks containing a claimed date of establishment usually indicate the late 19th or early 20th century. Height 16.6 cm. (Courtesy: City Museum & Art Gallery, Stoke-on-Trent)*

PLATE 236: *Large Wedgwood & Bentley black basalt ewer of helmet shape, sprigged with groups of putti, c.1770–80. The large size and the fact that this partnership did not normally make utilitarian wares suggest that this was intended more for ornament. Impressed mark 'WEDGWOOD & BENTLEY'. Height 28.6 cm. (Courtesy: Christie's, London)*

PLATE 237: *Fine quality Wedgwood black basalt jug, decorated with sprigging and engine-turning, c.1780–90. Impressed mark 'Wedgwood'. (Courtesy: Christie's, London)*

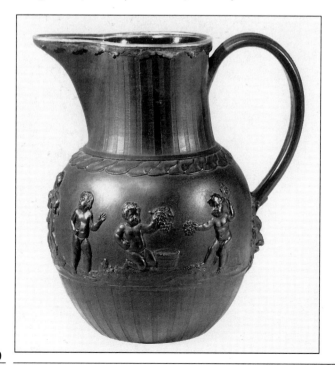

PLATE 239: *Fine quality blue jasper dip jug with white sprigs made by William Adams, c.1790–1800. Impressed mark 'ADAMS'. Height 18.4 cm. (Courtesy: City Museum & Art Gallery, Stoke-on-Trent)*

PLATE 242: *Another good quality Turner stoneware jug with brown neck, c.1790–1805. Impressed mark 'TURNER'. Height 25.7 cm.*

PLATE 243: *Turner jug of cream-coloured stoneware with brown neck, fitted with a heavily tarnished metal lid, c.1790–1800. Impressed mark 'TURNER'. Height 24 cm. (Courtesy: City Museum & Art Gallery, Stoke-on-Trent)*

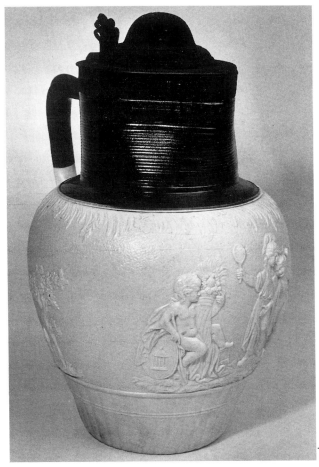

PLATE 241: *Turner stoneware jug with brown ring-turned neck, sprigged with a scene of huntsmen in front of an inn, c.1795–1810. Impressed mark 'TURNER'. Height 20.1 cm.*

PLATE 244: *Another cream-coloured stoneware jug by Turner, c.1790–1800. The low creamer-like shape belies its size. Impressed mark 'TURNER'. Height 17.3 cm.* (Courtesy: City Museum & Art Gallery, Stoke-on-Trent)

Right:
PLATE 247: *Stoneware jug with a black neck and foot, very similar to examples by Turner, but this one by William Adams, c.1800–10. Impressed mark 'ADAMS'. Height 26.6 cm.* (Courtesy: City Museum & Art Gallery, Stoke-on-Trent)

PLATE 245: *Impressive Turner jug of light-cane coloured stoneware with a moulded serpent handle and spout, c.1785–95. Impressed mark 'TURNER'. Height 20.3 cm.*

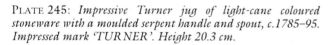

PLATE 246: *Low Turner stoneware jug with brown background to the sprigged border around the neck, c.1790–1800. Impressed mark 'TURNER'. Height 10.1 cm.* (Courtesy: City Museum & Art Gallery, Stoke-on-Trent)

PLATE 248: *Typical early 19th-century sprigged stoneware jug, this one by Benjamin Adams, c.1810–20. Impressed mark 'B. ADAMS'. Height 16.6 cm.*

PLATE 250: *Typical early 19th-century sprigged stoneware jug with brown enamelled neck, this one by Thomas & John Hollins of Shelton, c.1805–15. Variants of this hunting scene were commonly used by many other potters. Impressed mark 'T & J Hollins'. Height 13.3 cm.*

PLATE 251: *Another stoneware jug with the common sprigged hunting scene, this one by Davenport, c.1810–20. Note the gilded rim and the additional brown line round the foot. Impressed mark 'Davenport' over an anchor. Height 16.1 cm.*

PLATE 249: *Rare marked stoneware jug by Wedgwood & Co., probably made at Burslem, c.1790–5. The felspathic body has been engine-turned, and the ringed neck is enamelled with brown and yellow bands. Impressed mark 'Wedgwood & Co'. Height 10 cm.* (Courtesy: Jack Hacking)

White stoneware jugs with coloured necks were made well into the nineteenth century, although later examples usually have a more noticeable smear glaze, giving a sheen to the surface. Typical examples were made by T. & J. Hollins (Plate 250), Davenport (Plates 251–2), Ridgway (Plate 253) and Spode (Plate 254). Many are decorated with a common hunting scene, although with detailed differences, and attributions on the basis of this scene are dubious. Even the Spode version, apparently quite distinctive, was used at other factories.

It was not long before coloured bodies were introduced, some developed fairly early by Samuel Hollins, who often used a metallic process to simulate metal mounts. His jugs still have sprigs in the same colour as the main body, as does an example by Spode (Plate 255), but the decorative potential of contrasting colours was soon exploited. One interesting example with white sprigs on a marbled body was made at the Herculaneum Pottery (Plate 256).

PLATE 254: *Spode's variant of the hunting scene on a typical jug with a brown enamelled neck, c.1810–20. Note the stippled surface. Even this relatively distinctive version was used by other potters. Impressed mark 'SPODE'. Height 15 cm.*

PLATE 252: *This Davenport jug with a brown neck is sprigged with a scene of Topers, c.1805–25. Both this and the previous hunting scene are relatively common, and must have been a standard production line. Impressed mark 'Davenport' above an anchor. Height 16.3 cm.* (Courtesy: Jack Hacking)

PLATE 253: *The common sprigged hunting scene again, this jug made by Ridgway, c.1815–25. The rim is black and the shape of the top of the handle, which can just be seen, is quite distinctive. Impressed mark 'Ridgway'. Height 13.6 cm.*

PLATE 255: *Sprigged jug of glazed drab-coloured earthenware, made by Spode, c.1805–15. Once again, the sprigged design of Bacchanalian Boys, based on a Bartolozzi engraving, was used at several other factories. A strainer spout suggests there may once have been a matching lid. Impressed mark 'SPODE'. Height 13.3 cm.*

PLATE 256: *Distinctive sprigged jug by the Herculaneum Pottery of Liverpool, c.1800–10. The oval body is marbled using cream and brown clays. Impressed mark 'HERCULANEUM'. Height 17.2 cm.* (Courtesy: Jack Hacking)

Jugs like this were largely superseded by the 1830s, partly by competition from blue-printed wares and partly by the rise of relief-moulding (see Chapter 8). However, sprigging never died out and one interesting jug by G. F. Booth & Co. of Hanley was published as late as 1839 (Plate 276). By this time sprigging was mostly out of favour, but some lower-quality earthenwares were still made, such as a pouch-shaped jug from Swansea (Plate 277).

PLATE 257: *Typical fine quality white felspathic stoneware jug with brown ground behind the sprigs, c.1800–10. Many unmarked and unattributed wares like this have survived. Height 20.8 cm.*

PLATE 258: *Stoneware jug with brown ground, this one by David Wilson of Hanley, c.1800–15. Marked wares of this type are uncommon. Wilson is better known for his solid colour jugs – see, for example, Plates 260 and 261. Impressed mark 'WILSON'. Height 12.9 cm.*

Contrast was more commonly achieved using coloured backgrounds. A matt brown ground was perhaps the most usual, followed by blue, and very rarely green. Jugs of this type are almost invariably unmarked (Plate 257), but a few were marked by David Wilson of Hanley (Plate 258). The same type of decoration was also used on simpler earthenwares, such as one small jug by Wood & Caldwell with an olive-green ground (Plate 259). These earthenware versions appear relatively crude and unsatisfactory, largely due to their overall glaze.

A more definite contrast could, of course, be achieved more easily with coloured bodies rather than coloured grounds, and Wilson used this style to great effect. He produced fine-quality jugs, usually in drab or shades of brown, many of which are clearly marked (Plates 260–1, Colour Plate 12). Others can be attributed with a fair degree of confidence (Plate 262). Similar jugs were made by Ralph & James Clews (Plate 263), Ridgway (Plates 264–5, Colour Plate 13), Spode (Plate 266) and in the early 1830s Minton (Plates 267–9). These all feature white sprigs but others, equally attractive, can be found with coloured sprigs, including again jugs by Minton (Plate 270), Ridgway (Plate 271), Spode (Plate 272), Wedgwood (Plates 273–4), and a particularly rare example by Davenport (Plate 275).

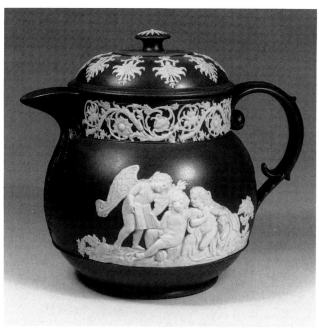

PLATE 259: *Glazed white earthenware jug with drab olive-green ground and white sprigs, by Wood & Caldwell, c.1810–18. Sprigged earthenwares like this are of poor quality compared to the more suitable stoneware bodies. Impressed mark 'WOOD & CALDWELL'. Height 9.6 cm. (Courtesy: Jack Hacking)*

PLATE 262: *Brown stoneware jug with white sprigs, white slip interior and strainer spout with matching lid, c. 1800–15. Although unmarked, this shows all the characteristics of jugs made by Wilson. Height 17.9 cm.*

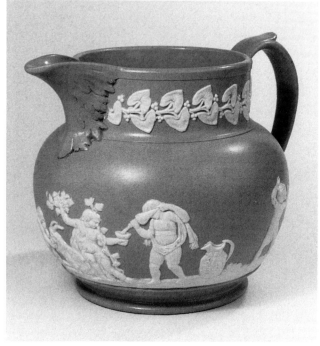

PLATE 260: *A typical solid colour stoneware jug with white slip interior, sprigged in white with cupid scenes by David Wilson of Hanley, c.1800–15. This example is drab in colour and the design matches the brown background jug in Plate 258. Impressed mark 'WILSON'. Height 16.9 cm.*

PLATE 263: *Grey stoneware jug with white sprigs by Ralph & James Clews of Cobridge, c.1815–25. This sprigged design was also used by other potters, particularly Ridgway (see Plates 265 and 271). Impressed mark 'CLEWS'. Height 15.6 cm.*

Left:
PLATE 261: *Smaller Wilson jug in dark reddish-brown stoneware with white slip interior and white sprigs, c.1800–15. Wilson made a large number of these jugs in various shapes, colours and sizes. Impressed mark 'WILSON'. Height 10.1 cm.*

PLATE 264: *Very typical Ridgway straw-coloured stoneware jug with white sprigs, c.1815–25. This Gryphon design appears on other shapes and also on china (see Plate 284), but jugs of this type were made by other potters. Rare impressed mark 'Ridgway'. Height 13.1 cm.* (Courtesy: Jack Hacking)

PLATE 266: *Brown stoneware jug with white sprigs by Spode, c.1810–30. The design of Bacchanalian Boys was used by several other makers – see, for example Plate 274. Impressed mark 'SPODE'. Height 17.8 cm.*

PLATE 267: *Grey stoneware jug with white sprigs by Minton, c.1830–1. This jug design is also found with sprigged and printed designs relating to the coronation of King William IV and Queen Adelaide. Applied white moulded scroll mark with model 'No. 14' and cursive initial 'M'. Height 18.3 cm.*

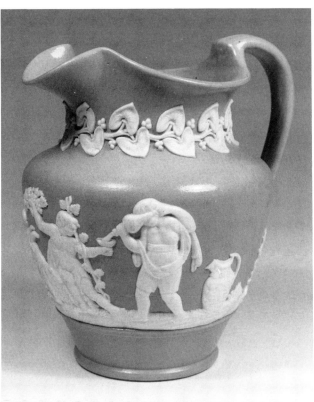

PLATE 265: *Another Ridgway stoneware jug, this one in grey with white sprigs, c.1815–25. This design is common, see also Plates 263 and 271. Applied white lozenge mark containing model number '37', which may well be incorrect; this colour combination should be numbered 229. Height 13.7 cm.*

PLATE 268: *Uncommon Minton grey-green stoneware jug with white sprigs, c.1835–40. Applied white moulded scroll mark with model 'No. 145' and cursive initial 'M'. Height 16.7 cm.*

PLATE 269: *Minton jug in sage green stoneware with white sprigs, c.1830. This is one of the earliest designs in Minton's model numbering sequence and was made in several colour combinations. Applied white moulded scroll mark with model 'No. 7' and cursive initial 'M'. Height 19.1 cm.*

PLATE 271: *Ridgway jug in straw-coloured stoneware with brown sprigs, c.1815–25. This is an unusual colour combination of the design in Plate 265. Applied brown lozenge mark containing model number '228'. Height 13.6 cm.*

PLATE 272: *Brown stoneware jug with white slip interior and blue sprigs, by Spode, c.1810–20. Note how some of the sprigs have broken away, making this an unusual faulty product from a normally excellent factory. Impressed mark 'SPODE'. Height 13.4 cm.*

PLATE 274: *Unusual Wedgwood jug in yellow jasper with black basalt sprigs, c.1805–20. This design is more common in ordinary earthenwares and stonewares, and was also used by other factories (see Plate 266). Impressed mark 'WEDGWOOD'. Height 18.5 cm.* (Courtesy: Jack Hacking)

PLATE 273: *Wedgwood jug in drab stoneware with very pale blue, almost white sprigs, c.1810–20. Impressed mark 'WEDG-WOOD'. Height 11.4 cm.*

Right:
PLATE 275: *Two views of a rare Davenport jug in white stoneware with blue sprigs, c.1810–30. This is an unrecorded design and the first to be found with coloured sprigs. Impressed mark 'DAVENPORT' over an anchor. Height 13.9 cm.*

PLATE 276: *White stoneware jug of unconventional design published by the little known G. F. Booth & Co. of Hanley in 1839. The blue sprigs include one Aesop's Fables subject, but another similar jug has been noted with an unidentified portrait medallion. Blue applied mark beneath handle 'PUBLISHED BY G.F. BOOTH & Co / HANLEY, STAFFORDSHIRE, / MAY 23 1839'. Height 12 cm.*

A large proportion of the jugs made before 1830 do not bear makers' marks. They include most colour combinations, some plain (Plate 278), some white with coloured sprigs (Plate 279) and others with both body and sprigs coloured (Plate 280). One interesting variation is a set of three felspathic stoneware jugs with brown backgrounds to the common hunting scene, but with the entire design enamelled in colours (Plate 281).

The Ridgway jugs included above are mostly from a range of wares in either stoneware or china, usually sprigged but sometimes moulded or ring-turned, often marked with an applied lozenge containing a model number (Plate 282). The attribution to Ridgway is discussed in *Staffordshire Porcelains* by Geoffrey Godden, who holds an original matching pattern book. The previous examples (Plates 265 and 271, Colour Plate 13) are potted in stoneware, while several others from the same series were made in china, usually with either blue or lavender sprigs (Plate 283). Another jug of this type bears a relatively rare impressed mark (Plate 284), the design matching a similarly marked stoneware example (Plate 264). The combination of white china with lavender or blue sprigs was fairly common in the second quarter of the nineteenth century, and some wares are of relatively low quality (Plate 285). Others can be superb, like one marked Spode example shown here (Plate 286), and another unmarked jug from the same factory (Plate 287).

PLATE 278: *Unusual biscuit-like stoneware jug, c.1780–1800. The amusing scene shows four corpulent Georgian gentlemen in a strong wind, one losing his wig. Height 13.9 cm.* (Courtesy: City Museum & Art Gallery, Stoke-on-Trent)

PLATE 277: *Glazed blue earthenware pouch-shaped jug with white sprigs made at Swansea, c.1845–50. Moulded scroll cartouche mark containing 'CYMRO/STONE/CHINA'. Height 14.6 cm.* (Courtesy: Jack Hacking)

PLATE 279: *Attractive but unattributed white stoneware jug with the common hunting scene in blue, c.1815–30. Inverted variants of this simple floral border appear on sprigged wares by Spode and Hackwood. Height 17.5 cm.*

PLATE 280: *Unattributed jug in cane stoneware with brown sprigs, c.1815–30. This hunting scene, while encountered less frequently than the very common version, was still used by several different makers. Height 15.8 cm.*

PLATE 281: *Set of three jugs in white felspathic stoneware with a brown ground, sprigged in white with the common hunting scene, c.1810–20. The sprigs have been enamelled in green, yellow, brown, grey, ochre and orange. Heights between 9 cm and 13.6 cm.*

PLATE 282: *Typical applied lozenge-shaped pad mark used for sprigged and other stonewares and china by Ridgway in the 1815–30 period. The range of model numbers exceeds 500. Similar marks were used by the Don Pottery, with 'DON' in the centre, by the Scotts of Sunderland, with 'Scott' in the centre (see Plate 671), and by a French manufacturer.*

PLATE 286: *Fine quality Spode china jug of low Dutch shape with blue ground and added gilding, c.1810–20. The sprigged design is based on 'The Dead Hog', one of the firm's Indian Sporting patterns, better known on blue printed earthenwares. Red-painted mark 'SPODE'. Height 14.9 cm.*

PLATE 283: *Impressive Ridgway covered jug in white china with lavender sprigs, c.1820–30. Applied white lozenge mark containing model number '468'. Height 23.8 cm.*

PLATE 284: *Ridgway jug of a relatively common design, this example in white china with a lavender-blue ground, c.1815–20. A similar marked jug in stoneware is shown in Plate 264. Impressed mark 'Ridgway'. Height 13.3 cm.*

PLATE 287: *Similar but unmarked Spode jug with a chocolate brown ground and added gilding, c.1810–20. The sprigs feature figures by Lady Templetown and are certainly not unique to Spode. Height 10.2 cm.*

PLATE 288: *Typical applied flower-shaped pad mark found on sprigged and relief-moulded stonewares from the 1815–35 period. For convenience, the unidentified maker has been dubbed the Chrysanthemum factory. The model numbers range up to at least 97.*

Returning to the stonewares, unmarked examples are frequently attributed to Ridgway, although many were made by other unidentified potters. Several makers adopted applied 'pad' marks containing model numbers, one common example being in the shape of a flower-head with a number in the centre (Plate 288). The maker is not known but for convenience the name Chrysanthemum factory has been coined. The wares date mainly from the period 1815–35 and are typified by

one characteristic jug with a serpent handle and spout made in various colour combinations (Plates 289–90). Different colours bear different model numbers, and other designs shown here are numbered between 5 and 54 (Plates 291–6). One jug numbered 43 has been reported with the gilt date 1828.

Although the last of these is sprigged, the main body is ornately moulded, and the factory went on to produce a range of relief-moulded jugs with model numbers ranging up to 97. These moulded wares seem to dominate from model number 61 onwards and the shift away from sprigging probably dates from around 1830. Some unmarked jugs exhibit all the characteristics of the marked wares, and two shown here appear to be from this Chrysanthemum factory (Plates 297–8).

Another pad mark from this period features two angels holding a banner bearing a model number (Plate 299). This is again found on sprigged stonewares (Plates 300 and 659), but in this case also on china (Plate 301). Yet another applied mark has a model number circled by the trade name 'Imperial Stone' (Plate 302). Three drab stoneware examples are shown here, numbered 24, 26, and 31 (Plates 303–5). A similar jug which appears to come from the same series (Plate 306) bears an ornate scroll mark with the wording 'Imperial Stone, Royal Clarence' (Plate 307).

PLATE 289: *Characteristic jug design from the Chrysanthemum factory, c.1815–25, sprigged with a hunting scene already seen in Plate 280. This example has a strainer spout and matching cover and is in cane-coloured stoneware with white sprigs. Applied white chrysanthemum pad mark containing model number '15'. Height 18.4 cm.*

PLATE 290: *The same Chrysanthemum factory jug design, this example in brown stoneware with white sprigs, c.1815–25. Applied white chrysanthemum pad mark containing model number '20'. Height 14.6 cm.*

PLATE 291: *Impressive and good quality covered jug by the Chrysanthemum factory in blue stoneware, c.1815–25. These white classical figure sprigs are commonly found. As with almost all covered jugs, there is a strainer behind the spout. Applied white chrysanthemum pad mark containing model number '5'. Height 21.4 cm.*

PLATE 292: *White classical figure sprigs again feature on this cane-coloured stoneware Chrysanthemum factory jug, c.1815–25. Applied white chrysanthemum pad mark containing model number '9'. Height 23.3 cm.*

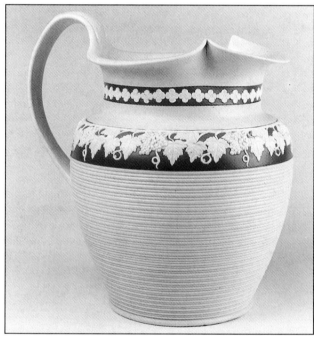

PLATE 293: *Simple but very effective jug by the Chrysanthemum factory, c.1815–25. The body is ring-turned in light cane-coloured stoneware with blue grounds to the white border sprigs. Applied white chrysanthemum pad mark containing model number '12'. Height 22 cm.*

PLATE 294: *Another typical Chrysanthemum factory jug, again decorated with white classical figure sprigs, c.1815–25. The cane-coloured stoneware body is engine-turned around the base, a characteristic also visible in Plates 289–91. Applied white chrysanthemum pad mark containing model number '16'. Height 18.6 cm.*

PLATE 295: *Blue-stoneware jug of large creamer-type, Chrysanthemum factory, c.1820–30. The white sprigged border is of a typical design (see also Plate 291), and the lyre-like sprigs around the neck occur on other maker's wares – see, for example, Plate 303. Applied white chrysanthemum pad mark containing model number '37'. Height 10.5 cm.*

PLATE 297: *Impressive jug in blue stoneware with white sprigs, c.1815–20. The reverse has a scene identified as 'Grouse Shooting in the Forest of Bowland', used by several manufacturers. Although unmarked, this jug exhibits several Chrysanthemum factory characteristics; compare it with Plates 289–91. Height 19 cm.*

PLATE 298: *Another unmarked jug possibly made by the Chrysanthemum factory, c.1815–25. This combination of white stoneware with a glazed blue ground is found on marked examples; compare it also with Plates 291 and 294. Height 10.1 cm.*

PLATE 296: *Typical mid-period Chrysanthemum factory jug in blue stoneware with ornately moulded body and white sprigs, c.1825–30. Applied white chrysanthemum pad mark containing model number '54'. Height 19.5 cm.*

PLATE 299: *Another pad mark found on sprigged stonewares and also china from the 1815–35 period. It has been called the Angels with Banner mark, or more simply the Angels pad mark. The model numbers range up to at least 115.*

Above:
PLATE 300: *Small but typical stoneware jug bearing the Angels pad mark, c.1815–30. The grey stoneware body has been ring-turned and engine-turned. Note also the impressed herring-bone pattern beneath the white border sprig. For a related example see Plate 659. Applied white Angels pad mark containing model number '68'. Height 9.7 cm.*

Above Right:
PLATE 301: *White china jug with blue sprigs, also bearing the Angels pad mark, in this case containing the model number '87'. Height 15 cm.* (Courtesy: Jack Hacking)

Right:
PLATE 302: *Another pad mark found on an interesting range of sprigged stonewares by an unknown maker from the first quarter of the 19th century. Known model numbers are low, ranging up to only 31.*

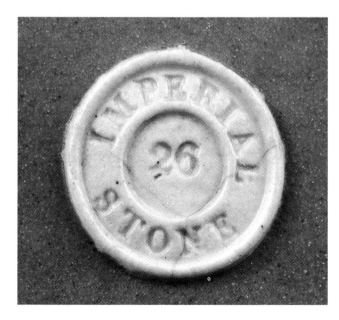

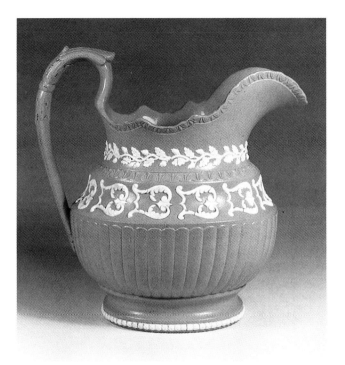

PLATE 305: *Good-quality Imperial Stone jug in drab stoneware with white Aesop's Fables sprigs, c.1820–30. Again the body is of moulded form, and the same basic design appears in china with adjacent model number 30 on an oval pad mark. Applied white circular pad mark with 'IMPERIAL STONE' around the model number '31'. Height 17 cm.*

PLATE 303: *Drab stoneware jug of excellent quality by the Imperial Stone factory, c.1820–30. The body is slightly oval, moulded and applied with white sprigs and beading. Applied white circular pad mark with 'IMPERIAL STONE' around the model number '24'. Height 21.3 cm.*

PLATE 304: *Another Imperial Stone jug in drab stoneware with white sprigs, c.1820–30. Although of lesser quality than the previous example, this jug provides a link to a range of sprigged china wares with an oval pad mark; the same basic design appear in china with adjacent model number 27. Applied white circular pad mark with 'IMPERIAL STONE' around the model number '26'. Height 19.5 cm.*

PLATE 306: *Although with a slightly different form of mark, this drab stoneware jug must originate from the same factory as the previous three examples. Applied white ribbon mark with trade name 'Imperial Stone' and title 'Royal Clarence' (see Plate 307). Height 18.4 cm.*

107

PLATE 307: *Scroll variant of the 'Imperial Stone' pad mark on the drab stoneware jug shown in Plate 306.*

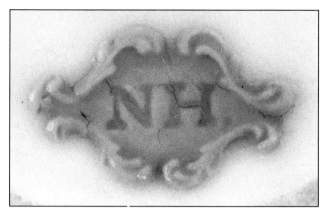

PLATE 308: *Uncommon pad mark with initials 'NH' within a scroll cartouche. This mark appears on the jug in Plate 309. Although for obvious reasons it has been linked with the New Hall factory, recent discoveries include jugs with similar marks containing N1 and N2.*

Most of the pad-marked jugs previously discussed are stoneware, but a fair number were made of china. One group, usually found with lilac-coloured sprigs, have an oval-shaped pad mark, and since the designs appear to be closely related to the 'Imperial Stone' examples, with adjacent model numbers, they may well have been made at the same factory. Other pad marks are shield or star-shaped, and one which has aroused much speculation features the initials 'NH' in a scroll cartouche (Plate 308). It has been suggested that these stand for New Hall, but there are significant doubts. The jug shown is very typical (Plate 309).

One final group of pad-marked stonewares bear a rectangular mark (Plate 310). The example shown here in model 115 is typical, in white stoneware with blue sprigs (Plate 311), and another unmarked jug may be related (Plate 312). The numbers recorded to date range between 114 and 209, and since the designs do not correspond with the Ridgway pattern book, we must look elsewhere for the manufacturer.

Another group of well-known but unidentified jugs are of the common octagonal form associated with Mason's ironstone, although these are impressed 'Oriental'. They are usually in grey stoneware with white or blue sprigs (Plate 313, Colour Plate 14), although other colours are occasionally found, as are examples in white china with lavender-coloured sprigs. The name 'Oriental' is a widely used trade name for this jug shape, but the significance on these wares is unclear. Interestingly enough a similarly marked matching covered sucrier is in the author's collection, so the name appears to refer to the general design rather than just the jug shape. Several potters made similar octagonal jugs, including Spode (Plate 314, Colour Plate 15) and one unidentified potter whose jugs have survived in significant numbers (Plate 315).

PLATE 309: *White china jug with lavender-blue sprigs by an unknown maker, c.1815–30. The main floral spray sprig appears on other jugs of a similar shape but with a different handle, some bearing the Angels pad mark, others a shield-shaped mark. Applied lavender-blue scroll cartouche mark containing initials 'NH' (see Plate 308). Height 12.7 cm.*

PLATE 310: *Less commonly encountered rectangular pad mark found on some sprigged stonewares from the 1815–30 period. At the time of writing few examples have been recorded, but model numbers range between 114 and 209.*

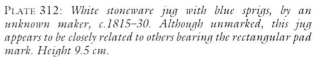

PLATE 312: *White stoneware jug with blue sprigs, by an unknown maker, c.1815–30. Although unmarked, this jug appears to be closely related to others bearing the rectangular pad mark. Height 9.5 cm.*

PLATE 311: *The most common design of jug found with the rectangular pad mark, always in white stoneware with blue sprigs, c.1815–30. The same sprigs appear on a Dutch-shape jug with model number 160. Applied blue rectangular pad mark containing model number '115'. Height 11.1 cm.*

PLATE 313: *Two very typical octagonal grey stoneware jugs bearing the unexplained impressed mark 'ORIENTAL'. The example on the left has blue sprigs and an impressed number '1', the other has white sprigs and number '66'. At least thirteen different figure sprigs are known. Similar examples in white china with lavender-blue sprigs are impressed '77'. Heights 12.1 and 11 cm.*

PLATE 314: *Spode octagonal jug in drab stoneware of unusually poor quality, c.1810–25. The same basic design in contrasting colours can be seen on two jugs of much higher quality in Colour Plate 15. Impressed mark 'SPODE'. Height 12.4 cm (size 30).*

PLATE 315: *Another frequently encountered octagonal jug, c.1820–30. These are in a heavy yellow-drab stoneware with turquoise sprigs, always unmarked, and are distinguished by the small foot rim, unusual on jugs of this common shape. Height 21.7 cm.*

The move away from sprigged decoration around 1830 was probably inspired in part by the high wages commanded by skilled workmen. Relief-moulding was easier and cheaper. However, the change was a gradual process and some attractive hybrid jugs were made, basically relief-moulded but with additional sprigged decoration. Examples from the Chrysanthemum and 'Imperial Stone' factories have been mentioned (Plates

296, 303–6), and two jugs by Wedgwood are shown here (Plates 316–17). These are both moulded with a hunting scene and sprigged with a grapevine border, although the shapes and colours differ.

Another puzzling name, rather akin to 'Oriental', which appears on sprigged jugs made in the third quarter of the nineteenth century is 'Milan'. These jugs are of a distinctive shape although several different versions are known, each with the impressed name and a model number. The most common are in heavy white stoneware with a ring-turned body and white sprigs on a jasper-dip neck (Plate 318), but other variants occur (Plate 319). One example is particularly unusual with a dense terracotta body and black sprigs (Plate 320). These jugs have been the subject of much speculation, including one popular attribution to Dudson. However, one example with a rouletted rather than sprigged neck is impressed with initials 'T.B. & S', possibly relating to Thomas Booth & Sons (Plate 321).

This leads us to wares known to have been made at the Dudson factory, which can be traced back to the beginning of the nineteenth century. Few early products have been identified but by 1850 or so the firm was producing a wide range of goods, still mainly unmarked but fortunately recognized through the pioneering work of Audrey Dudson and her book *Dudson, A Family of Potters Since 1800*. The firm specialized particularly in sprigged and moulded wares, and jugs formed a large proportion of the output. Many are recognizable by their ubiquitous tankard shape, and by the use of incised numbers on the base. It is convenient to consider these as model numbers, although they were probably used in the production process, perhaps to identify which sprigs should be applied. Whatever the reason, the numbers are distinctive and are generally acceptable for attribution purposes.

PLATE 316: *Drab stoneware moulded jug with white sprigged border by Wedgwood, c.1820–30. This design must have been popular, as several variants were made in different colours. Impressed mark 'WEDGWOOD'. Height 20.6 cm.*

PLATE 317: *Wedgwood moulded jug of similar design to the previous example but of a different basic shape, c.1815–30. This one is in white stoneware with blue sprigged border. Impressed mark 'WEDGWOOD'. Height 11.8 cm.*

(Right):
PLATE 318: *White stoneware jug with ring-turned body and white sprigs on a blue neck, c.1870–80. This is a typical example from a series of jugs by an unknown maker, all impressed with the mystery name 'MILAN', possibly relating to the shape, along with a model number, in this case '47'. This side shows the Archery Lesson, copied from a much earlier Turner sprig design. Height 19.4 cm (size 12).*

PLATE 319: *Another 'Milan' jug, this one with overall dark-blue jasper dip, c.1870–80. The sprig shown depicts Samuel and Eli; the reverse has Hamlet. Impressed mark 'MILAN' with model number '52'. Height 19.3 cm (size 12).*

PLATE 320: *Untypical 'Milan' jug of the usual shape but with red terracotta body and black sprigs, c.1870–80. This example has the impressed mark 'MILAN' but the adjacent model number is indistinct, possibly '164'. Height 20.1 cm.*

PLATE 321: *This typical 'Milan' jug is decorated with a rouletted design rather than sprigs around the neck. In addition to the usual name 'MILAN' with model number '50', it is also impressed with the trade name 'PATENT MOSAIC' relating to the rouletting technique, and initials 'T.B & S'. These have not yet been positively identified, but may relate to Thomas Booth & Sons. Height 14.5 cm (size 30).*

Lower numbers appear on some attractive jugs in a straw-coloured stoneware with contrasting sprigs (Plates 322–3), or on jugs decorated with white sprigs on a jasper dip ground (Plate 324). The latter are often of tankard shape with a small overhang at the base (Plate 325). The later, more standard tankard shape is straight at the base, either covered with jasper dip (Plates 326–7) or of solid-coloured stoneware, most commonly brown or green, but sometimes grey, black or blue. The handle is usually a twisted rope design, but a crabstock handle also occurs (Plate 328). Some other shapes were also made (Plates 329–30). A very wide range of sprigs were used, many also found on wares from other factories. Attribution on the basis of sprigs alone would be inadvisable, but some unmarked jugs are almost certainly of Dudson origin (Plate 331).

The firm's customers included other potters who presumably found it cheaper and easier to subcontract orders for jugs. This explains the presence of the initials of the Brownhills Pottery Company on some obvious Dudson wares (Plates 327, 332–3). Another interesting collaboration concerns a design registered by Ridgway but manufactured by Dudson (Plate 334). Some jugs also bear impressed names which have not yet been explained, although they may relate to retailers. One such customer named Paxton must have been important, since many examples have survived (Plates 328 and 335).

Many of these sprig-decorated tankard jugs were produced by Dudson, but some other firms made them. As a general rule they are unmarked, but one has an impressed mark for Adams & Bromley (Plate 336). If it were not for the mark, this jug would probably be attributed to Dudson, although on close examination both the handle shape and the colour vary slightly from known Dudson pieces.

Dudson did not corner the market for sprigged wares entirely at this period; major competitors were Copeland and Wedgwood. Copeland produced tankard and other shaped jugs in a style which is quite distinctive (Plates 337–8). Earlier examples are in grey, sage green or caramel-coloured stoneware with white sprigs (Plate 339). Others are often cream-coloured with white sprigs on a blue jasper-dip ground (Plates 340–1). The production of these continued into the twentieth century, and some of the later examples are heavily glazed with a dark green background.

PLATE 322: *Attractive straw-coloured stoneware jug with alternate blue and white sprigs, attributed to Dudson, c.1845–55. Many Dudson jugs have a distinctive incised number on the base, in this case '443'. Height 16.6 cm (size 24).*

Opposite Bottom Left:
PLATE 323: *Another Dudson straw-coloured stoneware jug with alternate blue and white sprigs, c.1845–55. In this case the body is moulded with a design of tall columns. Incised number '448'. Height 15.8 cm.*

PLATE 324: *Attractive and good quality Dudson claret jug with white sprigs on a dark blue jasper-dip ground, c.1845–60. The unmarked metal lid is silver-plated, which is relatively uncommon; most lids at this period were made of Britannia metal. Incised number '395'. Height 22.5 cm (size 12).*

PLATE 325: *This unmarked Dudson jug displays an early version of the common tankard shape, with a small overhang above the footrim, c.1845–60. The ground is a green jasper-dip. This side is sprigged with a scene from Hamlet; the reverse includes the figure of Minerva. Height 16.9 cm (size 24).*

Bottom Right:
PLATE 326: *Dudson stoneware jug of the standard tankard shape, c.1850–70. The lower body is ring turned, and the blue jasper-dip neck is finely sprigged in white. The small holes around the rim indicate a missing metal lid. Incised number '904'. Height 14.8 cm (size 30).*

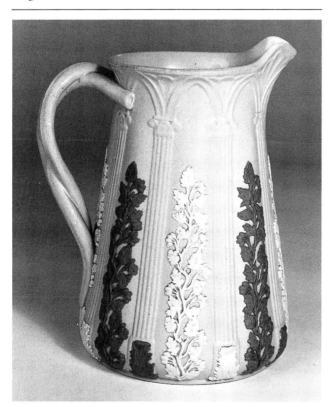

113

PLATE 327: *Another Dudson blue jasper-dip tankard jug, this one made for the Brownhills Pottery Co., c.1870–90. Dudson used very many different sprigs, but this Domestic Employment figure is uncommon. Incised number '3006' and faintly impressed initials 'B P Co'. Height 15 cm.*

PLATE 328: *Dudson tankard jug in solid brown stoneware with white sprigs, 1880. This crabstock handle is less common than the usual twisted rope design. Incised number '1530'; also impressed name 'PAXTON' and date code for May 1880. Metal lid marked 'B. GRAYSON / SHEFFIELD'. Height 22.8 cm (size 12).*

PLATE 329: *Dudson jug in light brown stoneware with white sprigs, c.1870–90. This shape is much less common but still typical. Compare the sprigged design with the much earlier Ridgway jug in Colour Plate 13. Again, the holes around the rim indicate a missing metal lid. Incised number '1205'. Height 16.4 cm (size 24).*

PLATE 330: *Unusual Dudson jug, moulded in brown stoneware with white dragon sprigs and mythical bird handle, c.1850–70. Incised number '1405'. The Britannia-metal lid is not marked. Height 20.7 cm.*

PLATE 333: *Another green stoneware jug made by Dudson for the Brownhills Pottery Co., c.1890–1900. This sprig of a corpulent toper is one of many which were revived from 18th-century Turner designs. Incised number '3650' and impressed initials 'B P Co'. Metal swing lid missing. Height 10 cm.*

PLATE 331: *Attractive ring-turned tankard jug in white stoneware with blue jasper-dip neck sprigged with two portrait medallions, c.1855–80. Although unmarked, this was probably made by Dudson. Height 19.2 cm (size 12).*

PLATE 334: *Distinctive brown stoneware jug made by Dudson to a design registered by Ridgways in 1882. Incised number '1688', black-printed registration diamond for 10 November 1882, and impressed date code for October 1882. Height 19.3 cm (size 12).*

PLATE 332: *Blue-green stoneware jug made by Dudson for the Brownhills Pottery Co., c.1888–1900. Several different attractive bird sprigs were used. Incised number '3535' and impressed initials 'B P Co'. The metal swing lid with flower finial is marked 'MARTIN / HANLEY / Rd No 101287'. Height 16.1 cm (size 24).*

PLATE 335: *Another Dudson tankard-shaped stoneware jug with a blue jasper-dip ground, 1879. This is one of several designs often found marked Paxton, possibly a customer's name. Incised number '1621' and impressed name 'PAXTON' with date code for September 1879. Height 19.6 cm (size 12).*

PLATE 336: *Tankard-shaped stoneware jug very like the Dudson examples, but made by Adams & Bromley of Hanley, c.1875–85. Neither the shape of the handle nor the brown colour quite match the Dudson products. Impressed 'ADAMS & / BROMLEY'. Height 15.8 cm (size 24).*

PLATE 337: *Two Copeland jugs of a common design, the tankard shape sprigged with the ubiquitous hunting scene, c.1880–1910. The left hand jug, in light-green stoneware has an unmarked metal swing lid and is impressed 'COPELAND'. The right hand jug, in cream stoneware with white sprigs on a blue* *ground, has a matching stoneware lid and a brown printed 'COPELAND / late / SPODE' seal mark along with an impressed mark 'COPELAND' with 'ENGLAND'. Heights 15.8 cm (size 24) and 18.4 cm (also size 24).*

PLATE 338: *Two more Copeland jugs of another standard design with a different stag-hunting scene, c.1880–1910. The left hand jug, in cream stoneware with white sprigs on a blue ground, has an impressed mark 'COPELAND' with 'ENGLAND'. The right-hand jug, in caramel-coloured stoneware with white sprigs, is impressed simply 'COPELAND'. The second jug has a hole burnt right through the base during firing. Heights 15 cm (size 9) and 10.4 cm (size 30).*

PLATE 340: *Simple but very attractive cream stoneware tankard jug by Copeland, c.1875–95. Once again the white sprigs are backed with a blue jasper-dip ground. The classical designs are taken from 18th-century originals, this side showing the goddess Diana. Impressed mark 'COPELAND'. Height 15.9 cm.*

PLATE 339: *Attractive caramel-coloured stoneware jug by Copeland, 1890. The sprigged classical figures are common. Note the excellent turned design around the base. Impressed mark 'COPELAND' and date code for May 1890. Pivoting metal lid not marked. Height 15.4 cm (size 30).*

117

PLATE 341: *Impressive cream stoneware jug with white sprigs on a blue ground, again by Copeland, c.1890–1910. The scene depicted is Columbus landing at San Salvador. Impressed mark 'COPELAND' and 'ENGLAND'. Height 21.1 cm.*

7.

Pratt Ware

With the development of finer earthenwares and porcelain during the eighteenth century, sophisticated painted decoration became practical. Most painted wares used overglaze enamel colours, but the same impetus which inspired potters to develop underglaze printing techniques also led to a search for colours which could be painted under the glaze. As with printing inks, the main difficulty was manufacturing colours capable of withstanding high temperatures in the kiln used to fire the glaze. This problem was overcome by the mid-1780s with the development of so-called 'Pratt' colours. These were all derived from metallic oxides which produced a distinctive palette including various shades of green, orange, blue, yellow and brown.

The first use of these colours was probably straight-forward hand-painting, such as on one typical late eighteenth-century jug, simply but elegantly decorated with a floral design (Plate 342). They were also quite widely used for colouring Toby jugs around the end of the eighteenth century (Plate 343), although this rather specialist subject is covered in more detail in Chapter 13 (see Plates 630 and 632). However, the colours have come to be associated particularly with a range of relief-moulded creamwares and pearlwares which are widely known as Pratt ware. The term covers hollow items such as jugs, mugs and teapots, and decorative pieces such as figures and plaques, although some unusual objects such as money boxes, bird feeders and coiled pipes were also made. Some of the jug designs are very simple, such as one with pineapple moulding (Plate 344), although the most common are pictorial designs featuring domestic and country scenes, classical figures, famous personalities and events of the day. The whole subject has been admirably covered by John and Griselda Lewis in their definitive work *Pratt Ware, English and Scottish Relief-decorated and Underglaze Coloured Earthenware, 1780–1840*.

The term Pratt ware derives from two jug designs marked with the simple impressed name 'PRATT'. These were almost certainly made by William Pratt at Lane Delph, probably in the 1790s. One design is moulded with the Sailor's Return (Plate 345), and has the corresponding Sailor's Farewell on the reverse. The other features Britannia. While these two jugs have given rise to the term Pratt ware, similar wares were made elsewhere in Staffordshire, Yorkshire, Liverpool, the north-east of England, and also in Scotland; Pratt was

PLATE 342: *Unattributed late 18th-century creamware jug with engine-turned base, hand-painted underglaze in green, orange, blue, yellow and brown. Height 17.1 cm.*

probably not the most significant manufacturer. However, while the term is unfortunate, not least due to conflict with the much later multi-coloured underglaze printed wares also associated with the Pratt family, it goes back many years and is widely accepted.

While examples have been recorded with the marks of more than twenty different potters, such pieces are rare. Inevitably, not all are jugs, but six clearly marked examples are illustrated here. Amongst the Staffordshire makers was Walter Daniel whose firm was potting at Burslem from the early 1780s until 1804. His impressed name appears on a jug featuring a bust of Captain Trollop, depicted with the figure of Clio, the Muse of History, and with a similar bust of Admiral Duncan on the reverse (Plate 346).

Perhaps the most famous Staffordshire name to be found is the simple impressed word 'WEDGWOOD'. This mark appears on two jugs shown here (Plate 347), one with designs of Smokers and Drinkers, the other featuring another portrait of Admiral Duncan, this time with Flaxman's Offering to Ceres on the reverse. The maker has been the subject of much discussion, and current opinion tends to discount the main Josiah Wedgwood firm in favour of Ralph Wedgwood. He was potting at Burslem in the 1790s before moving to Yorkshire for a brief association with the Knottingley Pottery at Ferrybridge.

The fact that the Yorkshire factory made Pratt ware is clear from jugs with the impressed name 'FERRY-BRIDGE'. This seems to date from 1805, some five years after Ralph Wedgwood's departure, and appears on a range of jugs of a rather squat shape moulded with several different scenes. One example has a design of huntsmen (Plate 348), with Toby Fillpot on the reverse, while others feature Venus, a version of the Sailor's Return, and Old Mother Slipper Slopper from the traditional song and nursery rhyme recounting the story of Daddy Fox and the Grey Goose.

PLATE 344: *Unattributed pineapple-moulded earthenware jug of a type popular in the early 19th century. The moulding has been picked out with underglaze colours of brown, blue, green and orange. A similar jug decorated with silver lustre can be seen in Plate 516. Height 12.9 cm.* (Courtesy: Jack Hacking)

PLATE 345: *Marked underglaze-coloured pearlware jug of the type which has given the name to Pratt ware. This side depicts the Sailor's Return, the reverse has the Sailor's Farewell. Impressed mark 'PRATT'. Height 15.6 cm.*

PLATE 343: *Toby jug of traditional type decorated with typical underglaze colours, c.1800. Other Toby jug designs can also be found with Pratt-type colouring. Height 25 cm.* (Courtesy: Sotheby's, Sussex)

PLATE 346: *Two views of a pearlware jug by Walter Daniel of Burslem, c.1797–8. In this case the colouring is predominantly brown and green. The portraits are titled 'CAPTAIN TROLOP' [sic] and 'ADMIRAL DUNCAN'. Impressed mark 'W. DANIEL'. Height 19.5 cm.*

PLATE 347: *Two different Wedgwood-marked pearlware jugs, c.1790–8. The left-hand jug has two scenes of smokers and drinkers; the right hand example shows 'ADMIREL [sic] DUNCAN' with Flaxman's Offering to Ceres on the reverse. Probably made by Ralph Wedgwood while he was potting at Burslem. Both with impressed mark 'WEDGWOOD'. Heights 15.8 cm and 13.9 cm.*

PLATE 348: *Pearlware jug decorated with typical underglaze Pratt colours by the Ferrybridge Pottery, c.1805–10. This side is moulded with huntsmen at a meet; the reverse has the popular Toby Fillpot figure. Impressed mark 'FERRYBRIDGE'. Height 11.6 cm.*

Several other Yorkshire potteries made similar wares, including the Hawley family who worked at Kilnhurst and Rawmarsh at the end of the eighteenth century. Several pieces bearing the impressed mark 'HAWLEY' are known, including one jug featuring a bust of the Duke of York (Plate 349), with the Royal Sufferers on the reverse. This jug dates from about 1795 and could have been made by either Thomas Hawley at Kilnhurst or William Hawley at Rawmarsh. John and Griselda Lewis illustrate several other similarly marked pieces, including one richly-coloured Bacchus jug.

Another important pottery centre which produced these wares was the city of Liverpool, one jug design being known with the impressed mark of the Herculaneum Pottery (Plate 350). This would date from before 1810 and features on one side a group of peasants drinking, derived from an original painting by David Teniers the Younger, widely used at Liverpool on early black-printed wares. The reverse shows a group of village musicians. Both subjects can also be found on sprig-moulded jugs by Turner and other Staffordshire potters.

While these marked examples are of considerable interest, similar unmarked jugs exist in large numbers, although few of them can be attributed with any certainty. Amongst them is one jug with a shooting scene (Plate 351), with a pair of gardeners on the reverse. Although unmarked, the same design was later reproduced by the Seniors at Leeds, and since they based much of their output on moulds from the original Leeds Pottery, an attribution to Leeds for this early nineteenth-century jug must be considered reasonable.

The remaining jugs shown here are all unmarked and no satisfactory attributions have emerged. They include another jug moulded with a scene from Daddy Fox and the Grey Goose (Plate 352); an apparently unrecorded

pot-bellied jug with scattered figures, all of which are known on sprig-moulds of the period (Plate 353); and a military review jug similar to another example shown by John and Griselda Lewis (Plate 354). One particularly attractive unmarked jug is moulded with a rustic scene featuring a windmill, with a group of birds on the reverse (Plate 355). Another attractive jug is moulded simply with a patriotic design of roses, thistles and shamrocks, shown alongside a fascinating and rare bird drinking pot (Plate 356).

Although most Pratt ware jugs are unique in their design, some are identical to others decorated in other ways. One example is the ovoid jug moulded with heart-shaped reserves containing children at play representing 'Sportive Innocence' (Plate 357), with 'Mischievous Sport' on the reverse. This design is quite commonly found in felspathic stoneware of the so-called Castleford type, sometimes plain but usually decorated with sparse overglaze enamels, particularly blue-lining. The same scenes are also found on other Pratt ware pieces, including a mug and a flask.

PLATE 349: *Portrait of the Duke of York on a pearlware jug potted by one of the Hawley family in Yorkshire, c.1795. The impressed mark 'HAWLEY' could relate to either the Kilnhurst Pottery or the Rawmarsh Pottery, both near Rotherham. The reverse depicts the Royal Sufferers. Height 13 cm.*

Opposite:
PLATE 350: *Two views of a pearlware jug decorated underglaze in yellow, orange, green, blue and brown, by the Herculaneum Pottery at Liverpool, c.1796–1810. The Teniers drinking scene on the left is commonly found on Liverpool ceramics, and both scenes were used on sprigged wares by Turner and others. Impressed 'HERCULANEUM'. Height 16.3 cm.*

PLATE 351: *Unmarked early 19th-century pearlware jug with scenes depicting shooting and gardeners. Possibly made at the Leeds Pottery since the same subjects were later used by the Seniors, who based many of their designs on earlier Leeds wares. Height 15.3 cm.*

PLATE 352: *Unattributed Pratt-style jug, c.1800–10. The design is based on the folk tale of Daddy Fox and the Grey Goose, the figures visible being Old Mother Twiddle-Twaddle (or Slipper-Slopper) releasing the ferocious dog, while Farmer John stands nonchalantly by with his pitchfork. Height 17.8 cm.* (Courtesy: Christie's, London)

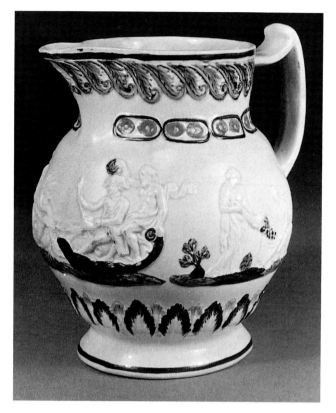

Below:
PLATE 354: *Military review jug by an unknown maker, c.1800. The scene depicts cavalrymen practising their sword exercises on horseback, and two further figures with a gun and ladder. A nice touch is the border of spearheads and cannons around the shoulder. Height 19 cm.* (Courtesy: Sotheby's, Sussex)

PLATE 353: *Another unattributed pearlware jug decorated in green, brown, blue, orange and yellow, c.1805–10. The figures, all copied from popular sprig moulds of the period, include Hope and Plenty, the Apotheosis of Nelson, and Britannia. Height 15.9 cm.*

Below:
PLATE 355: *Two views of an attractive and good quality under-glaze coloured pearlware jug, c.1800–10. Despite the distinctive handle, no attribution has been forthcoming. Height 15.6 cm.*

Left:
PLATE 356: *An unusual early 19th-century patriotic jug by an unknown maker. The union design features a rose and thistle spray on each side, below a shamrock border. Height 15 cm.* (Courtesy: Sotheby's, London)

Below:
PLATE 357: *Unattributed ovoid-shaped jug decorated in typical Pratt palette, c.1795–1800. This relatively common design depicts children at play, titled 'Sportive Innocence'; a similar subject on the reverse is titled 'Mischievous Sport'. The same subjects appear on other wares, including Castleford-type stonewares, sometimes decorated with overglaze enamels. Height 15.3 cm.* (Courtesy: Sotheby's, Sussex)

The last two jug designs both feature political subjects. The first is moulded with busts of Henry Brougham and Thomas Denman, both Members of Parliament who were prominent in the defence of Queen Caroline during her trial in 1820 (Plate 358). It was suggested by the Lewises that this jug might exist with underglaze Pratt colours, since they illustrated a very similar jug moulded with a bust of Caroline herself, although they were able to show only an overglaze enamelled version. Another example of this design with overglaze enamels but with the addition of pink lustre is shown here (Plate 359).

The remaining jug features a bust of Sir Francis Burdett, who was also a Member of Parliament. He had a somewhat stormy career which included imprisonment on two occasions, in 1810 and 1820, the first of which resulted in a stay in the Tower of London. Two versions of the jug are known (Plate 360), one moulded in creamware decorated with typical Pratt colours, the other, which has been turned to show the reverse design titled 'Liberty', of green-glazed earthenware. It appears that both were made from the same mould, but as with most of these Pratt wares, the maker has not been identified.

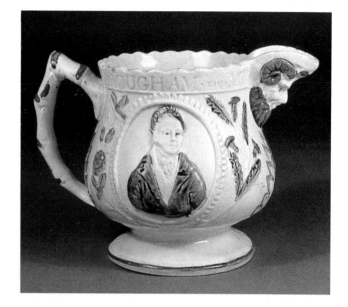

Above:
PLATE 358: *Two views of an unattributed jug moulded with portraits of Henry Brougham and Thomas Denman, underglaze coloured in blue, brown and orange. The two MPs were active in the defence of Queen Caroline in 1820. Height 11.2 cm.*

PLATE 360: *Two jugs by an unknown maker, featuring Sir Francis Burdett who was imprisoned in the Tower of London in 1810. These two jugs are taken from an identical mould. The left-hand example is green-glazed and reversed to show a figure titled 'LIBERTY'; the other is creamware decorated with typical underglaze colours. Height of each jug 14.5 cm.*

PLATE 359: *The same moulded jug design but produced in earthenware decorated with overglaze enamels and pink lustre. Height 15 cm.* (Courtesy: Sotheby's, Sussex)

8.

Relief-moulding

lthough sprig-moulding proved very successful, one disadvantage was its requirement for skilled workers. Commercial pressures inevitably led to more extensive use of moulds, and fully-moulded jugs were a natural development. While moulds could produce pots of many different shapes, they also offered the ability to cast decoration on the surface. Wares of this type are widely described as relief-moulded. The Pratt wares discussed in Chapter 7 are relief-moulded, as are thinly cast felspathic stonewares of the Castleford type which are often attractively enamelled (Plates 361–2). Some earthenwares were relief-moulded in the first quarter of the nineteenth century, but usually highlighted with enamelling or lustre. Some are commemorative (Plate 670) while others emulate sprigged jugs of the period, including one by Rogers (Plate 363). A few other jugs derived from sprigged versions were moulded in china (Plate 364), but these are unusual.

PLATE 362: *Felspathic stoneware jug of very fine quality, enamelled in blue, greens, purple and brown, c.1795–1805. This hunting scene is accompanied on the reverse by a similar shooting scene. Height 21.6 cm.* (Courtesy: Jack Hacking)

PLATE 361: *Typical thin-felspathic stoneware jug of Castleford type but probably made elsewhere, c.1795–1805. The slip-cast design depicting the Judgment of Paris is crudely enamelled in blue, brown, green, turquoise and maroon. The reverse has a hunting scene. Height 12.2 cm.*

The thin felspathic stonewares did not remain in production for long, and neither ordinary earthenware nor china proved ideal for relief-moulding, probably for reasons of durability, cost, or the fact that glazing tended to obscure the moulded details. The solution proved to be a utilitarian fine-bodied stoneware and relief-moulded jugs in this material began to appear in the 1820s. However, it was a gradual process and some of the sprigged jugs discussed earlier feature relief-moulded bodies.

No purely relief-moulded wares are known from the 'Imperial Stone' manufacturer but most jugs recorded have quite decoratively moulded bodies (Plates 303–6). The so-called Chrysanthemum factory also made sprigged jugs with moulded bodies (Plate 296) but went on to make fully-moulded jugs (Plate 365). The Wedgwood factory made similar wares including one hunting design issued both with and without sprigged border decoration (Plates 316–17 and 366). Wedgwood made other early fully-moulded jugs, including a naturalistic 'leafage' jug, although these were mostly enhanced with coloured enamels.

PLATE 363: *Glazed white stoneware jug with brown enamelling by John Rogers & Son of Longport, c.1820–30. This example is moulded but is very much in the style of earlier sprigged jugs. Impressed mark 'ROGERS'. Height 13.8 cm.*

Right:
PLATE 364: *Spode jug relief-moulded in bone china with green enamelled neck and gilt lining, c.1817–25. Red-painted mark 'SPODE' with pattern number '2686'. Height 19.9 cm.*

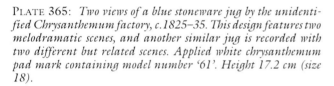

PLATE 365: *Two views of a blue stoneware jug by the unidentified Chrysanthemum factory, c.1825–35. This design features two melodramatic scenes, and another similar jug is recorded with two different but related scenes. Applied white chrysanthemum pad mark containing model number '61'. Height 17.2 cm (size 18).*

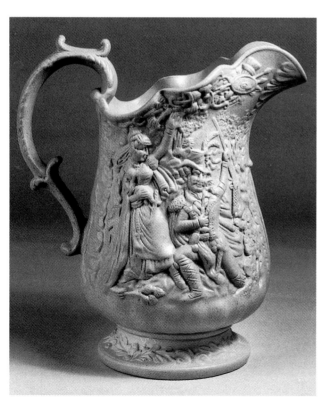

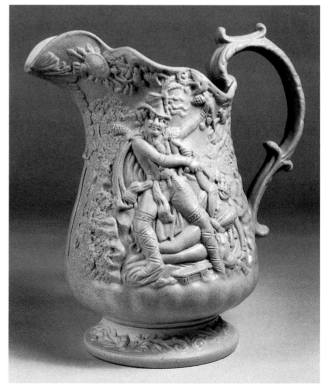

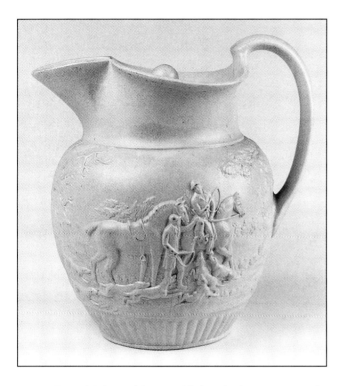

PLATE 366: *Wedgwood jug moulded in drab stoneware with a matching lid, c.1820–30. This same hunting design was also issued with a sprigged border around the neck (see Plate 316). Impressed mark 'WEDGWOOD'. Height 20.3 cm.*

A vast number of relief-moulded jugs were produced and generalizations are difficult. However, in the earlier years up to about 1855, quality tended to be good and many interesting designs were made, often pictorial in nature, some modelled in high relief. From about 1850 quality steadily deteriorated and designs became less inspiring, typically simple floral or geometric patterns in low-relief. A truly comprehensive review of the subject is not possible here, but specialist books are available; the current author's *Relief-moulded Jugs 1820–1900*; Kathy Hughes's two volumes titled *A Collector's Guide to Nineteenth-Century Jugs*; and Jill Rumsey's exhibition catalogue *Victorian Relief-moulded Jugs*. In order to avoid duplication most illustrations here have been selected to complement my earlier volume, although some designs are repeated to ensure a representative survey.

Possibly the first firm to make relief-moulded stoneware jugs was Phillips & Bagster, potting in Hanley between 1818 and 1823. They issued one jug with animal hunting scenes (Plate 367), and a further floral design titled 'Ivy' was produced by the succeeding partner, John Denton Bagster, before 1830. The new decade saw several major manufacturers issue jugs, amongst the most important being Ridgway and Minton, soon followed by Samuel Alcock, Charles Meigh, and a lesser known partnership between Elijah Jones and Edward Walley. With the exception of Alcock, jugs by these manufacturers are well illustrated, so just a few examples including new discoveries should suffice.

The Animal Hunting scene made by Phillips & Bagster was probably modelled by Leonard James Abington. He went on to partner William Ridgway and the firm began to issue jugs in 1830 or 1831. One was a redesigned Animal Hunting scene, but others include the god Pan, the story of John Gilpin and several stylized floral patterns (Plate 368). Two previously unrecorded early jugs are shown here (Plates 369–70). These were followed by many attractive and popular designs featuring Tam o'Shanter, the Eglinton tournament, the Assyrian discoveries of Austen Henry Layard, the Dunmow Flitch, the Crimean War and Moses at Horeb. These can all be seen, along with several others, in the current author's earlier volume. Two extensively enamelled jugs feature the uncommon Nineveh and Alhambra designs (Plates 371–2).

Minton started to issue similar jugs at much the same time as William Ridgway; their most common early design is the Silenus jug (Plate 373). Most Minton jugs bear model numbers, initially within an ornately moulded cartouche but later, particularly on Parian, simply impressed. The Silenus jug is numbered 16 in light green stoneware or 19 in dark green. Later versions in Parian are numbered 261 and 264. The rare example illustrated is made of 'English Porcelain', and the initials 'WT' within the printed mark are believed to be those of Dr Wilton Turner who helped develop this experimental pre-Parian body. Fuller details can be found in Geoffrey Godden's *Minton Pottery and Porcelain of the First Period*. The Silenus design was copied by Mason and Doulton, amongst others.

PLATE 367: *Animal Hunting jug in buff stoneware by Phillips & Bagster of Hanley, c.1818–23. Although apparently unmarked, the maker's name is moulded on the collar of the dog forming the handle, and again on dog collars within the boar-hunting scene on the reverse. A variant of this design was made later by William Ridgway & Co. Height 21 cm.*

PLATE 368: *Arabesque and Vines jug in buff stoneware by William Ridgway, Son & Co. of Hanley, c.1840. This is a relatively late example of a design first issued in 1830 or 1831. Impressed mark 'RIDGWAY SON, & Co./HANLEY'. Height 28.5 cm (size 4).*

PLATE 370: *Glazed blue stoneware jug of an unrecorded design by William Ridgway & Co., c.1830–5. This is very similar to another design covered with daisy heads made by an earlier Ridgway partnership. Moulded urn and anchor mark with maker's name. Height 17.1 cm (size 9).*

PLATE 369: *Buff stoneware jug of hexagonal form moulded with a simple design of scrolls by William Ridgway & Co., c.1830–5. Moulded urn and anchor mark with maker's name, also a small impressed anchor. Height 15.8 cm (size 12).*

PLATE 371: *Distinctive but uncommon Nineveh jug, registered by Ridgway & Abington in 1851. This glazed white stoneware example is enamelled in blue and mustard yellow, and gilded. The design is based on Assyrian artefacts discovered at Nimrud and Nineveh by Austen Henry Layard. Moulded registration diamond for 16 August 1851. Height 24.3 cm.*

PLATE 372: *Unmarked stoneware jug of another uncommon design first issued by William Ridgway, Son & Co. in the early 1840s. The design, picked out here in underglaze blue with red enamel and gilding, is based on motifs from the palace of the Moorish kings at the Alhambra Palace, Granada. Unmarked except for the red-painted pattern number '2315'. Height 21.1 cm.*

PLATE 373: *Minton & Boyle jug in white unglazed 'English Porcelain', c.1839. This Silenus design was commonly produced in stoneware by Minton, and also by Mason and Doulton, but this version in the experimental pre-Parian body is rare. Blue-printed scroll mark with name of body, maker's initials and also 'WT' for Dr Wilton Turner. Height 14.8 cm (size 30).*

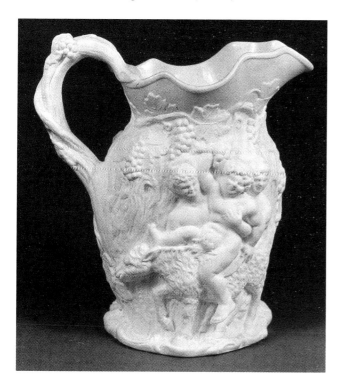

Other Minton designs include the famous Hop Jug designed by Henry Townsend (Plate 374); the award of the Dunmow Flitch (Plate 375); a hunting scene based on earlier sprig-moulded jugs (Plate 376); two impressive Parian jugs featuring cherubs (Plates 377–8); and three naturalistic patterns (Plates 379–81). A final example, although unmarked, is attractively potted in mid-blue stoneware enhanced with coloured enamels (Plate 382).

Long before relief-moulded jugs became collectable, the name Charles Meigh was synonymous with them. He made some notable jugs in the 1840s including the famous Apostle, 'York Minster' and Bacchanalian Dance designs (Plate 383). The earliest would appear to be the 'Julius Caesar' jug published in 1839, followed in 1840 by the ornate 'Roman' jug (Plate 384). The firm became Charles Meigh & Son in 1851 and although a few interesting designs appeared (Colour Plate 19), some were of lesser merit (Plate 385).

This trend appears to have been reversed when the firm became the Old Hall Earthenware Co. Ltd in 1861. Several better designs emerged, the first commemorating Prince Albert, who died late the same year (Plate 386). This jug was registered but others were not and are usually marked only with the firm's initials. Two examples are shown, the first depicting six of the Virtues (Plate 387), rather reminiscent of an earlier jug titled 'International' made by William Brownfield for the 1851 Great Exhibition. The other is a floral design typical of this later period (Plate 388). Since they were not registered these jugs are less easy to date, but they were probably made in the early 1860s.

PLATE 374: *Minton's famous Hop Jug designed by Henry Townsend and registered in 1847. This example, which is missing its matching lid, is in white Parian with a blue ground but other versions are known. The same design was also issued ornamented with additional figures. Moulded registration diamond for 14 May 1847. Height 19.9 cm.*

PLATE 375: *Blue stoneware jug with Minton's version of the Dunmow Flitch scene, c.1840. The same scene was later used on a different shape by Ridgway & Abington. Applied blue moulded scroll mark with model 'No. 134' and cursive initial 'M'. Height 17.3 cm (size 12).*

PLATE 377: *Porcelanous stoneware jug impressively moulded in high relief, registered by Minton in 1845. Designs of cherubs, putti or amorini were popular at this period. White moulded scroll mark with model 'No. 229' and cursive initial 'M'; also registration diamond for 20 March 1845. Height 26.8 cm.*

PLATE 376: *White stoneware jug with black glazed neck by Minton, c.1845. The two hunting scenes are adapted from earlier sprig designs used by other potters. The jug was issued in several variants, some with a moulded border around the neck. White moulded scroll mark with model 'No. 222' and cursive initial 'M'. Height 12.8 cm.*

PLATE 378: *Another Minton design with cherubs, this one dating from about 1849. Minton issued several similar designs usually made, like this example, in Parian with a distinctive dark blue ground. White moulded scroll mark with model 'No. 364' and cursive initial 'M'. Height 12.9 cm (size 24).*

PLATE 379: *This Minton jug, very similar to the design with cherubs in Plate 377, also dates from about 1845. Again it is made in white porcelanous stoneware with a blue ground. White moulded scroll mark with model 'No. 260' and cursive initial 'M'. The Britannia-metal lid is marked 'JAMES DIXON / & SONS'. Height 20.2 cm (size 24).*

PLATE 381: *Small decorative jug in Parian registered by Minton in 1857. This example shows quite clearly that Parian moulding is often not very crisp, in this case probably as a result of using a worn mould. Indistinct moulded registration diamond with impressed model number '530'. Height 11.5 cm (size 30).*

PLATE 380: *Impressive jug moulded with a design of vertical leaves registered by Minton in 1856. This example is in white stoneware and bears a date code for 1859. Moulded registration diamond for 23 January 1856 with impressed model number '526'. Height 24.7 cm (size 9).*

PLATE 382: *Unmarked jug in blue stoneware of a design introduced by Minton c.1845. This example bears a date code for 1851 and the moulding is picked out with green, red, pink, ochre and blue enamels. Pattern number '6750/7' painted in red. Height 18.6 cm.*

PLATE 383: *Bacchanalian Dance jug in white stoneware, regis-*
tered by Charles Meigh in 1844. This impressive design is based
on a painting by Poussin, now in the National Gallery. Ornate
applied mark with registration diamond for 30 September 1844
together with the date and maker's name. Height 19.5 cm.
(Courtesy: Lawrence Fine Art, Crewkerne)

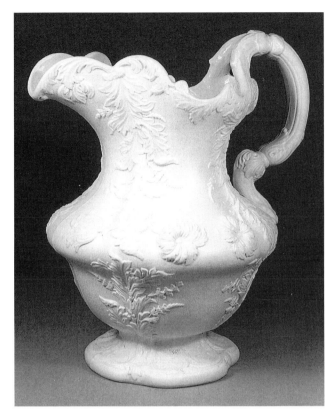

PLATE 384: *Ornately moulded grey stoneware jug of a design titled 'Roman', published by Charles Meigh in 1840. Moulded mark containing the inscription 'OCT. 1ST. / 1840. / PUBLISHED BY C. MEIGH / HANLEY. / ROMAN'. Height 26.3 cm (size 6).*

PLATE 385: *Simple and rather uninspiring jug in white stoneware with blue enamelled flutes, the design registered by Charles Meigh & Son in 1854. Moulded registration diamond for 9 June 1854. Height 17.3 cm (size 18).*

PLATE 386: *The 'Prince Consort' jug registered by the Old Hall Earthenware Co. Ltd not long after Prince Albert's death in December 1861. This example is in white Parian with a blue ground, but others are plain white or in stoneware. Moulded registration diamond for 9 April 1862 with maker's initials 'OHECL'. Height 23.8 cm (size 6).*

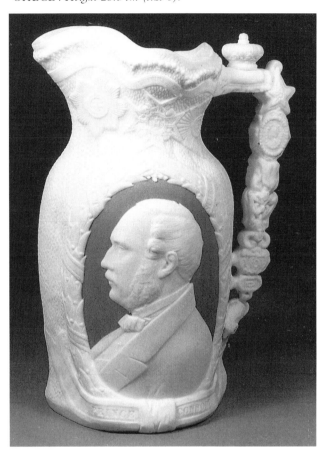

PLATE 387: *Attractive jug moulded in white stoneware with a blue ground by the Old Hall Earthenware Co. Ltd, c.1861–5. The classical figures represent six of the seven virtues, poor Charity is missing. Moulded roundel mark with initials 'OHECL' and address 'HANLEY'. Height 21.2 cm (size 12).*

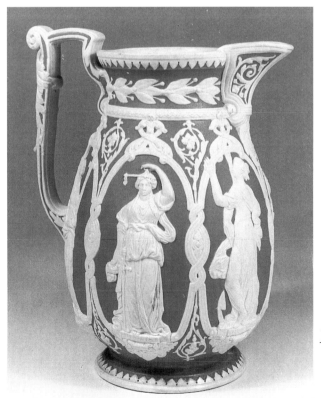

Left:
PLATE 388: *Another attractive design, this time of fuchsias, by the Old Hall Earthenware Co. Ltd, c.1861–70. This white stoneware example has an unusual dark red ground. Moulded roundel mark with initials 'OHECL' and address 'HANLEY'. The Britannia-metal lid is marked 'ATKIN BROTHERS / SHEFFIELD'. Height 19.8 cm.*

The company's jugs were sometimes unmarked and one magnificent example is a copy of their Wedgwood jug (Plate 389). This design, modelled by Henry Baggeley and possibly inspired by the unveiling of Wedgwood's statue at Stoke in 1860, is known with the 'OHECL' initial mark. A final unmarked jug with a design of swans shows all the signs of being by Meigh or his successors (Plate 390).

While the above firms are all well-known, the same is not true of Elijah Jones and Edward Walley. Jones probably started potting around 1830 and appears to have issued his first moulded jug in 1835. A design featuring coral followed in 1838 (Plate 391), and two more jugs appeared before 1841 when he was joined in partnership by Walley. They made at least two jugs together, titled 'Good Samaritan' and 'Gipsey' [*sic*], the latter also made by Samuel Alcock, but the partnership was short-lived. By 1845 Walley was potting alone.

He made a range of impressive jugs, mostly registered designs, and apart from a change of style to E. & W. Walley in the later 1850s, possibly to take his son into the business, he continued until at least 1859. One jug produced in large numbers around 1850 shows the Death of Abel, a design shared with Samuel Alcock, although the example illustrated here is of an unrecorded shape (Plate 392). Others are 'Ceres' dating from 1851 (Plate 393); 'Havelock' and 'Harvest', both from 1858 (Plates 394–5); and 'Enville' and 'Sportman', both from 1859 (Plates 396–7). The previously unrecorded 'Harvest' design is similar to a differently shaped jug titled 'Gleaner', registered on the same day.

PLATE 389: *Unmarked Parian jug commemorating Josiah Wedgwood, attributed to the Old Hall Earthenware Co. Ltd, c.1861–70. The design was modelled by Henry Baggeley and marked examples have been recorded. The reverse has a lion and crown with Wedgwood's dates, and the famous Portland Vase is depicted beneath the spout. Height 26.2 cm.*

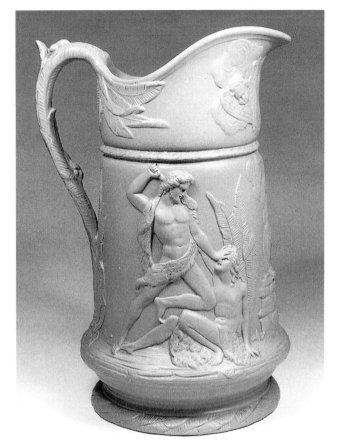

PLATE 390: *Unusual white stoneware jug with a design of a swan on a blue ground, c.1855–70. Although unmarked, this jug shows several characteristics associated with Charles Meigh and his successors. Height 22.3 cm (size 9).*

PLATE 392: *Rare variant of a design depicting the Death of Abel made by both Edward Walley and Samuel Alcock in the early 1850s. This green stoneware example by Walley is of an unusual shape; the common versions have a much more tapering body and do not have the cherubs visible beneath the spout. Black-printed Royal arms mark with maker's name and address. Height 27.2 cm (size 6 or 9).*

PLATE 391: *Squat jug in buff stoneware moulded with a design of coral published by Elijah Jones in 1838. Impressed mark 'PUBLISHED BY /E. JONES, / COBRIDGE, / SEPTEMBER 1, 1838'. Height 17.3 cm.*

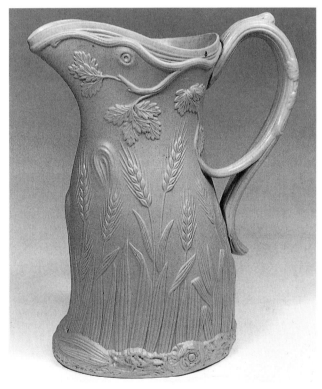

PLATE 393: *Another green stoneware jug by Edward Walley, this design titled 'Ceres' was registered in 1851. The holes in the rim indicate a missing metal lid. Black-printed royal arms mark with maker's name and address; also an applied green registration diamond for 26 April 1851 with the maker's name and address, the date and the title. Height 20.8 cm (size 18).*

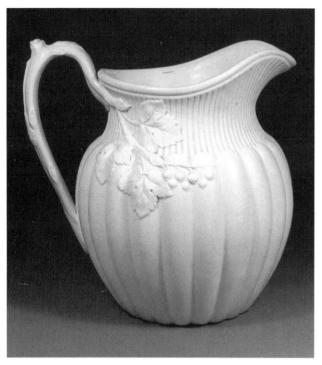

PLATE 394: *Simple but effective design titled 'Havelock' registered by E. & W. Walley in 1858. This is an example of Walley's Parian, previously unrecorded and rarely found. Sir Henry Havelock died during the Indian Mutiny in 1857. Applied white registration diamond for 29 January 1858 with the maker's name and address, the date and the title. Height 25.8 cm.*

PLATE 396: *Green stoneware jug moulded with hanging game, registered by E. & W. Walley in 1859. This design is titled 'Enville'. Applied green registration diamond for 7 May 1859 with the title beneath. Height 15.3 cm (size 36).*

PLATE 395: *A damaged but rare E. & W. Walley stoneware jug titled 'Harvest', registered in 1858. The same genre scenes appear on another more common design registered on the same day but titled 'Gleaner'. Applied registration diamond for 11 November 1858 with the maker's name and address, the year '1859' and the title. Height 21.9 cm (size 12).*

PLATE 397: *Green stoneware jug issued again by E. & W. Walley, under the title 'Sportman'. Applied registration diamond for 94 [sic] December 1859, surrounded by the year '1859' four times and with the title beneath. The Britannia-metal lid is marked 'T. BOOTH / HANLEY'. Height 17.8 cm (size 24).*

PLATE 398: *Two typical Parian jugs by Samuel Alcock & Co., c.1845. The two scenes depict 'The Sonah Wallah, or Itinerant Goldsmith of India' and 'Itinerant Musicians of India', both derived from Luard's* Sketches in India. *The larger example with* *lavender figures has a black-printed Royal arms mark with model number '101'; the smaller example, with lavender ground, has only the model number '114'. Heights 13.9 cm (size 30) and 22.3 cm (size 6 or 9).*

Unlike Jones and Walley, Samuel Alcock was a potter of some importance. His range of fine quality wares included a series of relief-moulded jugs, mostly potted in types of china or Parian. They are noted for a distinctive lavender colouring applied using a patent taken out by Richard Boote in 1843. Although Alcock's jugs are highly collectable, they are not well covered in existing literature, so a representative selection is shown in an attempt to redress the balance.

Most Alcock jugs bear a black-printed model number reflecting the design and colour combination. The numbering system began at 101 and ran through to at least 278, the last actually produced by Alcock's successor, J. S. Hill, who continued the sequence. It covers mainly relief-moulded wares, mostly jugs, although a few other items are known. Nearly half the numbers have been traced, including twenty-eight different jug designs in various colours. Some thirteen are shown here (Plates 398–410).

Several are not unique to Alcock. The scene showing Sir Sidney Smith at the siege of Acre (Plate 399) was copied by H. Mills; poor quality versions of the Portland Vase (Plate 400) were made by several potters; and the Babes in the Wood design (Plate 403) was used by Bradbury, Anderson & Bettany who also copied other Alcock designs. The earlier jugs were not normally registered but the Gypsy jug (Plate 408) was published in 1842 jointly with Jones & Walley. The highest recorded Alcock model number is 261 on one version of the Poppies design (Plate 406), but numbers 277 and 278 were used by J. S. Hill, so a few more might exist.

PLATE 399: *Relatively common jug in white Parian with lavender ground by Samuel Alcock & Co., c.1845. The scene depicts Sir Sidney Smith defending the breach at Acre in 1799, based on a painting by William Hamilton. Black-printed royal arms mark with maker's name and model number '116'. Height 19.3 cm (size 12).*

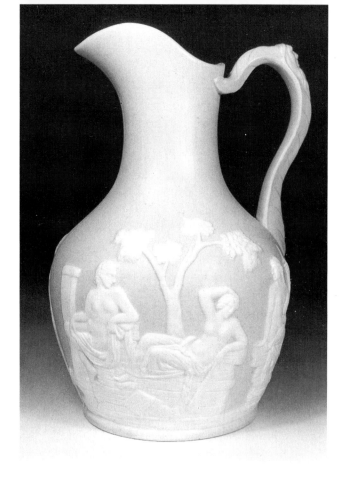

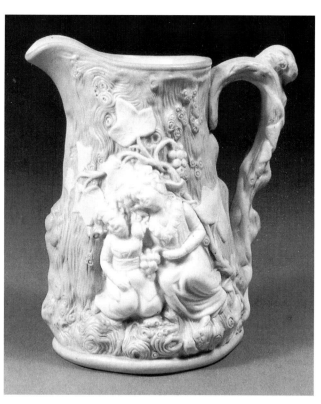

PLATE 400: *Another common Alcock jug in white Parian with a lavender ground, c.1845. This design is derived from the famous Portland Vase. Black-printed royal arms mark with maker's name and model number '118'. Height 20.5 cm (size 18).*

PLATE 403: *A popular design showing the Babes in the Wood, this Parian example with a lavender ground by Samuel Alcock & Co., c.1847. The design is based on a painting by J. H. Benwell and was copied by Bradbury, Anderson & Bettany, and Cork & Edge (see Plate 451). Black-printed royal arms mark with model number '143'. Height 11.4 cm.*

PLATE 401: *Two views of a rare Alcock Parian jug with a lavender ground, depicting the goddess Ariadne on a panther, c.1846. The design is based on a statue by Johann von Dannecker. Black-printed royal arms mark with model number '124'. Height 23.3 cm (size 6 or 9).*

PLATE 402: *Two views of an uncommon Alcock Parian jug moulded with a pair of medieval scenes picked out in lavender. Black-printed royal arms mark with model number '138'. Height 15.7 cm (size 30).*

PLATE 404: *Uncommon Alcock design featuring grapevines and a Bacchus mask spout, c.1847. This is an unusual example in white Parian with a lavender ground, most are plain white. Black-printed royal arms mark with model number '149'. Height 12.6 cm (size 36).*

PLATE 405: *Rare and very elegant Alcock jug, the outside covered overall in lavender, c.1849. Black-printed royal arms mark with maker's name and model number '191'. Height 23.2 cm (size 12).*

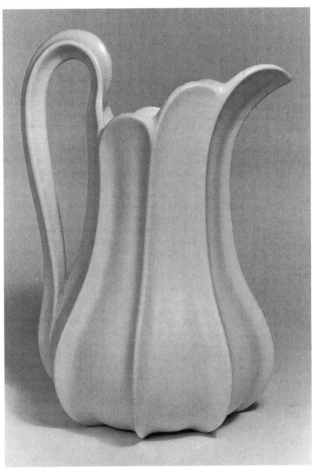

141

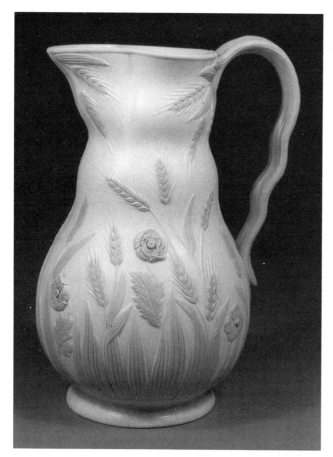

PLATE 406: *Attractive Alcock jug in white Parian with a design of poppies amongst the corn picked out in lavender, c.1849. This double-gourd shape is uncommon. Black-printed royal arms mark with maker's name and model number '194'. Height 19.6 cm (size 18).*

PLATE 407: *Another Alcock jug in white Parian with lavender moulding, c.1849. This uncommon design features Shakespearean characters framed in arches. Black-printed royal arms mark with maker's name and model number '196'. Height 16.7 cm (size 24).*

PLATE 409: *Popular jug with a design of ivy registered by Samuel Alcock & Co. in 1854. This Parian example has a blue ground but versions were also made plain white or coloured with lavender. Black-printed royal arms mark with maker's name; also registration diamond for 30 January 1854 and model number '253'. Height 15.2 cm (size 30).*

PLATE 410: *Alcock's Camel jug in white Parian with a brown
ground, c.1854. The design was first issued in other colours a year
or so earlier; the brown ground is a late Alcock feature not
commonly found. Black-printed royal arms mark with maker's
name and model number '259'. Height 22.1 cm (size 12).*

A short aside may be relevant here. Although Alcock's lavender colouring is distinctive, it was copied along with several jugs by Bradbury, Anderson & Bettany. They made a version of the Babes in the Wood jug (Plate 403), and both their Tasso & Ariosto jug (Plate 411) and their Ino jug (Plate 412) were derived from Alcock originals. Another design which appears to show Cleopatra's Needle does, however, appear to be original (Plate 413).

The firm's history is unclear but they were potting from about 1844. Their trading style became just Anderson & Bettany some time around 1851, and some initial marks clearly have the first B removed. One example is a dramatic design normally known as Feeding Time (Plate 414), also copied from an Alcock original. Another version was made by Cork & Edge under the title 'Keeper's Daughter' (Plate 453). One swan design, shown on a miniature jug, was probably also made full size (Plate 415).

Another related partnership was Bradbury, Mason & Bradbury who probably succeeded in around 1853 but survived for only a short time. The jug depicting hunting dogs or wolves appears to be the only known marked example of their work (Plate 416).

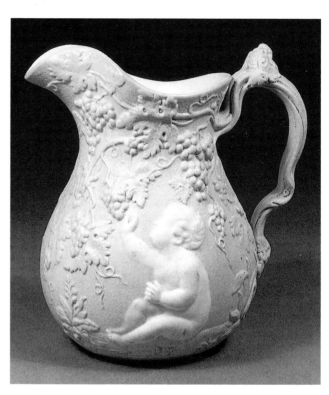

PLATE 412: *The Ino jug in white Parian with a lavender ground by Bradbury, Anderson & Bettany, c.1850. Again this design was also used by Alcock, and a similar jug was made by Charles Meigh. Black-printed royal arms mark with maker's initials. Height 13.2 cm.*

PLATE 413: *An apparently original design in white Parian with a lavender ground by Bradbury, Anderson & Bettany, c.1850. This side appears to feature Cleopatra's Needle; the reverse has a pavilion surrounded by military accoutrements. Black-printed royal arms mark with maker's initials. Height 17.7 cm.*

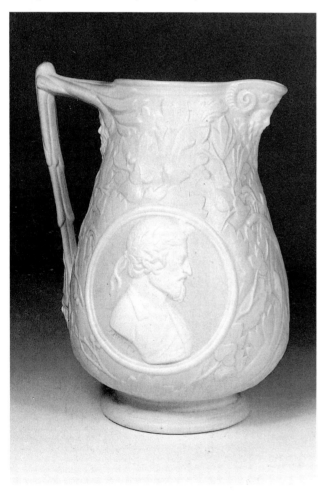

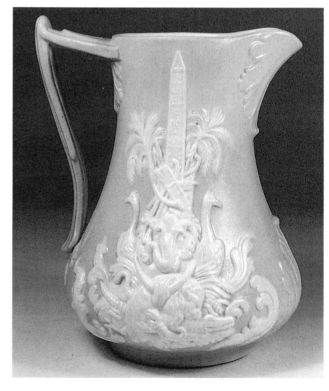

PLATE 411: *White Parian jug with lavender ground by Bradbury, Anderson & Bettany, c.1850. The design, featuring busts of the two Italian poets Torquato Tasso and Lodovico Ariosto, was also used by Alcock. Black-printed royal arms mark with maker's initials. Height 19.5 cm.*

PLATE 414: *This impressive jug in white Parian with a lavender ground is by Anderson & Bettany, c.1851–3. The design, usually known as Feeding Time, was originally made by Alcock, although it was also copied by Cork & Edge who titled it 'Keeper's Daughter' (see Plate 453). Black-printed royal arms mark with maker's initials. Height 22 cm.*

PLATE 416: *Rare marked jug by Bradbury, Mason & Bradbury, c.1853–5. This jug is in a hybrid Parian-like stoneware with a lavender ground, although the black-printed royal arms mark with maker's name and address describes it as ironstone china. Height 16.4 cm.*

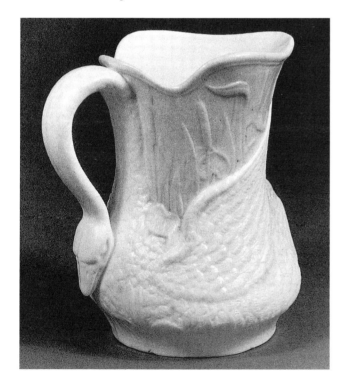

PLATE 415: *Attractive little jug based on the shape of a swan in white Parian with a lavender ground, by Anderson & Bettany, c.1851–3. Black-printed royal arms mark with maker's initials. Height 9.5 cm.*

Returning to major manufacturers, the next company to consider is Copeland. The famous firm founded by Josiah Spode became Copeland & Garrett in 1833 and W. T. Copeland in 1847. Apart from the china jug illustrated earlier (Plate 364) no true relief-moulded jugs appear to have been made during the Spode period and few appeared much before 1840. Copeland & Garrett made some designs which give the appearance of being sprigged, probably due to the use of sprigging in the manufacture of moulds for the distinctive lobed body (Plate 417). Another ornate Copeland & Garrett design was produced in white stoneware (Plate 418).

The firm made extensive use of Parian after its invention in the mid-1840s, with many jugs designed for the new body. Three typical examples include one registered in 1848 soon after Garrett retired (Plate 419) and two which are not dated (Plates 420–1). The Copeland firm also made a range of utilitarian jugs in more durable stoneware, but although they are workmanlike and functional, few are of real merit.

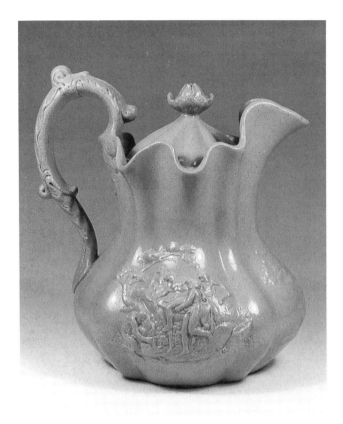

PLATE 417: *Ornate moulded jug in drab earthenware with a matching lid by Copeland & Garrett, c.1833–47. This lobed shape is quite common with a variety of different designs on the sides, all derived from earlier sprig moulds. Impressed mark with maker's name around 'LATE / SPODE'. Height 22.1 cm.*

PLATE 419: *Typical Parian jug by Copeland, registered in 1848. This design is commonly found with added enamel colouring. Moulded cartouche mark with maker's name, also registration diamond for 6 November 1848. Height 21.2 cm (size 18).*

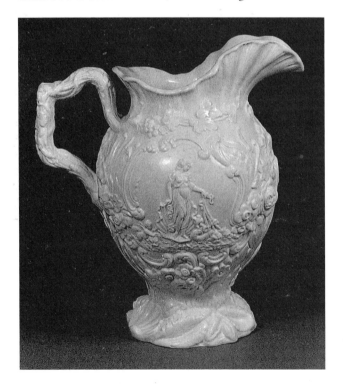

PLATE 418: *Another Copeland & Garrett jug, this one in white stoneware, c.1833–47. The reverse is similar but the panel contains the figure of Aurora. Moulded cartouche mark with maker's name. Height 19.3 cm (size 18).*

PLATE 420: *Another Copeland Parian jug, c.1848–55. An impressive design of basketweave and foliage but with no registration mark. Moulded cartouche mark with maker's name. Height 19.8 cm (size 9).*

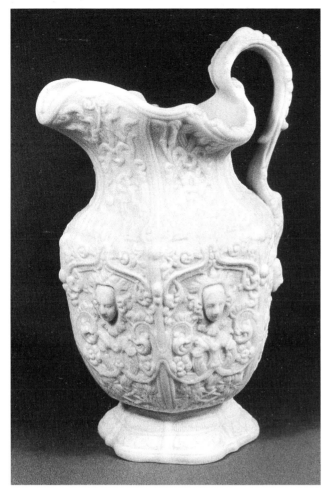

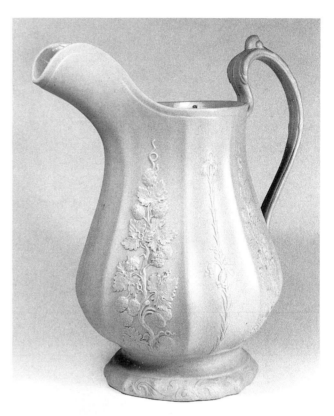

PLATE 421: *Ornately moulded Parian jug by Copeland, c.1848–55. Again there is no registration mark. Moulded cartouche mark with maker's name, which is also impressed. Height 16.5 cm (size 36).*

PLATE 422: *Unrecorded buff stoneware jug by Wood & Brownfield, published in 1841. The holes in the rim indicate a missing metal lid. Impressed mark 'PUBLIHSED [sic] BY / WOOD & BROWNFIELD / COBRIDGE / STAFFORD-SHIRE POTTERIES / JANUARY 1st, 1841'. Height 26.4 cm.*

From 1850 onwards pictorial designs became less common and floral or geometric patterns started to predominate. One of the better exponents was William Brownfield whose firm produced many jugs at Cobridge in the second half of the century, but it is now known that at least three jugs were made earlier by Wood & Brownfield. Two were published at the beginning of 1841, one a stylized naturalistic design (Plate 422), the other featuring a scene based on the Robert Burns poem 'Willie Brew'd a Peck o' Maut' (Plate 423). The latter subject was also used by J. W. Pankhurst & Co. and by Dudson (see Plates 436–7). These were followed a few months later by an impressive design based on one of the Rubens paintings which adorn the ceiling of the Banqueting House in Whitehall (Plate 424).

A decade later Brownfield produced what may have been the first of the long series of decorative jugs for which he is so well known (Plate 425). Initially they were issued mostly in plain stoneware, but coloured backgrounds soon became popular, followed by additional enamelling which was developed into quite a feature. Many designs have been illustrated before but others include two untitled jugs registered in 1855 and 1856 (Plates 426–7), and four later designs titled 'Donatello', 'Union', 'Marne' and 'Montana', registered between 1861 and 1883 (Plates 428–31). Another jug, marked only with the title 'Wicker', is an early design registered in 1855 (Plate 432).

PLATE 423: *Another unrecorded buff stoneware jug by Wood & Brownfield, again published in 1841. The scene from Burns' poem 'Willie Brew'd a Peck o' Maut' was also used by other makers (see Plates 436 and 437). Impressed mark 'PUBLIHSED [sic] BY / WOOD & BROWNFIELD / COBRIDGE / STAFFORDSHIRE POTTERIES / JANUARY 1st, 1841'. Height 18.1 cm.*

147

PLATE 424: *Fine quality and impressive buff stoneware jug published by Wood & Brownfield in 1841. The design is a copy of one of the Rubens panels, this one depicting King James I displaying the Judgment of Solomon, which adorn the ceiling of the* Banqueting House in Whitehall. Impressed mark 'PUBLISHED BY / WOOD / AND BROWNFIELD / COBRIDGE, STAFFORDSHIRE / POTTERIES SEPTEMBER 30th, 1841'. Height 22.8 cm.

PLATE 425: *Early design by William Brownfield, registered in 1851. The body is white stoneware but the dark blue ground has been poorly applied and is flaking off. Applied registration diamond for 16 October 1851. The Britannia-metal lid is not marked. Height 22.3 cm (size 12).*

PLATE 427: *Brownfield jug of an untitled design often referred to as Gothic Ivy, registered in 1856. This example is in white stoneware with a green ground. Moulded registration diamond for 30 April 1856. The Britannia-metal lid is not marked. Height 19.8 cm (size 24).*

PLATE 428: *William Brownfield's 'Donatello' jug in white stoneware with a lilac-coloured ground, registered in 1861. Donatello was a 15th-century Florentine sculptor. Moulded mark with title, registration diamond for 6 July 1861, and a Staffordshire knot containing the maker's initials. Height 17.5 cm (size 36).*

PLATE 426: *Plain white stoneware jug with matching lid by William Brownfield, registered in 1855. The same design was issued without the lid, and in other colours. Impressed registration diamond for 26 April 1855. Height 23 cm (size 12).*

149

PLATE 429: *Very attractive William Brownfield design titled 'Union', registered in 1861. This example is in white stoneware with a blue ground. Moulded mark with title, registration diamond for 4 December 1861, and a Staffordshire knot containing the maker's initials. Height 18.2 cm (size 30).*

PLATE 430: *William Brownfield's 'Marne' jug in white porcelanous stoneware with a blue ground, registered in 1870. Brownfield used several river names for his titles. Moulded circular mark with title and maker's initials and address, all around a registration diamond for 10 November 1870. Height 16.8 cm (size 12).*

PLATE 431: *Unusual jug design titled 'Montana' with a diamond-shaped cross-section, registered by William Brownfield & Sons in 1883. This white stoneware example has been picked out with orange enamel and gilding. Moulded twin-globe trade mark with registration diamond for 25 August 1883 and title; also impressed date code for December 1884. Height 17.5 cm (size 18).*

PLATE 432: *Attractive white stoneware jug titled 'Wicker' attributed to William Brownfield. Although this example has only a moulded title mark, the design was registered by Brownfield on 28 November 1855. Height 18.8 cm (size 18).*

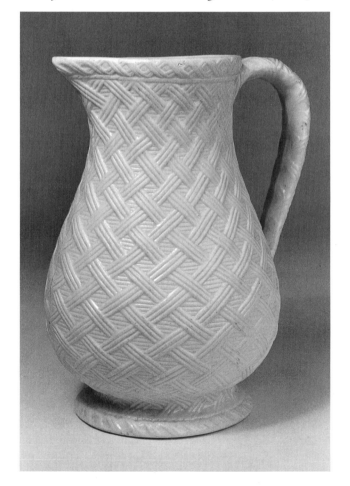

James Dudson of Hanley, along with his successors, produced utilitarian jugs in very large numbers. Many with sprigged decoration have been discussed in Chapter 6, but the firm also made extensive use of relief-moulding. Jugs were produced mainly in plain stoneware, and in comparison with the brightly enamelled jugs of William Brownfield they were presumably aimed at the cheaper end of the market. Dudson's jugs are featured by Audrey Dudson in her pioneering book *Dudson, A Family of Potters Since 1800*.

A Crimean War commemorative jug is impressive (Plate 433), but more mundane designs predominate including a previously unrecorded stylized geometric pattern probably issued twenty years or so later (Plate 434). The latter is typical of many Dudson jugs, with a bulbous body and flared spout, the same basic shape reappearing on a jug moulded with birds (Plate 435). As with several others, similar designs were used on sprigged jugs (Plates 328 and 332).

A final Dudson jug is unmarked but the design corresponds to shards excavated on the factory site (Plate

436). The scene is also taken from Burns's poem 'Willie Brew'd a Peck o' Maut', used earlier by Wood & Brownfield (Plate 423) and J. W. Pankhurst & Co. in the 1850s, although all three firms used different shapes. A jug of the Pankhurst shape is shown here with a fascinating and previously unrecorded incised mark for William Brunt (Plate 437).

The firms mentioned above all specialized to some extent in relief-moulded jugs. Ridgway, Meigh, Jones & Walley, Brownfield and Dudson concentrated on stoneware, whereas Alcock, Minton and Copeland are particularly noted for Parian. A few other major firms and a host of lesser potteries made jugs throughout the Victorian period, and the remaining illustrations represent just a small selection of their wares.

PLATE 433: *Two views of a rare and impressive drab stoneware Crimean War commemorative jug by James Dudson, c.1854–6. The design features the British coat of arms alongside those for France and Turkey, with Russian emblems on the reverse. Impressed mark 'DUDSON'. Height 21.5 cm.*

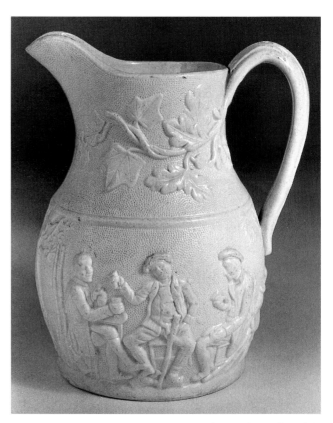

PLATE 436: *Although unmarked, shards matching this white stoneware jug were found during excavations on the Dudson factory site. The design probably dates from around 1860, and the same scene from Burns's poem 'Willie Brew'd a Peck o' Maut' was used by other potters (see Plates 423 and 437). Height 15.3 cm.*

PLATE 434: *Typical but previously unrecorded Dudson jug in white stoneware, c.1870–80. Impressed mark 'DUDSON'. Height 23.7 cm.*

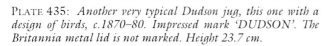

PLATE 435: *Another very typical Dudson jug, this one with a design of birds, c.1870–80. Impressed mark 'DUDSON'. The Britannia metal lid is not marked. Height 23.7 cm.*

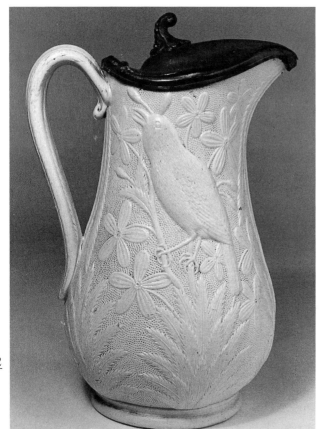

PLATE 437: *Another jug with the scene from 'Willie Brew'd a Peck o' Maut'. This version corresponds to the design registered by William Ridgway in 1851 but made by J. W. Pankhurst & Co., although this particular jug has an incised mark for William Brunt with an indistinct place name. Brunt may have been a workman at Pankhurst's pottery. Height 18.5 cm.*

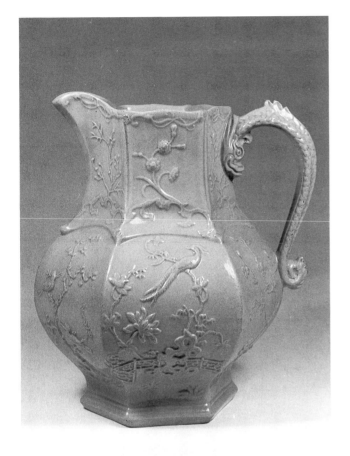

While the Mason name is synonymous with brightly coloured ironstone china (see Chapter 9), the firm also made some interesting relief-moulded jugs. They include a version of the popular Silenus jug more usually associated with Minton (Plate 373), a design of dogs in very high relief titled 'Toho', and a boar and stag hunting scene also made in brown stoneware by Doulton. Two others are shown here; a hexagonal jug moulded with a chinoiserie design (Plate 438), and a previously unrecorded jug with two unidentified classical scenes (Plate 439).

Although the connection is tenuous, the Mason firm was succeeded by Morley & Ashworth and then by G. L. Ashworth & Bros, who continued to produce ironstone china but also made moulded jugs. A previously unrecorded jug by Morley & Ashworth (Plate 440) is similar to a Minton design (Plate 379). The later Ashworth designs can be unusual but are often heavily enamelled and relatively undistinguished. Two typical examples are shown; one titled 'Dagmar' (Plate 441), the other 'Satyr' (Plate 442).

PLATE 438: *Hexagonal jug in drab stoneware by C. J. Mason & Co., c.1835–45. Other examples of this jug have slight variations in the moulded design. Black-printed crown and drape mark with maker's surname. Height 23.1 cm.*

PLATE 439: *Two views of a rare Mason's jug in blue stoneware, c.1840–5. The classical or biblical scenes have not yet been identified, although a double female head on the handle may provide a clue. Black-printed crown and drape mark with maker's surname. Height 16.8 cm.*

PLATE 440: *Rare but relatively poor quality jug in buff stoneware with a white slip interior, by Morley & Ashworth, c.1860. Note the similarity with the Minton jug in Plate 379. Impressed circular mark with maker's name and address. Height 16.8 cm.*

PLATE 442: *Another Ashworth jug, this one in white stoneware with brown ground, blue enamelling, and gilding, c.1865–70. This is a typically unusual Ashworth shape. Moulded circular mark with title 'SATYR' and maker's initials and address; also pattern number 'B/3615' painted in brown. Height 20.4 cm (size 24).*

PLATE 441: *White stoneware jug enamelled in green with orange ground to moulding, registered in 1868 by G. L. Ashworth & Bros. Moulded circular mark with title 'Dagmar' and maker's initials and address, all around a registration diamond for 31 December 1868; also impressed 'ASHWORTH'. Height 13.6 cm (size 36).*

The Mayer brothers are perhaps not so well known as Mason but their firm produced some fine wares in the mid-nineteenth century. Rather like Alcock they used a series of model numbers for moulded wares, mostly issued in several colour variants. Two typical designs are shown: one featuring convolvulus growing over a tree (Plate 443), the other depicting the popular story of Paul and Virginia (Plate 444). A third, moulded with cherubs, appears on two miniature jugs but was presumably also made full size (Plate 445). The Mayer firms were succeeded by Liddle Elliot in about 1860, and with his sons he also made a range of moulded jugs. They include one simple design with holly on a barrel (Plate 446). One feature noted on several Elliot jugs is a distinctive green background, which also appears on a fascinating jug depicting two of the nine worthies, Hector of Troy and King Arthur (Plate 447).

PLATE 443: *Convolvulus jug registered in 1850 by T. J. & J. Mayer of Longport. This jug is potted in a hybrid Parian-like stoneware, with a blue ground and turquoise leaves. Several other colour combinations were made. Moulded scroll mark with model 'No. 53'; also brown-printed royal arms mark with maker's name and address, along with registration diamond for 12 December 1850. Note the matching convolvulus knop on the unmarked Britannia-metal lid. Height 20.2 cm.*

PLATE 444: *Two Mayer jugs in white Parian with a dark pink ground. This popular design based on the novel* Paul and Virginia *was also registered in 1850. Both jugs have black-printed royal arms marks with the maker's name and address along with registration diamonds for 2 July 1850. The larger jug also has a moulded scroll with model 'No. 98'. Heights 18.7 cm and 20.1 cm (size 24).*

PLATE 445: *Two miniature Parian jugs with a design of cherubs by T. J. & J. Mayer, c.1845–55. The left hand jug is enamelled in green, turquoise, black, orange, pink, brown, yellow and purple, and has a moulded scroll mark with model 'No. 34'. The other has a brown-printed royal arms mark with the maker's name and address, and 'PRIZE MEDAL 1851' above. Heights 9.3 cm (size 36) and 9.1 cm.*

PLATE 446: *White stoneware jug registered by Liddle Elliot & Son in 1864. The simple barrel shape is draped with holly and mistletoe. Moulded registration diamond for 25 February 1864. Height 11.9 cm (size 12).*

PLATE 447: *Tall and impressive white stoneware jug with a green ground, potted in 1868. Although it is of a continental shape and unmarked, several attributes suggest that it may have been made by Liddle Elliot & Son. This side depicts King Arthur, while the reverse is similar but with Hector of Troy, another of the nine worthies. Impressed date code for January 1868 and pattern number '9372' painted in green. Height 26.3 cm.*

Although noted for fine porcelain, the famous Worcester factory made a few relief-moulded jugs in the second half of the nineteenth century. Parian examples include one based on Thorwaldsen's famous reliefs depicting Night and Morning (Plate 448), and another with a design of ivy (Plate 449). These both date from the Kerr & Binns period between 1852 and 1862, although the latter is uncommonly marked W. H. Kerr & Co. A so-called 'Shakspeare' jug, based on mid-eighteenth-century salt-glazed stoneware, was produced in earthenware at this period, and another slightly later design based on a pineapple is surprisingly made of stoneware (Plate 450).

The Staffordshire firm of Cork & Edge did not aspire to the heights of fine porcelain, but were always at the utilitarian end of the market. They owe their significance to engravings showing more than twenty jugs exhibited at the 1855 Paris Exhibition. Most of the designs are known only with the marks of other makers, particularly Alcock and Walley. This enigma still awaits a solution, but possibly the firm was acting as agents for other potters at the Paris show. Marked Cork & Edge jugs are uncommon but include a Babes in the Wood design (Plate 451), a fairly crude floral pattern (Plate 452) and an imposing design titled 'Keeper's Daughter' (Plate 453). This and the Babes in the Wood design are straight copies of jugs by Samuel Alcock (Plate 403), but both were also made by Bradbury, Anderson & Bettany (Plate 414).

Cork & Edge were succeeded about 1860 by Cork, Edge & Malkin and then in 1871 by Edge, Malkin & Co. Both made jugs typical of the period, including one attractive design with flowers above basketweave (Plate 454), a running plant pattern (Plate 455) and a later, undistinguished design titled 'Trentham' (Plate 456).

PLATE 448: *Worcester Parian jug potted in the Kerr & Binns period, c.1852–62. This side is based on Thorwaldsen's relief depicting Night, with the corresponding Morning on the reverse. Blue-printed circle mark. Height 15.9 cm.*

PLATE 449: *Hexagonal Parian jug with a design of ivy by W.H. Kerr & Co. of Worcester, c.1856–62. Blue-printed mark in the form of a crown within concentric circles inscribed with maker's name and address. Height 21.6 cm.*

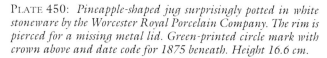

PLATE 450: *Pineapple-shaped jug surprisingly potted in white stoneware by the Worcester Royal Porcelain Company. The rim is pierced for a missing metal lid. Green-printed circle mark with crown above and date code for 1875 beneath. Height 16.6 cm.*

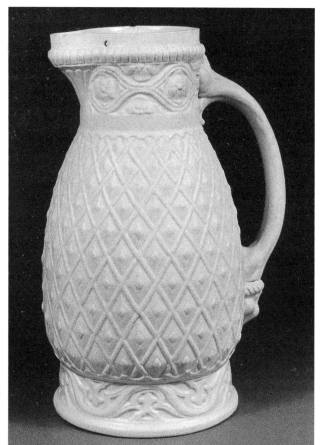

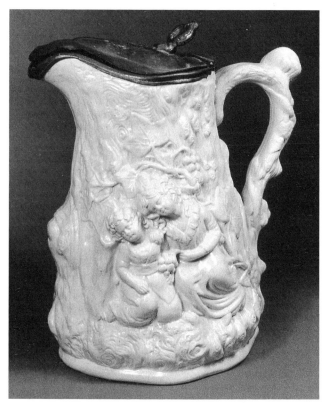

PLATE 451: *Popular Babes in the Wood jug in white stoneware by Cork & Edge, c.1850–60. The design was used by other potters (see for example Plate 403). Black-printed royal arms mark with maker's name. The Britannia-metal lid is not marked. Height 21.7 cm.*

PLATE 452: *Typically poor quality green stoneware jug by Cork & Edge, c.1855–60. Black-printed royal arms mark with maker's name. Height 15.5 cm.*

PLATE 453: *Although more impressive, this blue stoneware jug titled 'Keeper's Daughter' by Cork & Edge is still only of utilitarian quality. It is a copy of an earlier design by Samuel Alcock & Co. which was also used by Anderson & Bettany (see Plate 414). Moulded circular mark with title and maker's name. Height 23.1 cm.*

PLATE 455: *Another white stoneware jug by Cork, Edge & Malkin, c.1860–5. This design was not registered, and the turquoise ground is less common than blue. Moulded scroll mark with maker's initials. The Britannia-metal lid is not marked. Height 22.4 cm.*

PLATE 454: *Simple but attractive jug in white stoneware with a blue ground, registered by Cork, Edge & Malkin in 1861. Applied blue registration diamond for 31 May 1861, and separate mark with maker's initials. The Britannia-metal lid is marked 'THOMPSON'S PATENT'. Height 21 cm.*

PLATE 456: *Stoneware jug with blue ground in a design titled 'Trentham', registered by Edge, Malkin & Co. in 1874. Black-printed registration diamond for 17 June 1874 with title and maker's initials. Height 17.8 cm.*

Opposite:
PLATE 457: *Fine quality green and white stoneware jug made by T. & R. Boote in 1850 to commemorate the accidental death of Robert Peel. The combined colours are achieved by one of Boote's 'Patent Mosaic' processes. Ornate black-printed vignette mark with a lengthy eulogy and the maker's name. The Britannia-metal lid is marked 'J.F. PARKER / 12 MOOR ST / 7 LITTLE COMPTON ST / SOHO'. Height 23.3 cm.*

PLATE 458: *Although the maker's name is not present, this attractive turquoise and white Parian jug may also be by T. & R. Boote. Black-printed royal arms mark. Height 18.6 cm.*

Right:
PLATE 459: *The only moulded jug so far recorded by Thomas & John Carey of Lane End, c.1830–42. The overall pattern of daisy heads seen on this good-quality blue stoneware jug was a popular motif in the 1820–40 period. Moulded crown mark with thistle, rose, shamrock and maker's surname. Height 21.4 cm.*

The last firm to call for specific comment is T. & R. Boote of Burslem. Richard Boote patented several decorating techniques in 1843, including processes for producing coloured backgrounds or contrasting reliefs. One was adopted particularly by Alcock and also by Bradbury, Anderson & Bettany. The phrase 'Patent Mosaic' was coined and this appears on jugs by the Bootes, including a fine jug made by another of the processes and commemorating the accidental death of Robert Peel (Plate 457). It appears again on another jug which gives all the appearance of a Boote product (Plate 458). Unfortunately, the wording was also used for no apparent reason by Cork & Edge (Plates 451–2).

Relief-moulding was one of the most important methods for decorating utilitarian jugs from 1840 onwards and literally hundreds of designs appeared. Lack of space precludes many more illustrations, but a few may be appropriate. The opportunity lends itself to covering firms which have not previously been recorded as making these wares, some small and little-known but others quite important. Examples are shown without specific comment approximately in date order, including jugs by Thomas & John Carey (Plate 459), Sewell & Donkin (Plate 460), Samuel & John Burton (Plate 461), Elijah Hughes (Plate 462), Thomas Cooper (Plate 463), Bodley & Harrold (Plate 464), Charles Collinson & Co. (Plate 465) and Hall & Read (Plate 466). Three more jugs were made by Davenport (Plate 467) and F. & R. Pratt & Co. of Fenton (Plates 468–9), both famous names not normally associated with these wares.

PLATE 460: *Another rarity, this one in blue earthenware attributed to Sewell & Donkin of the St Anthony's Pottery at Newcastle-upon-Tyne, c.1830–40. The pattern is similar in style to the previous example but the jug is more closely related to an earlier design used by Ridgway and the Don Pottery. Applied white circular pad mark with maker's initials. Height 14.1 cm.* (Courtesy: Jack Hacking)

PLATE 461: *Glazed white earthenware jug by Samuel & John Burton, c.1832–45. The moulding is enhanced with gilding and a moulded mark with the maker's initials includes a model 'No. 6'. Height 16.3 cm.* (Courtesy: Jack Hacking)

Right Top:
PLATE 462: *Light grey stoneware jug of Dudson type but by Elijah Hughes of Cobridge, c.1860. Black-printed American eagle mark with maker's name. Height 18.4 cm.*

PLATE 463: *Two views of a rare and impressive Parian jug with a blue ground registered by Thomas Cooper of Hanley in 1862. The design commemorates the betrothal of Albert Edward, Prince of Wales (the future Edward VII), to Princess Alexandra of Schleswig-Holstein-Sonderburg-Glücksburg. They were married at Windsor on 10 March 1863. Moulded registration diamond for 9 December 1862. Height 29.6 cm.*

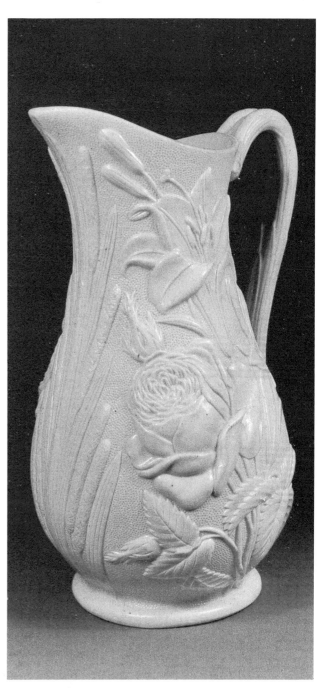

Below:
PLATE 464: *Stoneware jug with blue ground registered by Bodley & Harrold of Burslem in 1864. This is typical of very many designs made by minor potters in the third quarter of the 19th century. Moulded registration diamond for 28 October 1864. Height 19.8 cm.*

PLATE 465: *Attractive white stoneware jug of better than average quality registered by Charles Collinson & Co. in 1864. A metal lid is missing. Moulded registration diamond for 29 October 1864. Height 20.1 cm.*

PLATE 466: *White stoneware jug with blue ground and detailed gilding, registered by Hall & Read in 1883, very late for a pictorial design of this type. Moulded registration diamond for 22 February 1883. The Britannia-metal lid is not marked. Height 17 cm.*

PLATE 468: *Unusual and attractive chocolate-coloured stoneware jug registered by F. & R. Pratt & Co. in 1877. The moulding is picked out with blue, yellow, green, grey and red-brown enamels. Impressed registration diamond for 24 October 1877 with maker's initials. The Britannia-metal lid is marked 'THOMPSON'S / PATENT' and 'BROADHEAD & Co / SHEFFIELD'. Height 16.3 cm.*

PLATE 469: *White translucent stoneware jug with a design of ferns registered by F. & R. Pratt & Co. in 1866. Jugs of this standard type are not usually associated with the Pratt concern. Moulded registration diamond for 6 September 1866. Height 18.3 cm.*

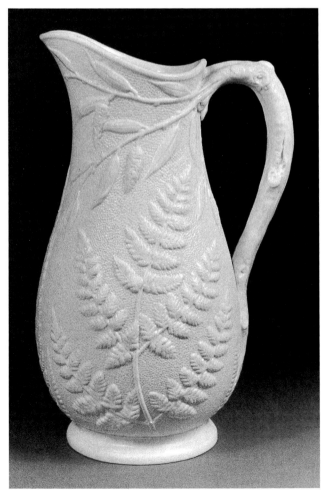

PLATE 467: *Rare buff stoneware jug by Davenport, c.1840. This is the only relief-moulded jug design known from this famous factory. Impressed mark 'DAVENPORT' above an anchor. Height 21 cm. (Courtesy: Jack Hacking)*

PLATE 470: *Glazed drab stoneware jug marked with unidentified initials. Designs featuring knights were popular around 1840 following the famous Eglinton tournament. Impressed initials 'M & C' over 'D'. Height 21.6 cm.*

Relief-moulded jugs offer a vast and fascinating field for study, and it seems quite appropriate to finish this chapter with a puzzle, a death and a rarity. The puzzle is a mystery initial mark found on at least two different jugs (Plates 470–1). They are both impressed 'M & C' over 'D' but no potter with these initials can be traced. The second design has a strong Irish flavour and it has been suggested these jugs they were made in Scotland for export to Ireland.

The death concerns a jug made in 1898 by Doulton to commemorate Gladstone (Plate 472). Although relief-moulding had largely been superseded by 1890 or so, it never entirely went out of fashion, and some interesting jugs were made even into the twentieth century.

The rarity is a magnificent jug covered with the coats of arms of nineteen nations represented at the Paris International Exhibition of 1855 (Colour Plate 20). This example is in porcelain, heavily gilt and enamelled, but others are known in stoneware, either plain white or green enhanced with silver. There have been suggestions that it was made by Alcock or modelled by Henry Baggeley, but in the true spirit of many of these jugs, the facts remain elusive.

PLATE 472: *Relief-moulded jug with a matt ivory glaze made by Doulton & Co. at Burslem to commemorate the death of Gladstone in 1898. The reverse has a coat of arms with crest and motto. Printed maker's mark with relevant registration number. Height 18 cm.* (Courtesy: Dreweatt Neate, Newbury)

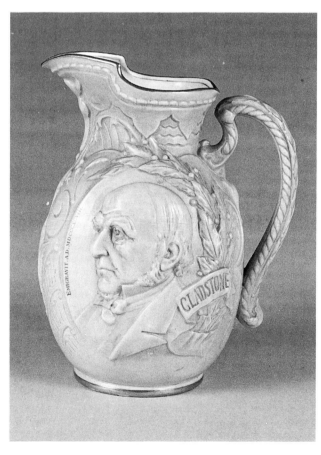

PLATE 471: *Another glazed drab stoneware jug with the same unidentified initials. It has been suggested that this design with a prominent harp may have been intended for the Irish market. Impressed initials 'M & C' over 'D'. Height 20.2 cm.*

PLATE 473: *Turner stone china jug with an Imari-type pattern, c.1800–5. This typical design features underglaze blue with iron-red, green and mulberry enamels and some gilding. Red-painted mark 'Turner's-Patent'. Height 12.1 cm.* (Courtesy: City Museum & Art Gallery, Stoke-on-Trent)

9.

Stone China and Other Coloured Jugs

The second half of the eighteenth century saw considerable improvements in pottery. Creamware, pearlware and fine-bodied stonewares all made a great impact, enabling. widespread production of attractive utilitarian wares. However, they had their limitations and there remained a need for a body stronger and more durable than earthenware but with the finer appearance of china. This emerged in the form of stone china, one of the most important developments of the early nineteenth century.

The Turners of Lane End took out a patent in 1800 for the use of a mineral which they incorporated in a stone china body called 'Turner's Patent'. This was used mainly for dinner and tea services and similar useful wares, but examples are uncommon and it was not in production for long. The jug shown is typically decorated with an Imari-type pattern in underglaze blue with overglaze red and green enamels (Plate 473).

Exactly what happened to Turner's patent when the firm went bankrupt in 1806 has been the subject of much speculation. However, in 1813 Mason introduced their famous 'Patent Ironstone China' and at about the same time Spode unveiled a similar body. Which came first is not clear, but while Masons promoted their patent particularly effectively, the Spode version is of higher quality.

Two typical Spode jugs dating from around 1812 have decoration of the same basic type as the earlier Turner jug. One incorporates the border from the blue-printed Grasshopper pattern (Plate 474); the other is a version of the factory's popular Cabbage pattern (Plate 475). Another similar Spode jug printed with the Marble pattern, carefully enamelled and gilt, is made of ordinary earthenware (Plate 476). All three are of the traditional Dutch shape. Similar Davenport jugs can be found, also potted before 1820.

Colourful patterns of this type are widely associated with stone china but were also used on earthenware and other bodies. Another Spode example, made of felspar porcelain, has the added feature of the body moulded with a spray of flowers (Plate 477).

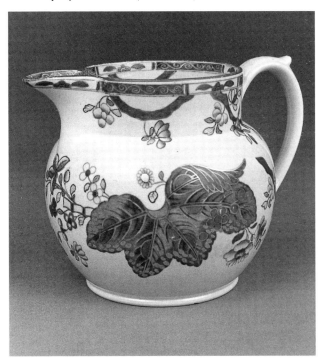

PLATE 474: *Spode stone china jug, c.1812–20. The underglaze blue design, enamelled in iron-red with some gilding and an ochre rim, includes the border from the blue-printed Grasshopper pattern. Printed 'Stone China' seal mark with pattern number '2086' painted in iron-red. Height 14.9 cm.*

PLATE 475: *Another Spode stone china jug, c.1812–20. This design, printed in underglaze blue and enamelled in iron-red, green and carmine with some gilding and an ochre rim, is known as the Cabbage pattern. Printed 'Stone China' half-seal mark with pattern number '2061' painted in iron-red. Height 12 cm.*

PLATE 476: *Covered earthenware jug by Spode, c.1822–25. The blue-printed Marble pattern is enamelled in yellow, pink and red, and gilded. Printed mark 'SPODE' on jug only; pattern number '3739/H' painted in red on both pieces. Height 18.4 cm.*

PLATE 477: *Spode jug moulded with flowers in felspar porcelain, c.1821–33. The typical outline print is enamelled in colours. Printed mark 'SPODE'. Height 30.4 cm (size 6).*

While Spode's stone china is particularly fine, Mason's version made a greater impact. Following their patent of 1813, the firm produced utilitarian wares in great quantity. Jugs were included, particularly the common octagonal 'Oriental' or 'Hydra' shape with a serpent handle. One popular pattern is a bright Japan-type design used also by Davenport (Plate 478). Another is an attractive Chinese garden scene (Plate 479), sometimes fitted with a crabstock handle (Plate 480). Many other patterns exist, frequently utilizing a printed outline colour filled with enamels (Plate 481).

PLATE 478: *Two octagonal stone china jugs of the common 'Oriental' or 'Hydra' shape, both decorated predominantly in red and blue with a popular Japan pattern, c.1815–30. The larger example is by Davenport with a printed 'DAVENPORT / STONE CHINA' arched anchor mark, the smaller one by Mason, impressed 'PATENT IRONSTONE CHINA'. Heights 11.5 cm and 7.4 cm*

PLATE 479: *Mason's ironstone octagonal jug of later date with a popular Chinese garden scene pattern. The design is printed in black and enamelled in reds, greens, yellow and blue with some peach lustre. Printed maker's crown and drape mark with pattern number 'C/107' painted in red. Height 17.5 cm.*

PLATE 481: *Another Mason ironstone jug with a typical later pattern, this one sparsely decorated with a maroon outline print enhanced with underglaze blue, red enamel and gilding. Printed maker's crown and drape mark. Height 15.1 cm.*

PLATE 480: *The same basic design as seen in Plate 479 but on two Mason ironstone jugs fitted with crabstock handles in place of the usual serpent. Printed maker's crown and drape mark. Heights 13.3 and 16.1 cm.*

Although colourful enamelled wares predominate, other distinctive designs include a dramatic red-enamelled dragon on a matt black background (Plate 482) and two with dark mazarine blue grounds (Plates 483–4). The latter are of fine quality but unmarked, and although considered to be by Mason, similar jugs were marked by Zachariah Boyle (see, for example, Northern Ceramic Society, *Stonewares and Stone Chinas of Northern England to 1851*, plate 295). An apparently similar Spode jug is made of bone china (Plate 485).

These octagonal jugs were a staple product for the Mason firm and its successors, and later examples often bear pattern numbers in addition to the usual Mason crown and drape mark. A few examples made by Ashworths are marked with their own name, typically decorated with outline prints roughly filled with coloured enamels (Plate 486). This jug has amusingly been fitted with a handle one size too small for the body.

While this 'Oriental' shape was made in great numbers, some others were also used. Two early hexagonal examples are shown (Plates 487–8), together with another octagonal shape known as 'Fenton' which was produced for some time (Plates 489–90). Most of these jugs are printed with outline designs which are enamelled over, although another example has sparser decoration which usually indicates a later date (Plate 491).

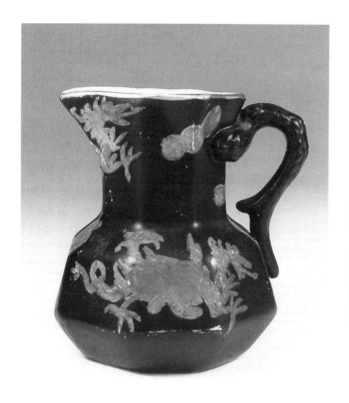

PLATE 482: *Mason's octagonal ironstone jug unusually decorated with a matt black ground, red dragons and a gilt rim. Printed maker's crown and drape mark with pattern number 'C/192/12' painted in red. Height 9 cm.*

PLATE 484: *Another unmarked ironstone jug with a mazarine blue ground, c.1820–30. The attractive design is gilded and enamelled in pale blue and white. Again attributed to Mason. Height 19.1 cm.*

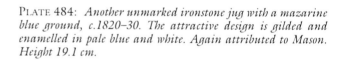

PLATE 485: *Although superficially similar to the previous example, this octagonal jug is by Spode and made in bone china, c.1820–25. The blue ground is gilded and enamelled in pink, yellow, blues and green. Red-painted mark 'SPODE' with pattern number '3420'. Height 13.8 cm.*

PLATE 483: *Octagonal ironstone jug with a mazarine blue ground finely gilt with a design of insects, c.1820–30. Unmarked, but attributed to Mason. Height 9.2 cm.*

PLATE 486: *Typical later Mason's ironstone china octagonal jug, but with an Ashworth mark, c.1862–80. The design is printed in black and enamelled in red, green, orange and carmine, with a peach lustre rim. Printed crown mark with maker's surname and address, also pattern number 'B/9447' painted in red. Height 16.7 cm.*

PLATE 487: *Mason's ironstone jug of a less common hexagonal shape, c.1825–40. The design features a blue ground, gilding and yellow, red, green and orange enamels over an outline print. Printed maker's crown and drape mark with pattern number '111/X' painted in red. Height 24.3 cm.*

PLATE 488: *Another uncommon Mason's hexagonal shape, c.1825–40. Again large areas of blue are enamelled in green, light green, red, yellow and ochre. Printed maker's crown and drape mark. Height 13.8 cm.*

PLATE 489: *This octagonal shape, known as Fenton, was produced for many years, this example probably c.1835–40. The Imari style pattern with gilt-framed panels again has a dark blue ground decorated in red and gilt. Height 24 cm. (Courtesy: Sotheby's, Sussex)*

171

The remaining Mason jugs are from the firm's earlier years, the first a fine example with an entwined handle rather reminiscent of eighteenth-century creamwares (Plate 492). The pattern matches one of the earlier illustrations (Plate 489). The remaining two are large water jugs, both with extra handles beneath the spout, one shown together with a matching footbath (Plate 493). The second is decorated with the same colourful Japan-type pattern (Plate 494).

The widespread adoption of stone china and its colourful Japan patterns had a great influence. The body was made in endless varieties, often promoted under trade names such as 'Real Stone China', 'Opaque China', 'Semi-China', and particularly 'Granite China' or 'White Granite'. Some of these were also misleadingly used on standard earthenwares.

While stone china itself was produced in large quantities, it also created a wider market for colourful wares. Around 1825–30 there was a fashion for enamelled jugs with prominent underglaze blue grounds. Two typical examples are shown; the first by a Longton firm, possibly Baggerley & Ball (Plate 495); the other by Mayer & Newbold (Plate 496). Similar jugs were made by other Staffordshire firms such as Lockett & Hulme, and at Bristol by one of the Pountney partnerships.

PLATE 493: *Large Mason's ironstone jug with matching foot-bath, c.1825–40. This colourful Japan pattern features vases and bowls of flowers. Note the usual serpent handle and the additional support on the front moulded as another grotesque creature.* (Courtesy: Lawrence Fine Art, Crewkerne)

PLATE 494: *Another large Mason's ironstone jug with the same Japan pattern, c.1820–30. The octagonal body is fitted with an unusual dolphin handle and again has an additional moulded support on the front. Printed maker's mark. Height 32.5 cm.* (Courtesy: Sotheby's, Sussex)

PLATE 495: *Simple earthenware jug printed underglaze in blue and enamelled in red, yellow, green and pink, c.1825–30. A printed 'Opaque China' mark includes initials 'B & B/L', possibly relating to Baggerley & Ball of Longton. Height 11.1 cm.* (Courtesy: City Museum & Art Gallery, Stoke-on-Trent)

PLATE 497: *Antique-shape jug by Spode, c.1820–33. The pattern is known as Tumbledown Dick but is unusually shown on a matt black ground enamelled in pink and red with some gilding. Impressed and printed marks 'SPODE'. Height 16.1 cm (size 12).*

PLATE 496: *Octagonal earthenware jug by Mayer & Newbold, c.1825–30. The decoration is of the same basic type as the previous example, in underglaze blue enamelled with iron-red, green, mulberry and ochre. Printed mark with maker's initials and trade name 'NEW/OPAQUE'. Height 11.3 cm. (Courtesy: City Museum & Art Gallery, Stoke-on-Trent)*

PLATE 498: *Tankard-like jug in Mason's Bandana ware, c.1835–45. The sheet design is black-printed and enamelled in red, yellow, blue, black and orange, with a gilt rim. Printed mark 'MASON'S' above a crown. Height 16.3 cm. (Courtesy: City Museum & Art Gallery, Stoke-on-Trent)*

Many other colourful wares were made at this period, often distinctive but difficult to classify. One example is a Spode antique-shape jug covered overall with a matt black ground and enamelled with birds and flowers in shades of pink and red (Plate 497). This is a variant of the popular printed Tumbledown Dick pattern, usually found with a cracked-ice or marble background. This jug was probably outline-printed before colouring.

Another development about this time was the introduction of sheet patterns, again printed and coloured. Mason's distinctive but rarely found Bandana ware is one good example (Plate 498), but more common are the many sheet floral patterns. A Spode jug of unusual shape, decorated with pattern number B241 in green, is a typical early example of this type (Plate 499). Although not strictly a sheet pattern, another jug made in the Copeland & Garrett period is similar (Plate 500). Like the genuine sheet patterns, the exact positioning of this print on the ware was not important to the overall result.

175

As the century progressed the popularity of wares printed in a single colour (see Chapter 5) steadily declined. Multi-colour printing was an obvious but technically difficult development, and other ways to satisfy the demand for colourful wares were sought. The easiest route lay in printing a design in outline and then using cheap unskilled labour to enamel it, rather like a child's colouring book. In practice, several earlier designs are of this type, including the four Spode jugs (Plates 474–7), but they are of high quality. Around 1840 the use of outline-printing became common in Staffordshire and elsewhere; typical examples include jugs by Twiggs of Yorkshire (Plate 501) and by the South Wales Pottery (Plate 502).

While these engravings were designed specifically to be colour filled, the same overglaze colouring technique was also applied to brighten up existing engravings. This is apparent on one large display jug with several scattered engravings (Plate 503) and on two jugs featuring animals alongside Grimaldi the clown. The first is unmarked but dated 1863 (Plate 504) while the second has a clear mark for Elsmore & Forster (Plate 505). Another unmarked jug of the same type is decorated with scattered agricultural motifs (Plate 506).

PLATE 499: *Spode earthenware jug of an unrecorded shape with a serpent handle, c.1827–33. The sheet pattern, number B241, is printed in green and picked out in red, yellow and blue. Printed mark 'SPODE'S NEW FAYENCE'. Height 12.7 cm.*

PLATE 500: *Angular Copeland & Garrett jug with mask spout, c.1833–40. This version of the Worcester Wheel pattern, number B336, is printed in brown and coloured yellow, blue, red and purple. A strainer behind the spout indicates a missing lid. Printed and impressed maker's 'LATE SPODE' marks. Height 20.3 cm.*

PLATE 501: *Earthenware jug with moulded octagonal body by the Twiggs of Yorkshire, c.1840–50. The design is outline-printed in brown and enamelled red, green, yellow, and blue. Impressed mark 'TWIGGS'. Height 23.1 cm.*

COLOUR PLATE 18: *Two views of 'The Royal Patriotic Jug' designed by George Eyre and registered by Samuel Alcock & Co. in 1854. This example has red and dark green enamelling but other variants are known. Ornate black-printed mark with title, designer's and maker's names, and registration diamond for 27 December 1854. Height 20.3 cm.*

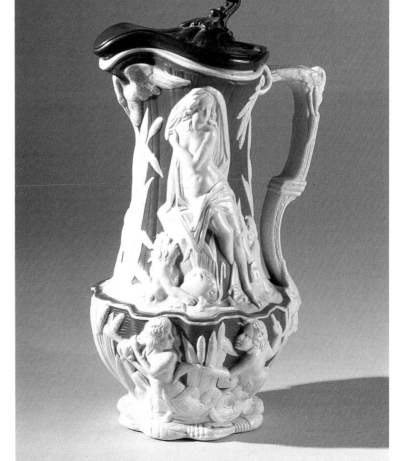

COLOUR PLATE 19: *Relief-moulded jug in white stoneware with a blue ground, registered by Charles Meigh & Son in 1856. This popular design depicts the goddess Amphitrite. Moulded registration diamond for 13 June 1856 with maker's name. The Britannia-metal lid is marked 'JAMES DIXON & SONS'. Height 21.3 cm (size 30).*

COLOUR PLATE 21: *Marbled or moonlight lustre earthenware jug with matching cup and saucer by Wedgwood, c.1810. The shades of colour are achieved using oxides of iron, platinum and gold. Impressed mark 'WEDGWOOD'. Height 14 cm.* (Courtesy: Trustees of the Wedgwood Museum, Barlaston, Staffordshire)

Opposite:
COLOUR PLATE 20: *Impressive but unattributed porcelain commemorative jug, superbly enamelled and heavily gilt. The design features the nineteen nations contributing to the Paris Exhibition of 1855, the name of each country appearing above its coat of arms. Height 38 cm.* (Courtesy: Sotheby's, London)

COLOUR PLATE 22: *Copper lustre jug with a pink wedding transfer of Queen Victoria and Prince Albert, probably Staffordshire, c.1840. The purple print is framed with pink lustre and surrounded by a yellow ground, unusual at this late date. Height 20 cm.* (Courtesy: Bonhams, Knightsbridge)

COLOUR PLATE 23: *Minton majolica jug in the Peasant Dancers pattern, dated 1868. This design is shape number 487. Impressed maker's mark with shape number and date code. Height 33 cm.* (Courtesy: Sotheby's, London)

COLOUR PLATE 24: *Wedgwood Vine jug with a design of vine leaves and bunches of grapes decorated with majolica glazes, c.1892–1900. Printed mark 'WEDGWOOD. ETRURIA. ENGLAND'.* (Courtesy: Trustees of the Wedgwood Museum, Barlaston, Staffordshire)

Opposite:
COLOUR PLATE 27: *A fine collection of nine puzzle jugs from the 18th and early 19th centuries. They include Liverpool delftware, pearlware, white salt-glazed stoneware with scratch-blue decoration, three in brown salt-glazed stoneware, another in pearlware, Bristol creamware, and Leeds creamware. Maximum height 31.5 cm.* (Courtesy: Sotheby's, London)

COLOUR PLATE 25: *Brown salt-glazed stoneware jug moulded as the head of the Duke of Wellington by Stephen Green of Lambeth, c.1830–40. The handle is moulded with military accoutrements. Moulded scroll frame containing maker's name and address. Height 18.9 cm.*

COLOUR PLATE 26: *Two early 20th-century Martin Brothers stoneware face jugs. Note the very different surface finishes. Smaller example with incised maker's mark 'R.W. Martin & Bros, London & Southall, 3.1911'; the larger jug with 'Martin Bros, London & Southall'. Heights 12 cm and 21.5 cm.* (Courtesy: Sotheby's, London)

COLOUR PLATE 28: *English delftware puzzle jug of the standard form, probably Liverpool, dated 1732. The body is painted in blue with the usual verse within a panel flanked by flowers. Height 18.4 cm.* (Courtesy: Dreweatt Neate, Newbury)

COLOUR PLATE 30: *Slipware scraffito puzzle jug made at the Ewenny Pottery, dated 1830. The body is inscribed: 'mary morgans ounr' with 'Thomas arthyr meker/june 19/1830'. Height 33 cm.* (Courtesy: Sotheby's, London)

COLOUR PLATE 29: *Another Liverpool delftware puzzle jug of similar form but later date, c.1760. This variant of the inscription is less common. Height 19.7 cm.* (Courtesy: Sotheby's, London)

COLOUR PLATE 31: *An attractive group of twelve late 18th-century Toby jugs of various types including the Thin Man, the Sailorman, and the Squire. Maximum height 29.2 cm. (Courtesy: Sotheby's, London)*

Below Left:
COLOUR PLATE 32: *Rare marked Ralph Wood Toby jug, finely modelled and decorated predominantly with green, brown, yellow, and blue glazes, c.1790. Impressed mark 'Ra. Wood Burslem' with mould number '51'. Height 24.8 cm. (Courtesy: Dreweatt Neate, Newbury)*

Below Centre:
COLOUR PLATE 33: *Admiral Lord Howe jug and cover decorated with typical coloured glazes, c.1780. The presence of an impressed mould number '63' suggests that it might be the work of Ralph Wood of Burslem. Height 25.5 cm. (Courtesy: Sotheby's, London)*

Below Right:
COLOUR PLATE 34: *Unattributed pearlware Toby jug of standard form but with unusual colouring, c.1800. Note the jug of ale inscribed 'SUCCESS TO OUR WOODEN WALLS'. Height 25.5 cm. (Courtesy: Dreweatt Neate, Newbury)*

COLOUR PLATE 35: *Earthenware jug made by Fieldings at their Crown Devon pottery to commemorate the planned coronation of Edward VIII, 1936. The design is moulded and colour enamelled. Note the union emblems on the handle. Height 20 cm.* (Courtesy: Bonhams, Knightsbridge)

COLOUR PLATE 36: *A display of nineteen Lotus and Isis jugs and vases in 'Bizarre' and 'Fantasque' designs by Clarice Cliff. All made by Wilkinsons in the 1930s and bearing various printed and facsimile signature marks. Typical height up to 29 cm.* (Courtesy: Christie's, South Kensington)

COLOUR PLATE 37: *Two Poole Pottery terracotta jugs painted in typical colours on white grounds, c.1925–35. The right-hand jug is shape number 303. Impressed factory marks with indistinct painted monograms. Heights 20.3 cm and 19 cm.* (Courtesy: Christie's, South Kensington)

Right:
PLATE 504: *Earthenware presentation jug inscribed 'John Matthews, Bricklayer's Arms, 1863'. The prints of Bewick's animals and Grimaldi the clown are hand-coloured. Although unmarked, this jug was probably made by Elsmore & Forster (see Plate 505). Height 22.5 cm. (Courtesy: Sotheby's, Sussex)*

PLATE 502: *Octagonal earthenware jug by the South Wales Pottery, c.1840–50. This 'Bombay Japan' pattern is outline-printed in brown and enamelled in red, blue, green, turquoise and pink. Printed vase mark with title and pottery name. Height 12.8 cm.*

PLATE 505: *Smaller earthenware jug, similarly decorated, by Elsmore & Forster, c.1860–5. The black prints are enamelled in red, maroon, green, yellow and blue, and picked out with peach lustre. Black-printed royal arms mark with maker's name. Height 19.3 cm.*

PLATE 506: *Dutch-shape earthenware jug, probably made in Staffordshire, c.1850–60. The scattered prints, mainly of agricultural implements, are coloured over and accompanied by gilt initials 'AN'. Height 15.9 cm. (Courtesy: Christie's, South Kensington)*

PLATE 503: *Large Dutch-shape display jug by an unknown maker, c.1830–50. The scattered engravings, including a cartoon and views of the Clifton suspension bridge, have been coloured over. Height 40.6 cm. (Courtesy: Christie's, South Kensington)*

Despite the words 'ironstone china' in the Elsmore &
Forster mark, these jugs are made in earthenware, and in
the second half of the nineteenth century the distinction
became rather blurred. A number of potters made wares
in a fine dense body which may best be described as
granite china, one high quality example being a large
water jug attributed to Charles Meigh or his successors
(Plate 507). This is part of a toilet set with matching
washbowl and other items. Such sets were popular and
wooden washstands of the time had suitable cut-outs for
the bowl, soap dish and other pieces.

While this granite china is clearly of stone china type,
the other extreme is simple earthenware, such as the
South Wales Pottery jug decorated with flowers on a
coloured ground (Plate 508). Between these two
extremes emerged a range of utilitarian bodies which can
be difficult to classify. Many later jugs are in variants of
this hybrid body, often decorated with outline prints and
added colouring. One decorative example with a
cheerful floral pattern is not marked (Plate 509) but
other designs were registered and can be dated.
Examples include jugs by Liddle Elliot & Son from 1869
(Plate 510), George Jones & Sons from 1881 (Plate
511), and Burgess & Leigh from 1896 (Plate 512).
Ornately moulded bodies, as on this last example, were
common in the late Victorian and early Edwardian
periods.

PLATE 508: *Octagonal earthenware jug of typical shape made
by the South Wales Pottery, c.1850–5. The flower pattern is in
underglaze blue enamelled in red, maroon and yellow, with a
green enamelled ground. Impressed initials 'SWP'. Height
20.8 cm.*

PLATE 509: *Typical but unattributed late Victorian jug with
an attractive floral pattern. The maroon outline-printed design
features areas of underglaze blue, enamelled in red, mulberry,
maroon, green, yellow and turquoise. Pattern number '7860'
painted in maroon. Height 16.9 cm.*

Left:
PLATE 507: *Heavy granite china ewer of fine quality, part of a
toilet set, c.1845–70. The pattern has a pink ground and is richly
gilt and enamelled in purple, red, greens, yellow and brown.
Unmarked but traditionally thought to be from the Old Hall
Pottery of Charles Meigh and his successors. Height 32.6 cm.
(Courtesy: City Museum & Art Gallery, Stoke-on-Trent)*

PLATE 510: *Simple earthenware jug with a 'Fern' design registered by Liddle Elliot & Son in 1869. The moulded body is underglaze printed in green and enamelled in green and red with some peach lustre. Printed registration diamond for 15 November 1869 with pattern title. The Britannia-metal lid has an indistinct maker's mark. Height 21 cm.*

Although not actually dated, the next jug is typical of the period around 1870 or so, in shape, decoration and quality (Plate 513). While clearly marked with initials B. & H., these could apply to several Staffordshire firms. The colouring includes a peach or apricot lustre, quite common on these later jugs.

The final example, made by F. Winkle & Co. of Stoke, probably dates from around 1910 (Plate 514). Although quality at this period was generally none too high, this brightly coloured jug in the traditional Dutch shape is both functional and attractive. It is interesting to note that the decoration still follows the common technique of outline-printing with overglaze colouring, so successful that it survived well into the present century.

PLATE 511: *Simple but attractive tankard shape jug with a design titled 'Ivy Bower' registered by George Jones & Sons in 1881. The pattern is outline-printed in brown and coloured green, pink and blue. Printed registration diamond for 29 September 1881; also printed maker's monogram mark with pattern title, and pattern number '6867' painted in red. Height 19.9 cm.*

PLATE 513: *Earthenware jug of a very common shape, possibly by Beech & Hancock, c.1870. The design is printed in green, coloured with red and green, and peach lustre. Printed trade mark with a swan, pattern title 'LYONS', and maker's initials 'B & H'; also pattern number '1245/H' painted in red. The Britannia-metal lid is not marked. Height 16.8 cm.*

Left:
PLATE 512: *Typical late Victorian jug with ornately moulded body, the shape registered by Burgess & Leigh in 1896. The 'Lilac' pattern is printed in brown and picked out in green, blue, pink and yellow. The handle is glazed brown. Printed mark with maker's initials, title and registration number '285772'; the latter also indistinctly moulded. Height 17.9 cm.*

PLATE 514: *Dutch-shape ironstone-type jug in 'Whieldon Ware' by F. Winkle & Co., c.1900–10. The design is outline-printed in black, enamelled in red, carmine, green, brown and blue, with some peach lustre and gilding. Printed mark with pattern title 'PHEASANT' and maker's name with 'ENGLAND'; also pattern number '6973/2' painted in red. Height 15.7 cm.*

PLATE 515: *Three typical early lustre jugs, all unmarked and unattributed, c.1810–25. The left-hand example is relief-moulded and coloured with pink lustre and green, red and blue enamels; the centre jug is decorated with silver resist; the right-hand jug is again relief-moulded but picked out with copper lustre and green enamel. Heights 14.5 cm, 14 cm, and 13.5 cm.* (Courtesy: Lawrence Fine Art, Crewkerne)

10.
Lustre

One of the most distinctive decorative techniques found on British ceramics is lustre. Although previously used elsewhere, particularly in the Islamic world, lustre did not appear in England until the beginning of the nineteenth century, and the English products are quite different in both manufacture and character. A detailed discussion of its development can be found in Geoffrey Godden and Michael Gibson's recent definitive work *Collecting Lustreware*.

Lustre jugs were made in large numbers, and while no one can doubt their decorative merits, they are among the most difficult of wares to categorize. As Godden and Gibson state in their introduction, clear factory markings are conspicuous by their extreme rarity. In the hunt for suitable illustrations for this book, apart from Sunderland jugs from the Garrison Pottery which sometimes used impressed marks or printed marks within the decoration, only one marked example has been unearthed. Lustre wares were widely produced in Staffordshire as well as the north-east of England, and also in reasonable quantity at Swansea and Leeds. Other areas almost certainly made use of the technique but the lack of marked examples makes attribution extremely difficult, if not impossible.

There are three main types of lustre found on British ceramics; silver, copper or gold, and pink or purple. Silver lustre is produced using platinum which, unlike silver itself, does not tarnish. Copper and gold lustre are variations of the same thing, using minute amounts of gold deposited on a dark, usually red or brown, ground. Pink and purple lustre also make use of gold, but deposited on a light background, usually white. The actual colours depend on the formula used, the temperature of the firing, and the number of coats applied. A single coat is adequate but a second produces a deeper, more lustrous finish. Two further types of lustre are much less commonly found. Orange lustre was achieved using iron, and while it can be thick and distinctive, its use on jugs is usually restricted to a peach or apricot sheen often found on cheaper jugs from the second half of the nineteenth century. Variegated or 'moonlight' lustre was also made, but with the possible exception of some wares by Wedgwood (Colour Plate 21) it is not often found on utilitarian jugs.

While it is convenient to consider lustred wares separately, the treatment could be used like any other overglaze colouring, and the amount varies from a few touches to a complete coating. Three jugs dating from around 1820 feature the three main types (Plate 515). The jugs on the left and right are picked out with pink and copper lustre respectively, in both cases used alongside coloured enamels to highlight the moulding. The centre jug has silver lustre applied with a resist technique to produce an attractive design.

Silver lustre, the first of the three main types, seems to have been confined largely to the earlier years of the nineteenth century. It was often used to decorate edges and rims, possibly as an alternative to gilding, but was sometimes applied more extensively. Some wares were entirely coated with the intention of emulating real silver, but this fashion was reserved mainly for tea and coffee wares. Some jugs have silver lustre as a major feature, including one where it has been used both to highlight pineapple-type surface moulding and as part of a hand-painted border (Plate 516). However, the most representative examples use the resist technique already mentioned.

PLATE 516: *Earthenware jug with pineapple moulding picked out with silver lustre, c.1810–20. The neck has a hand-painted silver lustre design with iron-red and orange touches. A similar jug decorated with Pratt colours can be seen in Plate 344. Height 12.9 cm.*

There were several versions of this process, but they all depended on protecting areas of the surface with a wax or oily coating to which the lustre would not adhere.

PLATE 517: *Four silver-resist lustre jugs, c.1810–20. The left-hand example has a blue-printed sporting scene, the next has a canary yellow ground. Oval reserves on the right-hand jug are printed in puce with landscapes. Heights between 12 cm and 14 cm.* (Courtesy: Sotheby's, Sussex)

This could be achieved by hand-painting, transfer, stencil or the use of paper cut-outs. These techniques were quite flexible and by using them with either the lustre or the resisting medium, designs could be produced with positive or negative images. Four typical jugs include one with lustre applied over a blue-printed hunting scene, two with simple floral bands, and a fourth with an oval reserve featuring a printed landscape (Plate 517).

Three more examples exhibit varying levels of sophistication. The first has a yellow ground relieved by a wide band of small flowers and leaves (Plate 518), while the second is covered with a prominent pattern of large leaves and stylized foliage (Plate 519). The third is of far superior quality with an attractive patterned resist ground, a coloured design of birds within a circular reserve, and an inscription on the front (Plate 520). The basic shape of these jugs is similar, with variations confined to the shoulder and handles, and they probably all date from before 1825.

PLATE 519: *This jug also has a canary-yellow ground but the leafy silver-resist pattern covers the whole surface. Unmarked and unattributed, c.1815. Height 17 cm.* (Courtesy: Christie's, London)

PLATE 518: *Another unattributed yellow-ground earthenware jug decorated with a band of continuous flowers in silver-resist lustre, c.1810–20. Height 12 cm.* (Courtesy: Lawrence Fine Art, Crewkerne)

PLATE 520: *Silver-resist lustre presentation jug of fine quality, c.1810–15. The quality of the design is apparent even from a photograph, but the enamelling on the birds is surprisingly crude. Height 22.2 cm.* (Courtesy: Christie's, London)

PLATE 521: *Another superficially similar jug but of somewhat lesser quality, c.1815–20. The chinoiserie scenes are outline-printed in black and crudely enamelled over in blue, green, yellow, red and maroon. Height 13.4 cm.*

The last silver lustre example features a chinoiserie scene outline-printed in black and crudely enamelled in colours (Plate 521). While this lesser quality jug might be a little later, silver lustre had largely been superseded by about 1830.

Copper lustre was less common in the earlier years although it later became widespread and very distinctive. Initially it appears to have been used mainly for highlighting moulded wares (Plate 515), or for broad borders (Plate 522). This latter example is a presentation piece with an inscription that helpfully dates it to 1824, and in view of the proximity of Stafford to the Potteries, also implies a Staffordshire origin. Another similar example dated 1819 with hand-painted decoration is shown elsewhere (Plate 37).

While relatively sparse use of copper lustre was not uncommon at this period, it soon became much more extensively used, often covering virtually the entire jug. Two early examples are shown, one with a green band featuring sprigged and enamelled animal emblems (Plate 523) and the other with a white band printed with a children's subject (Plate 524). These both date from around 1830 or so. The next jug (Plate 525) is typical of many copper lustre jugs made in the nineteenth century, of baluster shape with moulded handle and spout, and with a coloured band around the main body. This is a fine early example, with an attractive coloured floral border to the neck, but many similar jugs were produced, some extremely crude although still offering considerable charm.

PLATE 523: *Unattributed copper lustre jug, c.1830. The body is encircled with a green band sprigged with a winged horse picked out with black, grey, yellow, green and red enamels. Note the moulded animal-head spout. Height 16.8 cm.*

PLATE 522: *Earthenware jug with a broad copper lustre band around the neck and highlighted with blue enamel, inscribed and dated 1824. The sides are printed overglaze in purple with rural scenes, the reverse featuring a boy with a hoop, possibly copied from a Bewick woodcut. Height 14 cm.* (Courtesy: City Museum & Art Gallery, Stoke-on-Trent)

PLATE 524: *Another unattributed copper lustre jug, c.1830–45. A white band around the body is printed in black with 'THE LITTLE JOCKEY', a subject also known printed in red on a copper lustre mug. Height 15.8 cm.*

In view of the absence of marks, the dating of copper lustre can be problematical, although a few commemorative examples are helpful. The jug with the portrait of Queen Victoria and Prince Albert (Colour Plate 22) must date to their marriage in February 1840 or shortly thereafter, an unusually late use of a yellow ground. Both the shape and the ornate handle are typical of the period, and such characteristics can help to date other examples.

Copper lustre was sometimes used as a complete coating on relief-moulded jugs. One relatively common design featuring children is often referred to as 'Idle Apprentices' although they may well just be playing in a nursery (Plate 526). Most examples are in glazed blue stoneware, almost invariably unmarked although one is known with an impressed mark for John Ellis of Bristol. There have been doubts that lustre was made in Bristol, but Godden and Gibson document wares decorated with pink lustre which must have been made at the Bristol Pottery, and another Bristol firm, Joseph & James White, is recorded in directories as producing gold lustre during the 1840s. It is possible that this Idle Apprentices design was copied elsewhere, but could it be that John Ellis also used copper lustre?

PLATE 525: *Large and good quality, but otherwise typical copper lustre jug, c.1830–50. The enamelled band around the neck is less common but most examples have similar simple designs around the body. Height 33 cm. (Courtesy: Greenslade Hunt, Taunton)*

Right:
PLATE 526: *Well-known relief-moulded jug of a design known as the Idle Apprentices but covered in copper lustre, c.1855–65. This jug may have been made by John Ellis at Bristol. (Courtesy: Lawrence Fine Art, Crewkerne)*

The final example is one of a range of jugs featuring clock faces (Plate 527). These have given rise to many amusing folk myths about the times shown, including one fanciful story that they immortalize the time of death of some beloved relative. This can easily be discounted since the clock faces are often printed and no firm would have expensive copper plates engraved for every possible time of day. A few hand-painted examples exist, like the one shown here, but even this has different times on the two sides. Clock face jugs are frequently attributed to the South Wales Pottery, which certainly made some with printed faces, but they were also made elsewhere, particularly in Staffordshire.

While silver and copper lustre are each distinctive in their own way, it is perhaps pink lustre that offers most interest where jugs are concerned. The shade ranges from very light pink to dark purple and it is usually found in association with other forms of decoration, painted, printed or moulded. Although strongly associated with the north-east of England, particularly Sunderland, it was also widely used in Staffordshire.

The earliest examples use pink lustre to highlight relief-moulding. Three jugs shown with hunting scenes (Plate 528) and another particularly fine naturalistic example (Plate 529) are all unmarked, as are almost all jugs of this type. They are most commonly attributed to Staffordshire but another rare example (Plate 530) bears the impressed mark 'FELL', relating to Thomas Fell & Co. of the St Peter's Pottery at Newcastle-upon-Tyne. Other jugs like this may have originated in Sunderland or on Teesside.

Another type of decoration which emerged relatively early features naïvely-painted scenes of cottages, churches and similar buildings. One particularly fine example dating from around 1830 has two such scenes on an ornate shell-moulded body (Plate 531). Another example serves to represent the lower end of the scale, albeit still with considerable charm (Plate 532). This was probably made in the 1850s and the same basic shape can be seen on an example with printed and coloured

PLATE 527: *Copper lustre jug decorated on each side with a clock face enamelled in black, c.1850–80. The time on the reverse shows four o'clock. Probably made in Staffordshire, although superficially similar jugs with printed clock faces were made at Llanelly. Height 14.9 cm.*

PLATE 528: *A pair of relief-moulded pink lustre jugs with a standard hunting scene, flanking another similarly decorated jug with an unusual handle, c.1820–30. Heights 15.3 and 14 cm. (Courtesy: Christie's, South Kensington)*

PLATE 529: *Particularly fine earthenware jug, moulded with leaves picked out with pink lustre and green enamel, c.1820. Unmarked and unattributed. Height 14.4 cm.*

PLATE 530: *Rare marked lustre jug by Thomas Fell of Newcastle, c.1820. The moulded hunting scene with archers, repeated with slight differences on the reverse, is picked out with pink lustre and green enamel. Impressed mark 'FELL'. Height 14.6 cm.*

PLATE 531: *Earthenware jug with attractive shell-moulded body, washed and hand-painted in pink lustre, c.1815–25. A similar naïve scene on the reverse features a cottage in place of the church. One non-lustre jug of quite similar shape is recorded with an impressed mark 'WOOD'. Height 19 cm.*

patriotic decoration from the time of the Crimean War (Plate 533). The reverse of this jug is printed with a common 'Sailor's Farewell' scene, another version of which can be seen on another jug of more standard shape (Plate 534). This jug has a black-printed and coloured floral border both outside and inside the neck, a characteristic often associated with Scott's Pottery at Southwick, Sunderland.

Attractive pink lustre jugs are almost invariably described as Sunderland, but accurate attribution is fraught with difficulty. In a few cases the printed decoration includes a pottery name, but such names are engraved on the copper plates which could have been reused by subsequent owners. Two clear examples are shown here, one with a farmer's arms type print signed 'Dixon, Austin & Co., Sunderland' along with the engravers name 'Downing' (Plate 535), and another with an engraving of the 'Northumberland 74' signed 'Dixon & Co., Sunderland' (Plate 536). There can be little doubt that these two fine jugs were made at the Garrison Pottery, but it is not impossible that such copper plates could later have been reused elsewhere.

The style of these jugs, both with pink lustre dashes around the engravings and lining to the neck, spout and foot, is typical of the Garrison Pottery, but neither exhibit any of the famous splash lustre so closely associated with Sunderland. This effect was achieved by spraying or splashing oil on to the surface of the lustre when wet, the spreading oil creating a pleasing uneven design, apparent to good effect on the next jug (Plate 537). This also bears a print of the Northumberland 74, and like the previous example, this is accompanied by one of the popular prints of the cast-iron bridge at Sunderland. Many variations of this scene are recorded

by John Baker in *Sunderland Pottery*, but it must be emphasized that its appearance is no guarantee of Sunderland manufacture. The same scene was almost certainly used on Tyneside, and perhaps also on Teesside.

PLATE 532: *Squat earthenware jug, also decorated with a pink lustre naïve scene, c.1850–60. Compare the shape with the next example in Plate 533. Height 10.8 cm.*

PLATE 533: *Similar shaped pink lustre jug decorated with Crimean war subjects, c.1854–6. The reverse has a sailor's farewell scene and the black-printed designs are enamelled in red, yellow, blue, and green. This jug was possibly made by Scott's Southwick Pottery at Sunderland. Height 12 cm.*

Right:

PLATE 535: *Fine and clearly marked pink lustre presentation jug by Dixon, Austin & Co. of Sunderland, c.1820–6. The pottery's name and address can be seen beneath the farmer's arms, accompanied by the engraver's name 'Downing'. (Courtesy: Lawrence Fine Art, Crewkerne)*

PLATE 534: *Another pink lustre jug possibly made at the Southwick Pottery, c.1840–50. Again the black prints are enamelled in blue, red, yellow and green. There is a romantic seafaring verse on the front and a west view of the cast-iron bridge over the River Wear on the reverse. Height 19.1 cm.*

PLATE 536: *Sunderland pink lustre jug with a print of the 'Northumberland 74' signed by Dixon & Co., c.1826–40. The reverse has a view of the cast-iron bridge over the River Wear and beneath the spout is a framed verse and a black-painted inscription to a Mr George Wilds of Norwich. Height 21 cm.* (Courtesy: Sotheby's, Sussex)

PLATE 537: *Another pink-lustre jug with a print of the 'Northumberland 74', again accompanied by a verse and a view of the Wear bridge. Note the distinctive splash lustre. Height 20.3 cm.* (Courtesy: Christie's, South Kensington)

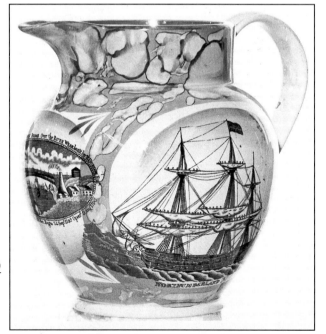

The next two jugs also feature the bridge, the first along with a sentimental poem (Plate 538). This is one of many commonly used romantic and religious verses, again mostly recorded in *Sunderland Pottery*. Another can be seen on a fine puzzle jug in Chapter 13 (Plate 610). The second jug has the bridge and another verse, along with an unusual lifeboat scene (Plate 539). This jug and particularly the next example (Plate 540), both exhibit some characteristics associated with Tyneside rather than Sunderland. These include the frames and dashes of coloured enamel around the prints, and the darker pink lustre which is smeared rather than splashed around the necks.

As with many pink lustre jugs, including some already discussed, the last two examples were both supplied to special order as presentation pieces. The first (Plate 541) bears an unusual name 'Perseller Edwards' enamelled on one side, whereas the other is inscribed 'Richard & Hannah Clark' and dated 1828 (Plate 542). This fine early example is probably a marriage jug, with prints including masonic emblems and a monument inscribed with the names of arts and sciences, including astronomy, music, geometry, arithmetic, logic and grammer [*sic*].

PLATE 538: *Prominent verse 'The Sailor's Tear' within a typical floral frame on an unattributed pink lustre jug, c.1830–40. The reverse has a west view of the Wear bridge. Height 13.2 cm.*

PLATE 541: *A typically inscribed unattributed pink lustre jug, possibly Sunderland, c.1830–50. Pious verses accompany the inscription and beneath the spout there is a sailing ship, flanked by a figure of Hope and a merchant with boxes and a barrel, all printed and coloured. Height 19 cm. (Courtesy: Lawrence Fine Art, Crewkerne)*

PLATE 539: *Pink lustre jug highlighted with coloured enamels, possibly made on Tyneside, c.1840–50. This unusual lifeboat scene is accompanied by a typical seafaring verse and a west view of the Wear bridge. Note the smeared lustre around the neck. Height 24 cm. (Courtesy: Sotheby's, Sussex)*

PLATE 540: *A similar jug to the last, also possibly made on Tyneside, c.1840–50. In this case there are two verses flanking a frigate in full sail. The panels are framed in iron-red and touched with green and yellow enamels. Height 24 cm. (Courtesy: Sotheby's, Sussex)*

PLATE 542: *Attractive and unusual pink lustre marriage jug, dated 1828. The sides are printed and hand-coloured with Hope and the Mason's Arms, and another Masonic print appears on the front. Note the hand-painted foliate border and framing. Height 24 cm. (Courtesy: Sotheby's, London)*

PLATE 543: *Unattributed green-glazed jug featuring Sir Francis Burdett, who was imprisoned in the Tower of London in 1810. The reverse is moulded with a figure titled 'LIBERTY'. The same design with typical Pratt-type underglaze colouring can be seen in Plate 360. Height 14.5 cm.*

11.
Majolica

Brightly coloured majolica was one of the great success stories of nineteenth-century ceramics. Coloured glazes were certainly not new. They had been widely used during the eighteenth century for naturalistic wares based on cabbages and cauliflowers, also for streaked agate-type wares, and later for figures and Toby jugs made by Ralph Wood and his contemporaries. A green glaze became popular early in the nineteenth century and remained in production well into the 1900s, but it was not hard-wearing and it was used mainly for dessert wares. A few jugs can be found, but they are uncommon (Plates 543–4). Similar wares were made with glazes coloured brown ('Rockingham') and blue, but neither these nor the green are directly related to true majolica.

PLATE 544: *Green-glazed earthenware jug featuring the American eagle, c.1815. The reverse is moulded with a flower spray. Once again the same design is known decorated with typical Pratt-type underglaze colours, and also with enamels and lustre. Height 15 cm.* (Courtesy: City Museum & Art Gallery, Stoke-on-Trent)

The subject of the invention, rise and decline of majolica in the second half of the nineteenth century is admirably covered by Victoria Bergesen in *Majolica: British, Continental and American Wares, 1851–1915.* It

was developed largely by Léon Arnoux working for Minton in 1849 and 1850 and was officially announced at the Great Exhibition of 1851. Initially, it was intended to imitate earlier Italian *maiolica*, although inspiration was taken also from Della Robbia and Palissy-type wares. However, these influences soon faded and it rapidly developed its own distinctive character. A definition of majolica is none too easy, but it encompasses mainly relief-moulded wares covered with colourful glazes, usually ornate or humorous, or both.

Majolica became hugely popular, despite the critics who disliked the very excesses which made it so distinctive. Following their 1851 Exhibition success, Minton soon faced competition from other potters, including Wedgwood, Copeland and even Worcester, and also a host of smaller firms who jumped on the band-wagon. The finest wares are magnificent, but some of the lesser pieces are equally dreadful. The craze lasted for some years but was eventually snuffed out by a depression of sales in the mid-1880s. Its popularity extended to several export markets, and British manu-facturers were joined by others from North America and mainland Europe, some of whom continued well into the twentieth century.

Any evaluation of majolica must start with Minton, the firm credited with its invention. They used a system of impressed shape numbers for their majolica, and Bergesen features a long but still incomplete list. Some twenty-four are described as jugs, four illustrated here together with another two which are not listed and one whose shape number, if any, is not known.

The first addition is shape number 474, a complicated design featuring a cherub, merman and mermaid, illustrated alongside two very ornate ewers, the smaller one of which is shape number 472 (Plate 545). In no way could either of the ewers be considered utilitarian, but many of Minton's pieces were obviously intended for decoration rather than use. The jug itself has a heavily moulded body with figures added separately. Although usable, even this would probably have been sold more as an ornament.

Another jug with a design of peasant dancers, numbered 487, has survived in quite large numbers and must have been popular (Plate 546, Colour Plate 23). One of the great benefits of studying Minton's wares is their clear use of date codes and this design has been noted with dates ranging from 1858 to 1873.

Above:

PLATE 545: *Minton majolica jug modelled in shape number 474 with a cherub, mermaid and merman, shown alongside two ornate ewers, the three pieces dated 1869, 1862 and 1870. Jug with impressed maker's mark, shape number and date code. Heights 31 cm, 44.4 cm and 34.3 cm. (Courtesy: Sotheby's, London)*

Below:

PLATE 546: *Three Minton majolica jugs dated 1864, 1873 and 1858 in the Peasant Dancers pattern, shape number 487. Impressed maker's mark with shape number and date codes. The two smaller jugs also have moulded registration diamonds. Heights between 24.5 and 25.4 cm. (Courtesy: Sotheby's, London)*

PLATE 547: *A pair of Minton majolica Toby jugs dated 1867, the gentleman of shape number 1140 and his lady companion numbered 1139. Impressed maker's marks with shape numbers and date codes. Heights 29.2 cm.* (Courtesy: Sotheby's, Sussex)

The final numbered design is a Tower jug of shape number 1231. Two examples date from 1870 and 1871, one fitted with a metal lid (Plates 549–50). The design itself is rather reminiscent of the Peasant Dancers jug, although modelled in much lower relief without the addition of separately moulded figures. It could possibly have been introduced as a cheaper version of the earlier jug. Note the fine majolica finial in the form of a jester's head on the metal lid.

The next two designs, shape number 1140 listed by Bergesen simply as a Toby, together with his unlisted female companion numbered 1139, are once again decorative rather than utilitarian (Plate 547). Examples noted have been dated 1865 and 1867, and some fitted with silver mounts are known. Although included here as majolica, they would equally feature as Toby jugs, covered in more detail in Chapter 13.

While the above jugs are all ornamental, the next example is refreshingly simple with a naturalistic body moulded from overlapping leaves and a stalk for the handle (Plate 548). This is shape number 1228, titled Water Lily. This example is dated 1869.

PLATE 549: *Minton majolica Tower jug of shape number 1231, fitted with a metal lid and dated 1870. Note the matching majolica jester on the lid. Impressed marks with date code. Height 33 cm.* (Courtesy: Dreweatt Neate, Newbury)

Left:
PLATE 548: *Attractive and restrained Minton majolica jug of shape number 1228, dated 1869. Impressed maker's mark with shape number and date code. Height 33 cm.* (Courtesy: Sotheby's, London)

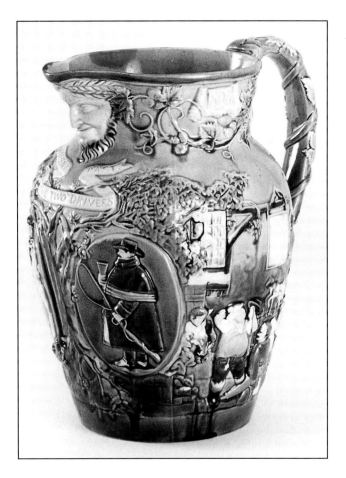

PLATE 550: *Another Minton majolica Tower jug, a slightly later example with no cover dated 1871. Impressed maker's mark with shape number and date code. Height 24.7 cm.* (Courtesy: Sotheby's, London)

PLATE 551: *Fine majolica version of Minton's rare 'Two Drivers' jug, originally modelled by Henry Townsend for Summerly's Art Manufactures scheme in 1847. This example was made in 1857. Impressed registration diamond. Height 23 cm.* (Courtesy: Sotheby's, Sussex)

The use of majolica glazes was associated particularly with moulded wares, and Minton, along with other manufacturers, reissued some earlier relief-moulded jug designs. Two notable Minton jugs are a design of hop-pickers and a coach and railway 'Two Drivers' jug, both designed by Henry J. Townsend for Summerly's Art Manufactures scheme. Although originally produced around 1847 in various forms of stoneware, both were later reissued with majolica glazes. An example of the latter dates from 1857 (Plate 551). It is not clear whether either design was allocated a shape number.

One of Minton's greatest competitors was Wedgwood, and although the famous firm did not introduce majolica until 1861, they may well have made more than any other manufacturer. They also numbered their products, although these are pattern rather than shape numbers. Some designs were issued in differently coloured variants, each allocated a different pattern number. Once again these numbers are listed by Bergesen.

Wedgwood's jugs are neither so ornate nor so commonly found as Minton's, but amongst the most popular must have been the Caterer jug, designed by Frederick Bret Russel and registered in 1867. It was issued in some twenty-one different versions, two of which are shown here (Plates 552–3). They are of strikingly different colouring and, like Minton's Tower

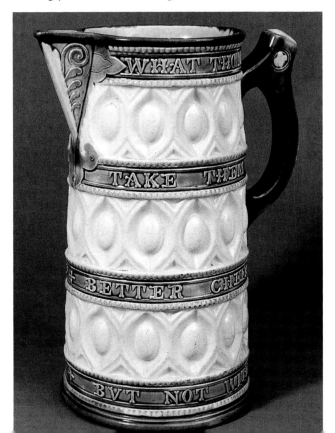

Right:
PLATE 552: *Wedgwood's popular Caterer jug sparingly coloured with majolica glazes. Impressed mark 'WEDGWOOD' with pattern number '964' painted in yellow. Height 21.8 cm.* (Courtesy: City Museum & Art Gallery, Stoke-on-Trent)

jug, the design was issued both with and without a metal lid. The inscription reads 'What tho' my gates be poor, take them in good part; Better cheer may you have, but not with better heart'.

Fortunately a comprehensive record of Wedgwood majolica has survived in the form of a set of pattern books and an extract from one depicts the firm's 'Athletic' jug in pattern 2836 (Plate 554). With its cricket and footballing associations, this jug would prove highly collectable. Note the detailed colouring instructions and the general description 'Argenta', meaning dark blue.

The next example is basically of traditional antique shape, moulded overall with grapes and vine leaves (Colour Plate 24). This is slightly later, probably from the 1890s when the majolica excesses had largely abated. In similar vein, the last Wedgwood jug illustrated exhibits admirable restraint. The classic bulbous body, fitted with a rope handle, is covered simply with brown and green streaked glazes (Plate 555).

Minton and Wedgwood were both eminent and renowned for other wares, but they were not the only British firms to manufacture majolica in quantity. Other well-known makers included Copeland, Worcester and Brownfield. A lesser-known potter who rose to prominence in this field was George Jones. Another Bergesen list includes several jugs with names such as 'Lotus', 'Eastern Plants', 'Foliage', 'Chestnut', 'Barrel', 'Holly Mask', 'Basket', 'Bamboo' and sounding rather like the last Wedgwood jug, 'Mottled Jug, Rope Handle'. Despite this list, Jones tended to concentrate, certainly in the later period, on more decorative pieces such as jardinières, comports, baskets and ornamental dishes.

PLATE 553: *Another version of Wedgwood's Caterer jug in notably darker colours. This example is also fitted with a Britannia-metal lid.* (Courtesy: Lawrence Fine Art, Crewkerne)

PLATE 554: *Detail from a page of one of Wedgwood's majolica pattern books, dating from the 1880s. The jug featured is the 'Athletic' jug, pattern number 2836, decorated with cricketing and footballing scenes.* (Courtesy: Trustees of the Wedgwood Museum, Barlaston, Staffordshire)

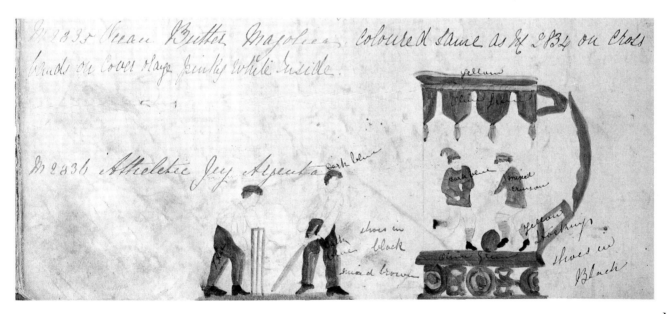

PLATE 555: *Simple but very effective Wedgwood majolica jug decorated with streaked yellow and brown glazes and a turquoise interior. Impressed mark 'WEDGWOOD' with an indistinct date code. Height 17.8 cm.* (Courtesy: City Museum & Art Gallery, Stoke-on-Trent)

PLATE 557: *Pair of majolica ewers with swan necks and handles, after Sèvres originals, c.1880. The main bodies are dark blue, the details are in naturalistic colours. Unmarked except for incised and black-painted numerals '414' and '32'. Height 44.5 cm.* (Courtesy: Sotheby's, London)

Opposite:
PLATE 556: *Ornate majolica ewer with an unusual relief-moulded discoidal body, c.1865. This design has been associated with George Jones, although there appears little to support such an attribution. Height 28 cm.* (Courtesy: Sotheby's, Sussex)

A very decorative flask-like jug (Plate 556) and a pair of extremely ornate ewers (Plate 557) have tentatively been attributed to George Jones, although both must be open to some doubt. As with Minton wares, these are in no way utilitarian, especially the swan-necked ewers derived from Sèvres originals.

George Jones's name has also dubiously been associated with the next jug (Plate 558). The design, featuring four military figures representing 'Our Army & Navy & Brave Volunteers', was originally registered by the little-known Sandford Pottery of Wareham in Dorset to commemorate reviews of the Volunteer Rifles held in London and Edinburgh during 1860. The jug is more commonly found in light buff-coloured earthenware, clearly marked with a registration diamond and the pottery's name. Some examples have an indistinct monogram within the moulded design, somewhat similar to the George Jones trademark. There seems little reason to link Jones with the Sandford Pottery, but it is interesting to see this good quality design decorated with majolica glazes, not previously associated with the Dorset firm.

PLATE 558: *Relief-moulded Volunteers jug decorated with majolica glazes. The design was registered by the Sandford Pottery in 1860 to commemorate Queen Victoria's two reviews of the Volunteer Rifles. The inscription on this example includes reversed letters N and S. Moulded registration diamond. Height 27.3 cm.* (Courtesy: Sotheby's, Sussex)

Existing relief-moulded jugs were often reissued with majolica glazes. Another example is a naturalistic design based on a corn-cob by James Ellis & Son of Hanley (Plate 559). This is more often found thinly potted in glazed Parian, and the majolica versions, although not uncommon, vary considerably in quality.

A slightly later jug by an unknown maker, still of moulded form but recorded only in majolica, shows a bewigged gentleman identified just as 'Dr K, MP' (Plate 560). This is reputed to represent Dr Kenealy, a local Staffordshire mayor who was elected to Parliament in 1875. Commemorative majolica jugs like this are uncommon.

The last jug illustrated is another novelty design, modelled in the form of a robed cleric with handle and spout rather incongruously adorning his back and chest (Plate 561). The figure's belt is inscribed with the date 1750, the significance of which is not apparent. The maker of this strange vessel also remains anonymous.

These last two unmarked jugs serve to represent many others of variable quality produced during the style's heyday in the 1860s and 1870s. Some are novel, some are highly decorative, a few are functional, but they are all colourful reminders of the eclecticism of taste in the second half of the nineteenth century.

PLATE 560: *Unattributed Staffordshire commemorative jug, c.1875. The earthenware body is decorated with yellow, brown and grey majolica glazes, with a pink interior. 'Dr K' is believed to refer to Dr Kenealy, a former local mayor elected to Parliament in 1875. Also known in a smaller size. Height 19.3 cm. (Courtesy: City Museum & Art Gallery, Stoke-on-Trent)*

PLATE 559: *Corn Cob jug registered by James Ellis & Son in 1869. Commonly found in plain white Parian but seen here in earthenware decorated with naturalistic green and yellow majolica glazes. Moulded registration diamond for 26 October 1869. Height 20.3 cm.*

PLATE 561: *Novelty jug by an unknown maker in the form of a robed cleric decorated with majolica glazes, c.1860–80. The unexplained date 1750 appears on his belt. Note the strange mask terminal on the handle. Height 30.5 cm. (Courtesy: Drewcatt Neate, Newbury)*

201

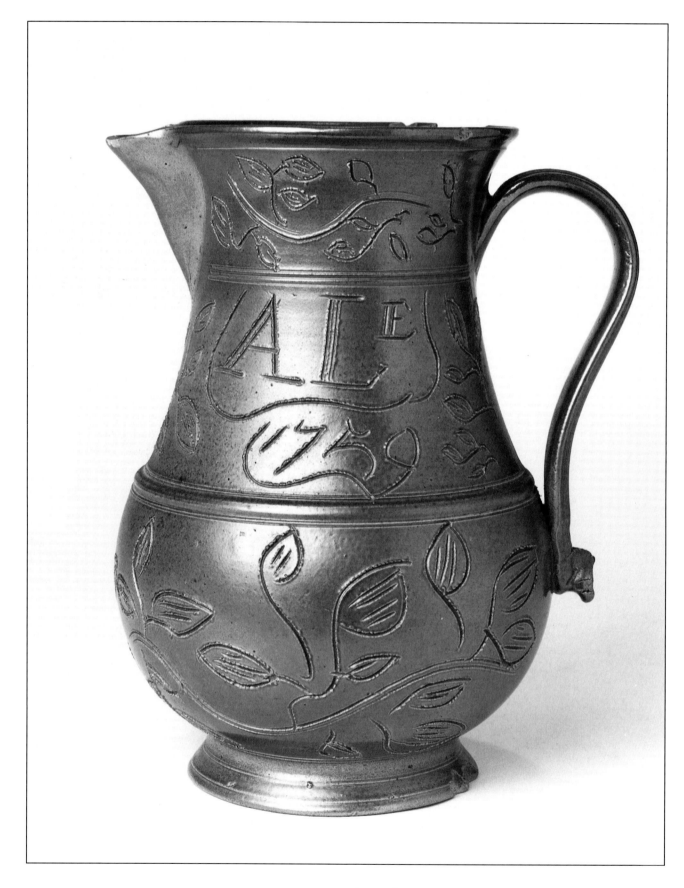

PLATE 563: *Stoneware ale jug made at Nottingham in 1759. The incised decoration, including an inscription 'ALE 1759', is typical, as is the surface finish. Height 24.5 cm.* (Courtesy: Phillips, London)

12.
Brown Stoneware

The production of brown stoneware in Britain is a fascinating subject extending over more than three centuries. It is basically a development of earthenware with additional ingredients, mainly sand. When fired to a higher than normal temperature the body vitrifies and becomes virtually impervious to liquids. Wares were generally glazed with salt which was added to the kiln at the highest temperature, the resulting vapour being deposited on the surface leaving a lustrous sheen, often with a distinctive orange-peel texture. Although somewhat coarse, the body is strong and durable, and until the middle of the nineteenth century it was used almost exclusively for utilitarian wares.

It seems to have made its first significant appearance in London, at the Fulham factory of John Dwight, in the early 1670s although earlier stoneware-type jugs are known (Plate 2). It was quickly copied elsewhere and by 1700 had been adopted in Nottingham, and soon also in Staffordshire. Although some early wares are quite distinctive, others can be extremely difficult to attribute, even to a general area.

Two typical eighteenth-century Nottingham jugs are illustrated. The first, in the form of a carved jug with the outer body decoratively pierced, was probably made soon after 1700 (Plate 562). Jugs of this type appear on a trade card used by James Morley of Nottingham in the 1690s, and at least one example dated 1703 is known. A later jug illustrates two other typical Nottingham features; incised decoration, in this case simply 'ALE' with the date 1759, and an iridescent sheen over the surface, achieved with a wash of ferruginous clay (Plate 563). The latter is particularly obvious on a puzzle jug of slightly later date (Plate 603).

Nottingham wares were rarely, if ever, dipped to achieve the two-tone appearance common elsewhere (Plate 564). This shape is typical of the late eighteenth century but remained popular for many years. Without the impressed inscription including the year 1792, the jug would be difficult to date. It probably originated in Staffordshire but similar jugs were made elsewhere. Note the fine orange-peel finish which later disappeared with the invention of more sophisticated glazes.

Although various types of decoration appear, the most characteristic jugs feature scattered sprigs. Early examples date from around 1730 but the style continued well into the twentieth century. One example, possibly made at Mortlake about 1800, features a main panel inspired

PLATE 562: *Brown salt-glazed stoneware carved jug made at Nottingham, c.1700. The body is double-walled with the outer layer pierced and incised with stylized plants. Note the orange-peel finish. Height 13 cm.* (Courtesy: Sotheby's, London)

by Hogarth's 'Midnight Modern Conversation' which had already been in use for many years (Plate 565). Another similar example with a different main subject has a silver lid hallmarked 1808 (Plate 566, left). The use of a prominent panel was later abandoned in favour of other sprigged scenes as seen on another jug with a lid hallmarked 1827 (Plate 566, right). These three jugs all have lids hallmarked in London, a small but possibly significant aid to attribution. Another common feature is the hunt running around the lower body. Similar sprigged hunting motifs remained popular, along with drinking scenes and rural subjects such as windmills, for all jugs of this type.

While sprigged ornament might be considered the norm, some jugs were relief-moulded in imitation of higher quality wares. One particularly fine example (Plate 567) is very much in the style of Pratt ware jugs made around 1800 (see Chapter 7). Another impressive but individual example modelled by J. Wetherill of Lambeth is heavily moulded with the Victorian Royal arms along with agricultural and other motifs (Plate 568).

PLATE 564: *Typical late 18th-century brown salt-glazed stoneware jug, this example dated 1792. The impressed inscription reads 'Wm Stone/Walton'. The orange-peel finish is very noticeable. Height 13.2 cm. (Courtesy: City Museum & Art Gallery, Stoke-on-Trent)*

Above Right:

PLATE 565: *Fine salt-glazed stoneware hunting jug, possibly made by Kishere at Mortlake, c.1800. The applied decoration includes a prominent and typical rectangular panel inspired by Hogarth's 'Midnight Modern Conversation'. The silver cover bears a London hallmark for 1689. Height 25.8 cm. (Courtesy: Sotheby's, Sussex)*

Below:

PLATE 566: *Two sprig-decorated salt-glazed stoneware jugs with silver lids. The lids bear London hallmarks for 1808 and 1827 respectively, the latter by William Ellerby. Note that the prominent panel on the earlier example has been replaced by more scattered sprigging on the later jug. Heights 21.5 cm and 23.5 cm. (Courtesy: Dreweatt Neate, Newbury)*

PLATE 567: *Two views of a good quality brown salt-glazed stoneware jug, c.1800. The relief-moulded style is very similar to the so-called Pratt wares of the period. Height 14.3 cm.*

PLATE 568: *Two views of an impressively modelled brown salt-glazed stoneware jug featuring the Victorian royal arms together with agricultural, nautical, and military motifs, c.1840. Marked 'Published / According to Act / of Parliament by / J. Wetherill / Modeler. No 1 / Cl...rer Street / Lambeth / London'. Height 25.1 cm.*

Another feature copied from finer wares is a sprigged hunting scene, many variants of which were used on earthenwares, stonewares and china by Staffordshire potters. One version appears on a jug impressed with initials WHR and the date 1843, and fitted with a correspondingly hallmarked silver lid (Plate 569). An inscription subsequently engraved on the lid shows that the jug was later gifted by WHR to JR on Christmas Eve in 1849. A truly delightful heirloom.

PLATE 569: *Unattributed brown salt-glazed stoneware jug of good quality, made in 1843. Note the common sprigged hunting scene. The body is impressed with initials 'WHR' and the date on the front. The silver cover, hallmarked at Sheffield in 1842–3, is engraved 'J.R. FROM W.H.R. – CHRISTMAS EVE / 1849'. Height 20.6 cm.*

The fact that this silver lid was hallmarked in Sheffield may suggest that the jug was made in the Midlands or the North of England rather than in London, but such clues only emphasize difficulties in attribution. Except when clearly marked, few jugs can be ascribed to an individual pottery with any certainty, and even the general area is often not apparent. Another later jug sprigged with common hunting and drinking scenes serves to emphasize this point (Plate 570). Despite being unusually dipped at the base rather than the neck, and having a less common rustic handle, the area of manufacture remains a matter of conjecture.

This is not always the case. One excellent example is a massive sprigged jug made at William Powell's factory in Bristol in 1840 (Plate 571). Even without the helpful inscription, a positive attribution would be straightforward. Two similar but slightly smaller jugs in the Bristol Museum were made in 1834 and 1844 to

commemorate the coming of age of Powell's two sons. The earlier example is very similar to this one, whereas the later of the two is covered with the newly developed leadless glaze which revolutionized stoneware production in Bristol and elsewhere. This vast jug was probably intended for display at an exhibition or important retail outlet. Whatever the case, not only is it an impressive example of the potter's skill, but it is also an important documentary piece. Many if not all of the sprigs applied to the surface originated elsewhere, and since they must have been available to Powell, they may well have been more widely used in Bristol than was previously thought.

William Powell had invented his leadless glaze by 1836, and he advertised himself as its sole manufacturer for more than a decade. Thereafter it was adopted by fellow Bristol potters and was also sold in bulk to other stoneware producing areas, so much so that it became known as the Bristol glaze. The city was a major stoneware centre throughout the nineteenth century and a vast range of wares was made, including some jugs. Most earlier examples bear impressed inscriptions relating to their purpose, usually for brewers, wine and spirit merchants, or public houses. Later examples have printed inscriptions (Plate 572). The two main firms, Price and Powell, were amalgamated in 1906 and continued to produce stonewares until the Second World War.

PLATE 570: *Unmarked and unattributed brown salt-glazed stoneware jug, c.1850–80. The reverse features the common Toby Fillpot figure. Note the unusual dipping at the base rather than the top. Height 21.7 cm.*

Another area which made stonewares in quantity was Derbyshire, and it has been suggested that the Prattware-style jug mentioned earlier (Plate 567) was potted at Brampton. Along with Chesterfield, Belper and Denby, Brampton formed an important area within which many interesting pots were made. It is particularly associated with cottage-style jugs (Plate 573) although production dates back to the early eighteenth century with wares similar to those made at Nottingham. A later jug sprigged with a hunting scene and a Union border was possibly made by Oldfield & Co., one of several Brampton firms (Plate 574). Like Bristol, production continued at Brampton until the Second World War.

Elsewhere in Derbyshire, Bourne's of Denby and Pearson's of Chesterfield were important manufacturers through the nineteenth and into the twentieth century. The quality of later wares declined considerably, indistinct sprigging often being obscured with a thick glaze (Plate 575).

Stonewares were also made in Scotland and some can be attributed with reasonable confidence. The Alloa Pottery near Stirling made some fine jugs with prominent applied ornament, including a running plant design of vines, in a style reminiscent of some continental stonewares (Plate 576). Another similar jug is illustrated by Oswald, Hildyard and Hughes in *English Brown Stoneware 1670–1900*. The significance of the incised initials found on these jugs is not known.

PLATE 571: *Very large sprigged stoneware display jug made by William Powell at Bristol in 1840. The sprigs include the Victorian royal arms and several designs copied from 18th-century originals commonly used in Staffordshire. Impressed mark 'W. Powell, Bristol, 1840' on the front. Height 111.8 cm. (Courtesy: Charles A. Whitaker Auction Co., Philadelphia)*

PLATE 573: *Brown salt-glazed stoneware jug of a popular 19th-century cottage form. Jugs like this are commonly attributed to Brampton in Derbyshire. Height 12.7 cm. (Courtesy: BBR Auctions, Barnsley)*

PLATE 572: *Pair of typical jugs made by Prices of Bristol for a Buckinghamshire publican, c.1890–1910. Jugs with similar black-printed inscriptions were commissioned by many firms associated with the drinks trade. Both with impressed maker's oval mark. Heights 19.9 cm and 16.4 cm.*

Right:
PLATE 576: *Mid-19th-century brown salt-glazed stoneware jug attributed to the Alloa Pottery near Stirling. Note the typical heavy applied decoration and the sprigged man on a barrel beneath the spout. Incised oval mark with initials 'GB'. Height 21.8 cm.*

PLATE 574: *Brown stoneware jug covered with a thick lustrous salt-glaze, possibly made by Oldfield & Co. at Brampton, c.1840–50. Note the sprigged hunting scene also found on finer stonewares made in Staffordshire. Height 25.3 cm.*

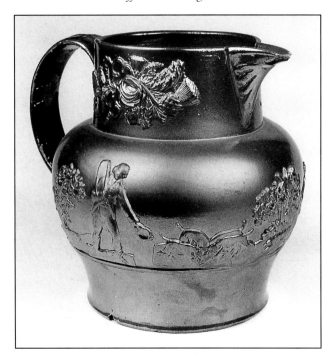

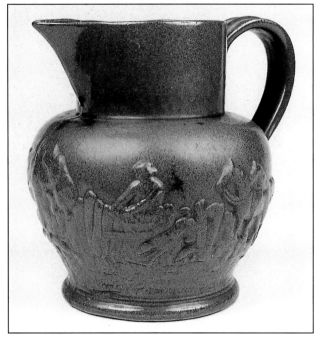

PLATE 575: *Poor quality brown stoneware jug covered with thick glaze, made by Pearsons of Chesterfield, c.1900. The design is based on the commonest of the sprigged hunting scenes. Black-printed mark with maker's name and address and date '1810' beneath. Height 16 cm.*

Although by far the bulk of stonewares are utilitarian, some more decorative pieces were made. These include the standard Toby, probably made in the early years of the nineteenth century at Brampton, although Nottingham should not be discounted (Plate 577). Other novelty jugs included caricatures, some possibly as early as 1800 (Plate 578). A fine example modelled as the head of the Duke of Wellington was made by Stephen Green at Lambeth, probably in the 1830s (Colour Plate 25), but most examples are anonymous and possibly somewhat later (Plates 579–80). The last of these, with its crude but strongly coloured features, exhibits considerable naïve charm.

The mention of decorative wares leads naturally to the famous Doulton factory and its artist decorators. The firm can be traced back to about 1815, and between 1820 and 1853 traded as Doulton & Watts. The art wares date from the time of Henry Doulton, who encouraged students from the local art school to join the firm's pottery studio at Lambeth. From the early 1870s many fine pieces were made, although they were mainly decorative rather than functional (Plate 581). Tankard-shaped jugs were made, often as part of lemonade sets, even by some of the more senior artists. Examples include four with silver mounts made between 1878 and 1881 by George Tinworth, Frances Lee and Edith Lupton (Plate 582), and two more of slightly later date by Florence Barlow (Plates 583–4).

PLATE 579: *Large 19th-century salt-glazed stoneware character jug. The modelling is none too successful since the subject has been variously identified as Mr Punch and the Duke of Wellington. Height 28 cm.* (Courtesy: Christie's, South Kensington)

PLATE 577: *Brown salt-glazed stoneware Toby jug of the traditional form, c.1800. This was probably made at Brampton in Derbyshire. Height 30 cm.* (Courtesy: Sotheby's, Sussex)

PLATE 578: *Early 19th-century brown salt-glazed stoneware caricature jug. Unmarked and unattributed. Height 12.2 cm.* (Courtesy: Dreweatt Neate, Newbury)

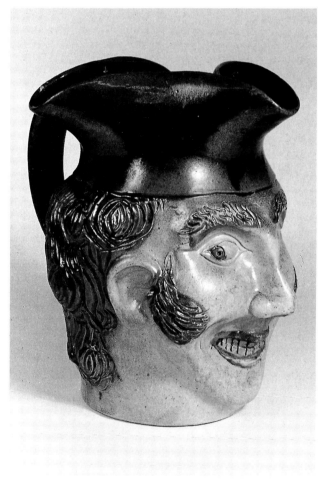

PLATE 580: *Naïve but charming brown salt-glazed stoneware character jug with coloured features. Neither the maker nor the subject has been identified. Height 21.9 cm.*

PLATE 581: *Doulton ornamental jug decorated by George Tinworth at Lambeth in 1874. The carved and incised decoration is typical of many of the Doulton artist-decorated stonewares. Impressed maker's mark with date and incised artist's monogram. Height 30.5 cm.* (Courtesy: Sotheby's, Sussex)

PLATE 582: *Four typical Doulton tankard-shaped jugs fitted with silver mounts. These were decorated by George Tinworth in 1878, Frances E. Lee in 1881 and Edith Lupton in 1879 and 1880. Impressed maker's marks with dates and incised artists' monograms. Heights between 23.5 cm and 26 cm.* (Courtesy: Sotheby's, Sussex)

PLATE 583: *Doulton tankard-shaped jug, decorated in the 1890s with a fieldmouse by Florence Barlow. The techniques used include pâte-sur-pâte and tube-lining, both over a stippled buff ground. Impressed maker's rosette mark with shape number '7967' and incised artist's monogram. Height 23.5 cm.* (Courtesy: Sotheby's, Sussex)

PLATE 584: *Another Florence Barlow decorated Doulton tankard-shaped jug, c.1890. This is a particularly charming example with vignettes of martins within beaded frames. Height 20.3 cm.* (Courtesy: Pretty & Ellis, Amersham)

PLATE 585: *Doulton stoneware jug made in 1890 to commemorate Stanley's expedition to rescue Emin Pasha. The sides show 'Enterprise' and 'Valour' with inscriptions listing those involved: E. M. Barttelot, W. Bonny, A. J. Mounteney-Jephson, W. C. Stairs, R. H. Nelson and T. H. Parke. Impressed maker's rosette mark with model number '1986'. Height 19.8 cm.*

Towards the end of the century Doulton issued several commemorative jugs in significant quantities. Examples include one inspired by Henry Morton Stanley's expedition to rescue Emin Pasha at Kavalli in 1889 (Plate 585), and two jugs marking the Boer War of 1900 (Plates 586–7). Although of similar shape, these last two show very different decorative styles, one glazed in greens, blues and browns, and the other very simply printed in black. Coloured glazes appear on many of the later jugs, including one decorated with sprigged golfing scenes (Plate 588). This is one of several sports featured, amongst which cycling also deserves mention.

Another Doulton fashion which emerged about 1880 was the decorative use of mottoes and sayings. A wide range exists, one of the most common featuring the quote 'Bread at Pleasure, Drink by Measure', often omitting the subsequent stern admonition 'If in doubt, Abstain' (Plate 589). Earlier examples are sprigged with coloured clays, but the idea remained popular for some years and later versions have printed inscriptions (Plate 590). Jugs of this type were probably the inspiration for a popular line of jugs specially made for pubs, brewers, distillers and similar trades. Such jugs are very collectable, and three typical examples advertising brands of whisky and beer are shown (Plates 591–3).

PLATE 586: *Stoneware jug decorated with coloured glazes made by Doulton to commemorate the hoisting of the flag at Pretoria in 1900. Impressed maker's mark. Height 21 cm.* (Courtesy: Phillips, London)

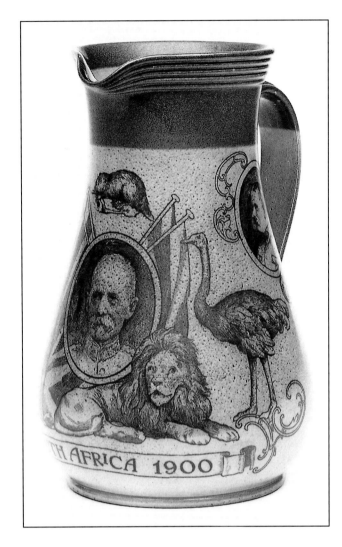

PLATE 589: *One of a series of brown stoneware motto jugs made by Doulton at Lambeth from the mid-1880s. This example reads 'Bread at Pleasure, Drink by Measure', the design and lettering applied using coloured clays. Impressed maker's rosette mark with date '1884' and various artists' and assistants' monograms, including one for Annie Milne. Height 19.8 cm.*

PLATE 587: *Another Doulton Boer War commemorative stoneware jug, 1900. This design is black-printed with patriotic portraits of three British leaders, probably Roberts, Kitchener and Baden-Powell, surrounded by flags and animals. Impressed maker's marks. Height 21 cm. (Courtesy: Sotheby's, Sussex)*

PLATE 590: *Typical later Royal Doulton stoneware motto jug, c.1910. In this case the inscription is black-printed and the neck is glazed a very dark brown. Impressed maker's lion and crown mark with model number '2242'. Height 22.8 cm.*

PLATE 588: *Attractive Doulton stoneware golfing jug, c.1900–10. The three reserves depict putting, driving and the lost ball. Note the coloured glazes typical of this period, used to enhance the foliate Art Nouveau borders. Height 22 cm. (Courtesy: Sotheby's, Sussex)*

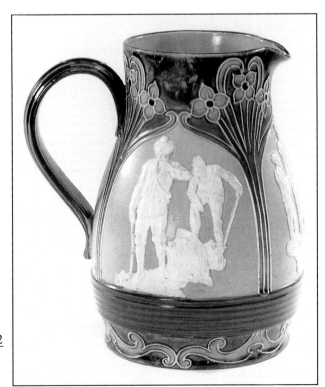

PLATE 591: *Brown stoneware jug made by Doulton to advertise Simpson's Scotch Whisky. The firm produced a long line of these 'pub jugs' in the early 20th century. Styles vary, this one having a deep blue neck. Doulton maker's marks. Height 15 cm.* (Courtesy: BBR Auctions, Barnsley)

PLATE 592: *Doulton stoneware advertising jug for Thorne's Scotch Whisky. This rare example is rather inappropriately decorated with scattered sprigs which include the common hunting motifs. Doulton maker's marks. Height 19.7 cm.* (Courtesy: BBR Auctions, Barnsley)

PLATE 593: *Royal Doulton stoneware pub jug, this one made for the Dartford Brewery Company. Although in any case a later example, presumably simple black-printed inscriptions like this were more affordable for the smaller firms. Royal Doulton maker's mark. Height 15.2 cm.* (Courtesy: BBR Auctions, Barnsley)

This brief review of Doulton jugs is concluded with two examples returning to the novelty theme. The first was modelled by Mark V. Marshall as a grotesque creature (Plate 594); the second as an owl with silver rim and rarely-found glass eyes (Plate 595). They have been included here to reflect the strong Doulton identity, although they could equally have been covered alongside other novelties in Chapter 13.

Doulton was by no means the only factory to decorate stoneware jugs to order, and many were made for individuals or local events. These are represented by one example bearing an 1895 electioneering inscription (Plate 596). Unfortunately, as with many stonewares, the jug is not marked, and the link with Cambridgeshire provides few clues to its manufacturer.

Although not noted for utilitarian jugs, any introduction to stonewares would be incomplete without mention of the Martin Brothers. The four brothers started potting in Fulham in 1873, and in 1877 established a workshop at Southall. They concentrated on studio pottery, particularly naturalistic vases, but also animals, birds, figures and other decorative wares. Some jugs were made, early examples often rather heavily potted with incised decoration (Plate 597). Particularly famous are R. W. Martin's grotesque bird and animal vases and his equally well-known face jugs. Four examples shown here date between 1898 and 1911 and are representative of a wide range of expressions and finishes (Plates 598–9, Colour Plate 26). Although not utilitarian, they represent the very best of British artist-made stonewares.

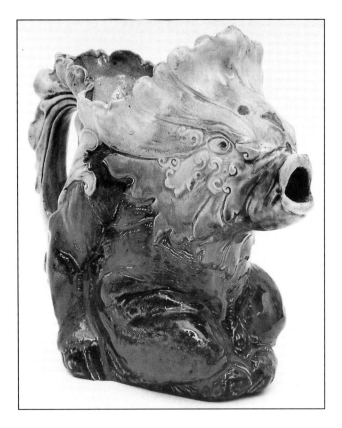

PLATE 594: *Stoneware jug made at Doulton's Lambeth studio by Mark V. Marshall. The fantastic creature, with a fish's head and boar's body, is glazed in mottled brown, pale green and blue. Impressed maker's rosette mark with incised artist's monogram and assistant's initials 'MH' and 'JBH'. Height 23 cm. (Courtesy: Lawrence Fine Art, Crewkerne)*

PLATE 596: *Unattributed brown stoneware electioneering jug, 1895. The blue incised inscription commemorates 'the signal Conservative success' in the Cambridgeshire election of July 1895, and features the names Giles, Greene, McCalmont, Jebb, Corst and Penrose-Fitzgerald. Height 15.2 cm. (Courtesy: BBR Auctions, Barnsley)*

PLATE 595: *Owl jug covered with thick brown glaze made by Doulton at Lambeth, c.1893. Note the glass eyes and silver beak. The silver mount made by Saunders and Shepherd is hallmarked 1893. Retailer's mark for Thornhill of Bond Street, London. Height 23.4 cm. (Courtesy: Sotheby's, London)*

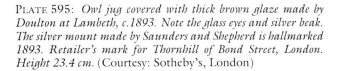

PLATE 597: *Early Martin Brothers stoneware jug made at London in November 1875. The heavy body is incised with a family of ducks and ducklings and glazed in blues, greens and browns. Incised mark '1717, R.W. Martin, London, 11-1875'. Height 19 cm. (Courtesy: Bonhams, Knightsbridge)*

PLATE 598: *Typical Martin Brothers stoneware face jug. This example, with its particularly happy face, has an overall white glaze. Incised maker's mark 'R.W. Martin & Bros, London & Southall'. Height 16 cm.* (Courtesy: Bonhams, Knightsbridge)

PLATE 599: *Another typical Martin Brothers face jug, dated 1898. Note the much darker matt colouring. Incised maker's mark 'R.W. Martin & Brothers, London & Southall, 1898'. Height 22.9 cm.* (Courtesy: Wintertons, Lichfield)

PLATE 600: *Staffordshire slipware puzzle jug possibly made by Ralph Simpson, dated 1709. The surface is decorated in cream and dark brown slip covered with a mottled golden glaze, the date flanked by the initials 'RS' and 'IHS'. Height 11 cm.* (Courtesy: Christie's, London)

13.

Puzzle Jugs, Toby Jugs and Other Novelties

W hile jugs are normally utilitarian and produced in large numbers, potters have never been slow to exploit any potential market. Despite poor working conditions, they had a keen sense of fun which emerges time and again in the subjects they used for decoration. It is no surprise that they also made pots which were deliberately humorous. This humour shows to good effect in novelties such as frog mugs, Toby jugs and puzzle jugs.

The classic puzzle jug has its neck pierced with a pattern of holes such that any attempt to pour will inevitably result in spillage. The secret lies in a series of three or more spouts fitted around the rim and connected to a hollow handle. The user needs to cover all but one of these and can then suck the liquid through the remaining spout. However, another small hole, typically beneath the handle, will frustrate such an obvious attempt unless it is also covered.

Exactly when this traditional form of puzzle jug

PLATE 601: *Unusual mid-18th-century slipware puzzle jug striated with brown and cream clays. Note the handle entwined with serpents. Height 21.5 cm.* (Courtesy: Christie's, London)

emerged is not known, but examples certainly date back into the seventeenth century. A fine collection of mainly eighteenth-century examples appears in Colour Plate 27 and others cover most of the early decorative types discussed in Chapter 1. These include one slipware jug dated 1709, possibly made by Ralph Simpson (Plate 600); a curious example in agate ware (Plate 601); one in white salt-glazed stoneware with scratch-blue decoration (Plate 602); and another dated 1788 in brown salt-glazed stoneware, possibly from Nottingham (Plate 603) *See Page 204*. Perhaps the most common early puzzle jugs are of tin-glazed earthenware with blue and white decoration, mostly attributed to Liverpool. Some are painted simply with flowers (Plate 604), but most feature a verse which typically reads:

> Here gentlemen come try your skill
> I'll hold a wager if you will
> That you don't drink this liquor all
> Without you spill or let some fall

Three such jugs made around 1750 are shown (Plates 605–6) along with another dated 1732 (Colour Plate 28). One less common verse refers to 'ale, wine or water' (Colour Plate 29), while another, shown on a jug with a cone-shaped interior strainer (Plate 607), reads:

> What tho I'm comon and well known
> To almost every one in town
> My hunsh to sixpence if you will
> That if you drink you some do spill

Puzzle jugs of this traditional type were produced well into the first half of the nineteenth century. A few rare examples are known in blue-printed earthenware and three other fine jugs are shown here. The first is a late creamware example made at the Bristol Pottery in 1819 (Plate 608) *See Page 21*. Although colourfully hand-painted in the style of William Fifield, it is signed with unidentified initials 'WD' on the base. The second commemorates the Great Reform Bill of 1832, black-printed with portraits of Earl Grey and Lord Brougham, enhanced with pink lustre (Plate 609). The third is a fine example with six spouts, decorated with splashed lustre and printed with a religious verse and a sailing ship (Plate 610). Although the shape of the Reform jug and the verse on the lustre example were both used by the Garrison Pottery at Sunderland, no attributions seem convincing.

PLATE 604: *Liverpool blue and white delftware puzzle jug dated 1766. The date is painted on the base. Height 24 cm.* (Courtesy: Christie's, London)

Right:
PLATE 607: *This blue and white delftware puzzle jug is also attributed to Liverpool but slightly later, c.1760. The interior is fitted with a cone-shaped strainer. Note also the different verse. Height 21 cm.* (Courtesy: Christie's, London)

PLATE 602: *White salt-glazed stoneware puzzle jug with scratch blue decoration of birds and flowers, c.1750. Note the distinctive pine-cone spouts and finial on the handle. Height 21.5 cm.* (Courtesy: Phillips, London)

PLATE 603: *Heavily glazed brown stoneware puzzle jug, possibly made at Nottingham, c.1770–80. Height 20.8 cm.* (Courtesy: City Museum & Art Gallery, Stoke-on-Trent)

Below:
PLATE 605: *A more typical Liverpool blue and white delftware puzzle jug, c.1750. This example is inscribed with the most common verse. Height 18.5 cm.* (Courtesy: Christie's, London)

218

Above:

PLATE 606: *Two further mid-18th-century Liverpool delftware puzzle jugs with the common verse. Heights 18 and 18.5 cm. (Courtesy: Sotheby's, London)*

Below Left:

PLATE 608: *Creamware puzzle jug made at the Bristol Pottery, monogrammed and dated 1819. The colourful design of flowers is enamelled in green, red, carmine, yellow, blue, maroon and brown. The style of painting is associated with William Fifield, but this jug is marked with unidentified initials 'WD'. Height 12cm.*

Above:

PLATE 610: *Rare and attractive pink lustre puzzle jug, possibly made at Sunderland, c.1820–30. This black-printed rhyme is accompanied by another on the front and a sailing ship on the reverse. Note the uncommon use of six spouts. Height 19 cm. (Courtesy: Sotheby's, Sussex)*

Bottom Right:

PLATE 609: *Creamware puzzle jug, printed in black with pink lustre, commemorating the Great Reform Bill of 1832. A floral wreath containing the word 'REFORM' is flanked by busts of Earl Grey, First Lord of the Treasury, and Lord Brougham and Vaux, Lord High Chancellor. Height 17 cm. (Courtesy: Phillips, London)*

Another contrasting jug from this period, made in 1830 by Thomas Arthur of Ewenny in Wales, is typical of unsophisticated but attractive slip-decorated jugs made at country potteries (Colour Plate 30). Puzzle jugs of the standard form were still being made in the twentieth century by potters such as those around Torquay in Devon. The West Country was famous for its slip-decorated motto ware, and the puzzle jug with its humorous verse was a natural product line.

Apart from country-made jugs, the traditional puzzle jug faded out of fashion towards the middle of the nineteenth century. Possibly they lost their novelty as the secret became widely disseminated, but the more dour tastes of the Victorian era following Prince Albert's death in 1861 may have contributed. It is perhaps surprising that they remained popular for so long.

Another, less obvious, form of puzzle jug emerged in the 1850s. Like frog mugs, these appear superficially normal, but the hollow handle is connected internally to a hole in the base. The fact that they will spill when poured is by no means apparent. Two examples are shown, one of a common relief-moulded design with hanging game (Plate 611), the other printed and coloured by Elsmore & Forster with a design featuring Grimaldi the clown (Plate 612), often found on ordinary jugs (see Plates 504–5). Other examples with personalized inscriptions are known. Humorous wares were ideal for less serious presentation purposes.

PLATE 611: *Mid-19th-century puzzle jug of unusual form with a hole in the base. This relief-moulded design is fairly common in both stoneware and earthenware with a greyhound handle (see Plate 672), but its use for a puzzle jug is rare. Height 22.3 cm. (Courtesy: Sotheby's, Sussex)*

PLATE 612: *Earthenware puzzle jug of the same type as the previous example but with printed and coloured decoration by Elsmore & Forster, c.1860–5. Compare with the jugs in Plates 504–5. Printed maker's mark. Height 22.5 cm. (Courtesy: Dreweatt Neate, Newbury)*

Another novelty which appeared in the eighteenth century is the bear jug. These strange objects, modelled in the form of a bear, usually covered with shredded clay to imitate fur, were first made of white salt-glazed stoneware around 1740 (Plate 613). The animal is usually clutching a cub or a dog and often has a chain through its nose. The head is detachable for use as a cup, and although the normal pose is seated, some are half-standing (Plate 614). Occasionally different surface finishes are found, such as one which has been incised and coloured (Plate 615). Unlike puzzle jugs, these novelties did not have a lengthy life, although one pearlware example, with the bear clutching a caricature of Napoleon Bonaparte, must date from the first decade of the nineteenth century (Plate 616).

PLATE 613: *Two typical Staffordshire salt-glazed stoneware bear jugs, c.1840. Note the detachable heads to be used as cups, the fur emulated by shredded clay, and the sparse decoration with iron slip. Heights 21.6 cm and 20.3 cm. (Courtesy: Christie's, London)*

PLATE 614: *Another Staffordshire salt-glazed stoneware bear jug and cover, c.1755. Although similar to the previous examples, the crouching pose is less common. Length 24 cm. (Courtesy: Christie's, London)*

The second half of the eighteenth century saw considerable advances in pottery manufacture, and the widespread adoption of fine-bodied creamware proved particularly significant. It was ideal for utilitarian wares, but with the development of semi-translucent coloured glazes, it also proved suitable for decorative figures. Complicated shapes could be reproduced using plaster moulds, and it was not long before the same techniques were applied to the manufacture of jugs. Notable amongst these were character jugs in the form of faces, heads, busts or even complete figures.

Two popular shapes were a satyr's head crowned with a dolphin spout and handle (Plate 617), and a similar head of Bacchus with a mask spout and a handle in the form of a figure clutching a bottle (Plate 618). These both date from the 1770s and are often attributed to Ralph Wood although relatively few marked examples exist. Another jug of similar type features a draped figure of Bacchus seated on a barrel, with a chained monkey handle and dolphin-like spout (Plate 619). Examples with coloured glazes again date from the 1770s but the design was widely copied and versions decorated with coloured enamels, possibly from Yorkshire, could have been made around 1800 (Plate 620).

PLATE 615: *Staffordshire salt-glazed stoneware bear jug and cover of very different character, c.1750–60. The patterned surface with coloured decoration is unusual.* (Courtesy: Christie's, London)

PLATE 616: *Although of traditional form, this bear jug and cover is made of pearlware, c.1810. Note the different treatment for the brown fur and also the clasped figure inscribed 'Boney' in place of the usual dog. Height 25 cm.* (Courtesy: Christie's, London)

PLATE 617: *Satyr jug of Ralph Wood type, c.1775. The dolphin spout and handle are glazed green, the face brown with grey beard and hair, and the scroll-moulded base is again green. Height 13 cm.* (Courtesy: Christie's, London)

221

PLATE 619: *Bacchus figure jug of a conventional form, c.1775. The figure is depicted seated on a barrel and holding a cornucopia supported by the chained monkey handle. The reverse has a faun. The dolphin spout is enriched in green and manganese. Height 30 cm.* (Courtesy: Christie's, London)

PLATE 618: *Bacchus mask jug, unattributed but again of Ralph Wood type, c.1775. Note the handle, which features a figure holding a bottle. Height 23.5 cm.* (Courtesy: Christie's, London)

Right:
PLATE 620: *Another Bacchus jug, probably made in Yorkshire, c.1800. This version is decorated with coloured enamels, predominantly blue and orange. Height 30.5 cm.* (Courtesy: Christie's, London)

three-cornered hat, holding a foaming mug of beer on his knee. The crown of the hat serves as both a lid and a small cup, but is often missing. A fine unmarked example decorated with coloured glazes (Plate 621) is similar to a rare marked example by Ralph Wood (Colour Plate 32). The latter also has an impressed model number, in this case 51, and although circumstantial, the presence of similar numbers on early examples could indicate a Wood origin (Colour Plate 33).

Other forms of Toby jug decorated with early coloured glazes include the Thin Man (Plates 622–3), the Squire (Plate 624 left), the Sailor (Plate 624 right), another version of which is known as the Planter, and Admiral Lord Howe (Plates 625–6, Colour Plate 33). Another early version is the Fiddler type, and a very rare example is shown with an inscribed mark for J. Marsh, possibly a forebear of the Jacob Marsh who was potting at Burslem by 1800 (Plate 627).

Several other Toby-type figures with overglaze enamel decoration are illustrated, mostly from the early nineteenth century. They include Falstaff (Plate 628), the Drunken Parson or Doctor Johnson (Plates 629 and 630, right) and the Hearty Good Fellow (Plate 631). Several designs were decorated with underglaze 'Pratt' colours including the Hearty Good Fellow (Plate 632) and a female figure depicting Martha Gunn (Plate 630, left). A rare figure is Drunken Sal, apparently made only by Davenport (Plate 633).

PLATE 621: *Good-quality but unmarked Toby jug of standard form, c.1780. This example is well-decorated with typical coloured glazes. Height 25 cm.*

Although the exact date remains unclear, the famous Toby jug emerged at about the same time as these three designs. Traditionally it was introduced by one of the Wood family of potters, and while this remains unsubstantiated, it soon became extremely popular (see Colour Plate 31). Many late eighteenth and early nineteenth-century firms issued versions, and the most common design has remained in production ever since. Unfortunately, most are unmarked, and although some can confidently be attributed to one area, such as Staffordshire or Yorkshire, few can be assigned to a particular potter. As a general rule earlier jugs were decorated with coloured glazes, but by about 1800 these had generally been replaced by overglaze enamels. Others were produced with the distinctive underglaze 'Pratt' colours (see Plate 343).

The standard Toby jug depicts a rather chubby seated figure, dressed in breeches, a long coat and a

PLATE 622: *Two early Toby-type jugs of a model known as the Thin Man. Both are covered with typical coloured glazes but one holds a pipe, the other a stirrup cup. Heights 24.1 cm each. (Courtesy: Christie's, London)*

PLATE 624: *Three unattributed but typical Toby-type jugs decorated with coloured glazes; the Squire, a standard Toby and the Sailorman. Note the shield just visible on the side of the centre jug, impressed 'It is all out then fill him again'. Heights 28.6 cm, 25.5 cm, and 31.8 cm.* (Courtesy: Christie's, London)

PLATE 623: *Another Thin Man Toby jug, c.1800. This figure holds a pipe and is coloured mainly in brown, blue and green glazes. Height 24 cm.* (Courtesy: Sotheby's, Sussex)

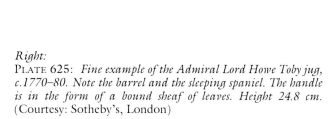

Right:
PLATE 625: *Fine example of the Admiral Lord Howe Toby jug, c.1770–80. Note the barrel and the sleeping spaniel. The handle is in the form of a bound sheaf of leaves. Height 24.8 cm.* (Courtesy: Sotheby's, London)

PLATE 626: *Another Lord Howe Toby jug of Ralph Wood type,
c.1780. The colouring is notably lighter than on the previous
example. Height 25.4 cm.* (Courtesy: Neales, Nottingham)

PLATE 628: *Large Toby-type jug of the Falstaff design, c.1800.
This example is attractively coloured with a yellow-edged black
hat, blue and yellow jacket and breeches, and a brown marbled
support. Height 40 cm.* (Courtesy: Christie's, London)

Left:
PLATE 627: *An extremely rare and documentary Toby jug of the
Fiddler type, inscribed 'J. Marsh, Folley' [sic]. A Jacob Marsh was
potting at Foley, near Burslem, in the early 19th century and this
jug may have been made by a predecessor. The head is a replace-
ment made in bell metal. Height 27.5 cm.* (Courtesy: Phillips,
London)

PLATE 629: *A traditional Toby, c.1800–10, and a Drunken Parson jug, c.1830, both decorated with coloured enamels. The latter is also sometimes referred to as the Doctor Johnson jug. Heights 25 cm and 21 cm.* (Courtesy: Sotheby's, Sussex)

PLATE 631: *Early 19th-century Hearty Good Fellow jug with a nicely modelled face. He is wearing a brown coat, green waistcoat and yellow knee breeches. Height 30.5 cm.* (Courtesy: Sotheby's, Sussex)

Left:
PLATE 630: *One of the few female Toby-type jugs, this one depicting the gin woman Martha Gunn, c.1790–1800, alongside another Doctor Johnson jug, c.1810–25. The Martha Gunn jug is decorated with typical Pratt-type underglaze colours. Heights 26 cm and 19 cm.* (Courtesy: Sotheby's, London)

Left:
PLATE 632: *Another Hearty Good Fellow jug, c.1800–10. This example is decorated with Pratt-type underglaze colours including a blue waistcoat and blue striped trousers. Height 26.5 cm.* (Courtesy: Sotheby's, Sussex)

Davenport also marked their version of the standard Toby, made in the 1830s, but few other firms marked their jugs. Amongst them are some rare late eighteenth-century examples by Neale & Co. (Plate 634, left). Another marked version in very different colouring is shown by Diana Edwards in *Neale Pottery and Porcelain*.

The two jugs shown in the last illustration would both be described as 'spotty faced', but the standard Toby is found in many variants with widely differing decoration. For example, the next three jugs differ markedly in the decoration of the tankard; one attractively enamelled (Plate 635), one a moulded foaming pot (Plate 636), and the third decorated with a painted chinoiserie scene (Plate 637). These probably date from the period between 1790 and 1810, as would the attractive Pratt ware version in Chapter 7 (Plate 343). One earlier example with coloured glazes has a plain mug although a shield at the side of the figure bears the bucolic inscription 'It is all out then fill him again' (Plate 624, centre).

PLATE 634: *Two Spotty-Faced Tobies with typical enamel colouring. The left-hand jug is a rare example by Neale & Co., c.1790–5, with impressed maker's mark. Heights 25 cm and 24.5 cm.* (Courtesy: Sotheby's, London)

Left:
PLATE 633: *Rare marked female jug known as Drunken Sal, made by Davenport, c.1830–5. The colouring includes black, pink, yellow, green, puce and brown. Impressed maker's mark with an anchor. Height 30.5 cm.* (Courtesy: Sotheby's, London)

Left:
PLATE 635: *Attractively coloured and finely detailed Toby of the standard type, possibly made in Yorkshire, c.1800. Height 25.5 cm.* (Courtesy: Dreweatt Neate, Newbury)

PLATE 637: *Early 19th-century Toby holding a mug painted with a Chinese landscape. The detail of the decoration is unusual, even the back of his chair is painted with a vase of flowers. Height 26 cm.* (Courtesy: Sotheby's, Sussex)

The mug on another example has an interesting inscription 'Success to our Wooden Walls', clearly referring to the naval events arousing great public interest around 1800 (Colour Plate 34). One design is commonly known as Admiral Lord Howe, after the great naval commander of the day (Plates 625–6), but one example of another design usually known as the Sailor actually bears the impressed name 'Lord Hou' [*sic*] (Plate 638). This is a specialist field and any interested collector would be well advised to refer to the appropriate literature.

PLATE 636: *Another Toby possibly made in Yorkshire, c.1790–1800. The colouring shows much less sophistication than on the previous example. Height 25.5 cm.* (Courtesy: Christie's, London)

PLATE 638: *Another version of the Sailorman jug shown in Plate 624, this example unusually inscribed 'Lord Hou' [sic]. Note the mottled colouring to the jacket, in grey and ochre, and the nicely lined trousers. Height 29 cm.* (Courtesy: Christie's, London)

PLATE 640: *Fine-quality Toby-type figure in majolica glazes. This Minton jug, of shape number 1140, is dated 1865. Another example of this design along with his lady companion can be seen in Plate 547. Impressed maker's mark with shape number and date code. Height 28 cm.* (Courtesy: Sotheby's, London)

Although the period up to about 1840 was the heyday of good quality Tobies, a large number were made later, many illustrated in Vic Schuler's *Toby Jugs*. Two from the second half of the nineteenth century are shown here; one a caricature of Mr Punch (Plate 639) and the other a high quality figure made in majolica during the 1860s by Minton (Plate 640). The latter is actually one of a pair (Plate 547).

The most notable of the later jugs are a set made by Wilkinsons depicting the allied leaders from the First World War (Plate 641). These were modelled by the political cartoonist Sir Francis Carruthers-Gould for sale

Left:
PLATE 639: *Typical Toby-type jug from the later 19th century, depicting the figure of Mr Punch. Note his seat consisting of three volumes of the popular journal. The colouring includes much prominent red. Height 24.8 cm.* (Courtesy: Christie's, South Kensington)

PLATE 641: *Set of eleven jugs depicting First World War leaders modelled by Sir Francis Carruthers-Gould and issued by Wilkinson Ltd, c.1915–19. The figures are President Wilson, Marshal Foch, Marshal Joffre, Lloyd George, Admiral Beatty, Admiral Jellicoe, Sir John French, Earl Haig, King George V, Lord Kitchener and General Botha. Printed maker's marks with facsimile signature and retailer's marks for Soane & Smith of Oxford Street. Heights 24.4 to 30.5 cm.* (Courtesy: Neales, Nottingham)

by the London retailers Soane & Smith of Oxford Street. There are eleven designs, issued individually in limited editions between 1915 and 1919. It has often been suggested that a twelfth was designed, but no matching figure has been recorded. One final Toby-type jug depicts another famous leader, this time Sir Winston Churchill during the Second World War (Plate 642). Made by the Wilkinson firm in 1941, it was designed by Clarice Cliff to show Churchill in his role as First Lord of the Admiralty, holding a battleship and seated on a bulldog draped with a Union Jack.

Jugs like this were never really intended for use, and their claim to inclusion here is marginal, although the same comment applies to most Tobies. They are representative of a large number of character jugs issued in the twentieth century, notably by Royal Doulton amongst others. Designed primarily as ornaments, they are outside the scope of this volume but interested readers may care to refer to Kevin Pearson's *The Character Jug Collectors Handbook*.

There is one other jug which, although not strictly a novelty, is normally decorated with early coloured glazes and is closely related to the early Tobies. This is a

Left:
PLATE 642: *Winston Churchill jug made by Wilkinson Ltd, c.1939–40. This was designed by Clarice Cliff to show the famous statesman as First Lord of the Admiralty. Printed maker's mark with facsimile signature. Height 30 cm.* (Courtesy: Sotheby's, London)

well-known jug designed by John Voyez, a modeller who worked for Wedgwood and other Staffordshire potters. It is of utilitarian shape but heavily modelled in the form of an oak tree with a standing figure on one side (Plate 643) and a rustic couple on the reverse (Plate 644). A notice above the couple reads 'Fair Hebe', and inscribed above the other figure is 'A Bumper, a Bumper'. They are frequently attributed to Ralph Wood, although examples dated 1788 with the Voyez name were made by both Robert Garner (his initials are visible on the bottle in Plate 643) and Richard Meir Astbury. A rare unmarked variant, decorated with coloured enamels, probably dates from 1789 when George III made his first recovery from mental illness (Plate 645). The usual inscriptions are replaced by 'Long Live the King' and 'GR. III Restor'd'. Another Garner example is shown alongside a later unrecorded version, heavily enamelled and surprisingly made by Copeland & Garrett (Plate 646).

PLATE 644: *The reverse of another Fair Hebe jug, also signed and dated 'I. Voyez 1788'. Height 25 cm.* (Courtesy: Christie's, London)

PLATE 643: *One side of a typical Fair Hebe jug decorated with blue, yellow and green glazes, c.1788–90. Note the initials 'RG' for Robert Garner visible on the bottle. The base is signed and dated 'I. Voyez 1788'. Height 24.5 cm.* (Courtesy: Christie's, London)

PLATE 645: *Unusual variant of the Fair Hebe jug, c.1789–90. Note the inscription 'GR. III RESTOR'D' in place of the usual 'FAIR HEBE' title. A similar modification on the reverse reads 'LONG LIVE THE KING'. Height 21.5 cm.* (Courtesy: Christie's, London)

Right:
PLATE 646: *Two Fair Hebe jugs, a Robert Garner version decorated with coloured glazes on the left shown alongside a rare and heavily enamelled example by Copeland & Garrett, c.1833–40. The latter with impressed maker's name around 'NEW / FAYENCE'. Heights 24.4 cm and 17.1 cm (size 12).*

PLATE 647: *Wedgwood Queen's Ware jug, c.1775–80. The elegant helmet shape is emphasized by the brown hand-painted broad and fine lines. Impressed mark 'WEDGWOOD'. Height 17.8 cm.* (Courtesy: Trustees of the Wedgwood Museum, Barlaston, Staffordshire)

14.
Miscellaneous Decorative Techniques

A ny attempt to classify objects as diverse as jugs will inevitably throw up inconsistencies. Some defy convenient classification, either being inappropriate to any of the obvious categories or fitting equally well into two or more. The following jugs represent several such miscellaneous types.

The most obvious group covers jugs with little or no decoration. One good example is an elegant Wedgwood creamware helmet-shape jug dating from about 1780 (Plate 647). Although it is hand-painted with brown lines around the foot, rim and handle, such restrained decoration would have been out of place in Chapter 2. An even better example is a mid-nineteenth-century stoneware jug which is totally plain except for two turned lines around the base and a blue jasper-dip neck (Plate 648). Despite the lack of decoration, this jug still holds some fascination with its impressed mark 'PATENT', as yet unexplained.

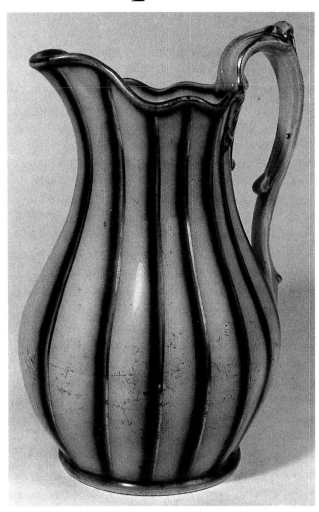

PLATE 649: *White stoneware jug by William Adams & Sons, c.1850–60. The lobed shape is gilded and highlighted with under-glaze flow-blue lining. Printed maker's mark with name and address, also gilt pattern number '3/917'. Height 20.9 cm.* (Courtesy: City Museum & Art Gallery, Stoke-on-Trent)

A third jug within this group is of similar date made by William Adams & Sons (Plate 649). While the lobed shape is both moulded and painted, a miscellaneous classification seems inevitable. A final jug to end this group is made of solid agate ware (Plate 650). As a general rule this technique was little used after the eighteenth century and this jug would be out of place in Chapter 1. Although grouped here under miscellaneous decoration, it is representative of several jugs which might be better classified by shape.

PLATE 648: *Unattributed plain white stoneware jug with blue jasper-dip neck. Unmarked except for impressed word 'PATENT'. Height 15.8 cm.*

233

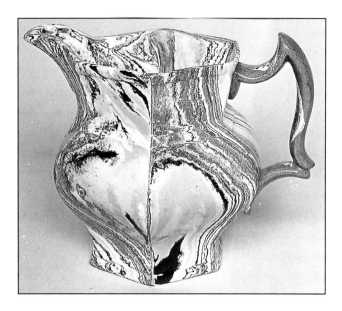

PLATE 650: *Unusual and unattributed mid-19th-century solid agateware jug. The hexagonal body is striated with brown, blue and cream clays. Height 15.2 cm.* (Courtesy: Dreweatt Neate, Newbury)

PLATE 652: *Mid-19th-century earthenware jug by an unknown maker. The buff body is banded with white slip and brown enamel lines, and features a blue dendritic Mocha design. A similar Mocha design on the reverse is in brown. Height 19.3 cm.*

Another colourful but simple jug of the barrel shape popular towards the end of the eighteenth century is decorated with simple painted bands and circular motifs (Plate 651). The precision of the banding suggests that it must have been turned while the paint was applied. Similar banding can be seen on a later jug introducing another distinctive decorative technique (Plate 652). The feathery Mocha decoration was achieved using a small drop of solution which spread dendritically when applied on to a wet coating of slip on the surface of the ware. A key constituent was apparently tobacco juice. Mocha decoration dates from the 1790s but most examples are from the mid-nineteenth century. It was simple to produce and widely used for cheaper utilitarian wares, particularly for public houses. This jug was probably made for milk or beer. The same design appears on the reverse, but in brown rather than blue.

Another relatively random technique involves the use of a sponge to apply colour. A good example is a late eighteenth-century pearlware jug a with nicely moulded mask spout (Plate 653). The process was particularly popular in Yorkshire, where sponged decoration was often used around the bases of Toby jugs and figures. It is just possible that this jug was made at Leeds.

Two fascinating pearlware jugs decorated with a related technique are presentation pieces, one dated 1807 (Plate 654), the other a year earlier (Colour Plate 11). The stylized geometric bands were possibly applied with a sponge, on the first jug just in blue, but on the other in blue, green and yellow. The latter seems quite unique with its hand-painted roundel containing eight Christian names from a family called Pomfret.

This form of decoration is most unusual, but a very common technique was engine-turning. This required a special lathe with an eccentric motion designed to cut regular patterns into the leather-hard clay before it was fired. The process was in use at Wedgwoods in the 1760s and was widely employed by many potters well into the nineteenth century. It is commonly found on unglazed stonewares, particularly black basalt (Plates 655–6). It often appears in association with sprigged ornament such as on two similar jugs by Turner, one basalt (Plate 657), the other caneware with an enamelled border inside the rim (Plate 658 *See page 90*).

Engine-turning can also be seen on many of the sprigged stoneware jugs shown in Chapter 6. Two jugs would be featured there except for a lack of the required sprigging (Plates 659–60). The first has an applied pad mark of the Angels type (see Plate 299) while the second has a moulded Minton scroll mark. The similarity of these two ring-turned jugs is remarkable but significant differences can be discerned.

PLATE 651: *Pearlware barrel-shaped jug, probably made in Staffordshire, c.1780. The body is painted with ochre concentric bands and blue medallions within green ribbed borders. Height 21 cm.* (Courtesy: Peter Wilson, Nantwich)

234

Above left:
PLATE 655: *Elegant helmet-shaped black basalt jug by Wedgwood, c.1790–1800. The body is decorated with a simple engine-turned pattern. Impressed mark 'WEDGWOOD'. Height 14.1 cm.*

Above Right:
PLATE 656: *Another black basalt jug decorated with simple engine-turning, this example by Elijah Mayer, c.1790–1800. Impressed mark 'E. Mayer'. Height 16 cm. (Courtesy: City Museum & Art Gallery, Stoke-on-Trent)*

PLATE 653: *Early pearlware jug, c.1780–90. The body has two green-glazed turned bands and is randomly sponged in purplish-blue. Note the finely moulded mask spout. Height 13 cm. (Courtesy: Jack Hacking)*

PLATE 654: *Barrel-shaped pearlware jug, inscribed and dated 'Danl. & Catherine Jackson 1807'. The body is hand-decorated in blue with an unusual stylized design probably applied with a sponge. Compare with another similar jug in Colour Plate 11. Height 26.2 cm. (Courtesy: Dreweatt Neate, Newbury)*

PLATE 657: *Good quality Turner basalt jug combining engine-turning with sprigged decoration, c.1800. Note the gilding and also the reticulated ground around the shoulder. Impressed mark 'TURNER'. Height 19.6 cm. (Courtesy: City Museum & Art Gallery, Stoke-on-Trent)*

PLATE 658: *Turner caneware jug of very similar design to the previous basalt example, c.1790–1800. The interior is lined with white slip and a border enamelled in green, mauve, and blue can be seen just inside the rim. Impressed mark 'TURNER'. Height 21.5 cm.* (Courtesy City Museum & Art Gallery, Stoke-on-Trent)

Another form of mechanical decoration adopted in the mid-nineteenth century is known as rouletting. In this process, a wheel bearing a repetitive pattern was pressed into the body of the vessel as it was turned on a lathe. The resulting indented band was then filled with coloured clay and the surface cleaned off to leave the contrasting pattern clearly visible. Several bands could be applied on the same pot. Examples often bear an impressed trade name 'Patent Mosaic', as on three typical jugs with different patterns (Plates 661–3). This shape with the snake-entwined handle is thought to have been made at the Dudson factory, which still holds corresponding roulette wheels. Impressed numbers

PLATE 659: *Drab stoneware ring-turned jug decorated with engine-turning, beading and a herringbone pattern around the neck, c.1820–30. Compare with the same jug featuring a sprigged border in Plate 300. Applied white Angels pad mark containing model number '53'. Height 11 cm.*

usually appear alongside the trade name, these three having '103', '23' and '253' respectively. The third also has the name 'Stourbridge', and another rouletted 'Patent Mosaic' jug has been seen with the name 'Delhi'. The significance of these names is not known. Yet another rouletted jug is impressed 'Tuscan' with the number '2' (Plate 664), but everything about this example is so different to those marked 'Patent Mosaic' that it was probably made elsewhere.

The phrase 'Patent Mosaic' dates from 1843 when Richard Boote invented various techniques for decorating pots with surface designs in contrasting colours. Whether he had any involvement with the rouletting process is unclear, but another of his techniques was adopted for use on relief-moulded jugs by Alcock and by Bradbury, Anderson & Bettany (see Chapter 8). A further process involving sprigged designs inlaid within the surface appears to have been used only by T. & R. Boote. Two distinctive and very typical jugs are shown, one in green with white figures (Plate 665), the other in white with drab figures (Plate 666). These are again marked 'Patent Mosaic', so the phrase covers at least three different techniques. It was also used for no apparent reason on ordinary sprigged and relief-moulded wares by Cork & Edge.

The mention of relief-moulding brings us to several jugs which, although moulded, do not comfortably fit within Chapter 8. The first two are ornately shaped but bear little or no relief design on the surface. The design registered by Jones & Walley in 1843 (Plate 667) was also made with printed and coloured decoration, often with a yellow ground. The second similarly ornate jug by the South Wales Pottery is described by Gareth Hughes and Robert Pugh in *Llanelly Pottery* as the Raglan shape (Plate 668).

PLATE 660: *An almost identical stoneware jug by Minton, c.1835–40. Despite the striking similarity, there are some subtle differences including the more prominent features on the mask spout. Applied white moulded scroll mark with model 'No. 135' and cursive initial 'M'. Height 15 cm.* (Courtesy: Jack Hacking)

PLATE 661: *White stoneware jug with blue and green rouletted bands, c.1870. These jugs are unmarked but tentatively attributed to Dudson. Impressed mark 'PATENT MOSAIC' with number '103'. The Britannia-metal lid is not marked. Height 18.2 cm (size 30).*

PLATE 663: *Similar jug in light grey stoneware with drab and blue rouletted bands and some gilding, c.1870. This example is impressed 'STOURBRIDGE' in addition to the usual mark 'PATENT MOSAIC' with number '253'. It also has a pattern number '2/4361' painted in red. Height 17 cm (size 30).*

PLATE 662: *Green stoneware jug with brown and white rouletted bands, c.1870. The design is basically the same as the previous example but the colours and patterning are different. Impressed mark 'PATENT MOSAIC' with number '23'. Height 20.7 cm (size 12).*

PLATE 664: *White stoneware jug with black, mauve and blue rouletted bands, c.1880. Although of the same basic type, this jug is very different to the three previous examples and is impressed 'TUSCAN' with number '2'. The Britannia-metal lid is not marked. Height 21.9 cm (size 18).*

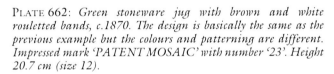

PLATE 665: *Green stoneware jug inlaid with white figures by T. & R. Boote, c.1845–50. The border is picked out with gilding. Black-printed royal arms mark with 'PATENT MOSAIC' above and maker's name beneath. Height 20.3 cm. (Courtesy: City Museum & Art Gallery, Stoke-on-Trent)*

PLATE 666: *White stoneware jug inlaid with drab figures by T. & R. Boote, c.1845–50. The design is picked out with gilding. Black-printed royal arms mark with 'PATENT MOSAIC' above and maker's name beneath. Height 21.4 cm. (Courtesy: City Museum & Art Gallery, Stoke-on-Trent)*

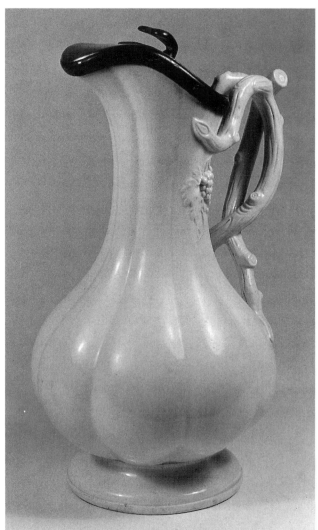

PLATE 667: *Glazed white stoneware jug of an ornately moulded form registered by Jones & Walley in 1843. Black-printed mark with 'REGISTERED No. 7122, 13 May 1843 By JONES & WALLEY, Staffordshire' between concentric circles. The Britannia-metal lid is not marked. Height 23.7 cm (size 12).*

PLATE 668: *Moulded and glazed drab earthenware jug of Raglan shape by the South Wales Pottery, c.1850. Impressed mark 'SOUTH WALES POTTERY'. Height 15.9 cm.*

This brings us to a group of jugs which are relief-moulded but for various reasons are best treated as exceptions. One is made of black basalt, and although moulded this would normally be collected for its body rather than the decoration (Plate 669). The next is relief-moulded in pearlware with busts of General Hill and Lord Wellington (Plate 670). This must date from the time of the Peninsular Campaign between 1809 and 1814 and is much more akin to Pratt ware (see Chapter 7) than the later relief-moulded jugs. With its early date and enamel colouring, it would feature in a collection of commemorative rather than moulded wares.

PLATE 671: *Unusual relief-moulded earthenware jug, probably made at Scott's Southwick Pottery, Sunderland, c.1840–50. The moulding is coloured with green and turquoise glazes combined with yellow, pink and black enamels. Applied white Ridgway-style lozenge mark containing maker's surname 'Scott'. Height 18.8 cm.*

PLATE 669: *Wedgwood black basalt jug moulded with a union design of shamrock, thistle, rose and harp, c.1825–50. Impressed mark 'WEDGWOOD'. Height 11.1 cm.*

PLATE 670: *Pearlware jug moulded and brightly enamelled with portraits of General Hill and Lord Wellington, c.1809–14. Unmarked and unattributed. Height 13 cm. (Courtesy: Sotheby's, Sussex)*

Three other jugs which are moulded but extensively coloured appear more relevant here. The first is decorated with a combination of enamels and coloured glazes and has a previously unrecorded applied mark bearing the name 'Scott' (Plate 671). It was presumably made by the Scott Brothers at Sunderland, not known for more traditional relief-moulded wares. The second is a well-known design of hanging game (Plate 672), more commonly found in coloured-body stoneware. Marked examples are recorded by the Chrysanthemeum Factory and also in the distinctively lacquered siderolith ware by the Schiller firm of Bodenbach in Bohemia, but the design was widely copied. A similar but unusual example was made in the form of a puzzle jug (Plate 611).

The third jug is also heavily coloured but was produced by the little-known Sandford Pottery, near Wareham in Dorset (Plate 673). This design is one of several, mostly commemorative, registered by the firm during 1860 and appears to have been intended to have a bust sprigged in the front panel. It has been suggested that this example was heavily coloured to disguise the fact that the sprigging had failed to adhere, but this is admittedly rather speculative.

Jugs which feature relief-moulding together with other forms of decoration are not uncommon. One good example, registered by Thomas Till & Son in 1852, is moulded with bulrushes around the base and handle, but the main surface is black-printed with a pair

PLATE 672: *Unattributed relief-moulded jug of a common Hanging Game design, c.1835–50. This earthenware version is enamelled in blue, yellow, grey, purple, orange, green and ochre, with gilt lining to the rim and foot. Compare with the similar puzzle jug in Plate 611. Height 20.5 cm.*

of classical figures (Plate 674). Another is moulded in white Parian with a design which features a reserve attractively hand-painted with a small vignette (Plate 675). Another example of the same jug has been noted without any painted scene, also regrettably unmarked.

In the same way as relief-moulding, sprig-moulding can also be found in combination with other decoration. One typical early Victorian jug has a small floral spray sprigged on to a coloured earthenware body and then crudely enamelled (Plate 676). The body itself is attractively ring-turned, with two bands of beading and a pineapple-moulded spout. Similar mugs and jugs are quite common, always unmarked, and although of no great quality they are workmanlike and quite charming.

Such charm is also found on so-called Measham wares, like the jug made for Mrs Bibby of Rishton in 1882 (Plate 677). This features crudely-coloured sprigging on a moulded body covered with a treacly-brown glaze. These wares are named after Measham, near Ashby-de-la-Zouch, where there was a shop supplying passing canal folk with personalized pots, made mostly at nearby Church Gresley. Rishton lies on the Leeds and Liverpool canal, between Blackburn and Accrington, and this jug may have been made for a boatman's wife normally based there.

240

PLATE 673: *Heavily enamelled white earthenware jug of a moulded design registered by the Sandford Pottery in 1860. The colouring features a green ground with highlights in yellow, pink, crimson and green, and added gilding. Moulded registration diamond for 6 July 1860 with maker's name beneath. Height 27.8 cm.*

PLATE 674: *Green stoneware jug registered by Thomas Till & Son in 1852. The simple but attractive design combines relief-moulding with black-printed classical figures. Impressed mark 'TILL' and printed mark with 'T. TILL & SON' above a registration diamond for 13 August 1852. Height 20.8 cm. (Courtesy: City Museum & Art Gallery, Stoke-on-Trent)*

PLATE 675: *White Parian jug with blue ground by an unknown maker, c.1850–70. Polychrome landscapes are hand-painted in the reserves on each side, but this feature is omitted on some examples. Height 22.7 cm.*

PLATE 676: *Attractive mid-Victorian drab earthenware jug of a common type. The floral design is sprigged and crudely enamelled in green, red, orange, yellow, blue and brown. Unmarked and unidentifiable. Height 16.7 cm.*

PLATE 677: *Typical Measham-ware jug, inscribed and dated 1882. The body is white earthenware covered with brown glaze, crudely sprigged and enamelled in green, red and blue. The impressed inscription reads 'MRS BIBBY / RISHTON / 1882'. Height 18.2 cm.*

The remaining jugs are also brightly coloured. The first is a fine Spode Dutch-shape jug made in dark brown earthenware (Plate 678). It is decorated with fine gilding and an unusual design of scattered roundels, apparently hand-painted in highly-raised enamels. A similar enamel pad appears on the base alongside the usual factory mark. Two more jugs by Spode might equally well have featured in Chapter 2 or Chapter 9. These are of the common octagonal shape, potted in redware which is glazed inside, and enamelled with prominent flowers (Plate 679, Colour Plate 16). The two patterns were introduced in about 1820 and 1837 respectively, and if they were not by Spode would probably be collected more for their body than their decoration.

It is often not easy to decide whether such designs are outline printed or painted freehand, and another jug made in redware is decorated with a multi-coloured design of flowers which appears to have been transferred in some way (Plate 680). Although unmarked, this jug was made by Dudson, also responsible for three tankard-shaped jugs with a shiny black Jackfield-type glaze over a terracotta body (Plate 681). The right-hand example is decorated with the same technique as the redware jug just discussed, but the other two are enamelled by hand.

PLATE 678: *Good quality but very unusual covered jug by Spode, c.1815. The dark brown earthenware body is finely gilt but strangely decorated with raised enamel pads. A similar enamel pad appears on the base alongside the impressed mark 'Spode', with pattern number '2370' painted in red. Height 16.6 cm. (Courtesy: City Museum & Art Gallery, Stoke-on-Trent)*

PLATE 680: *Terracotta jug with glazed interior, attributed to Dudson, c.1865–80. The floral design in white, green, carmine, yellow and peach enamels seems to have been applied by some transfer process. Pattern number '3/9288' painted in white. Height 18.1 cm (size 12).*

PLATE 679: *Octagonal jug in dark redware by Spode, c.1820. The floral design is enamelled in blue, green, white, yellow and carmine. Impressed mark 'SPODE' with pattern number '3339' painted in black. A similar jug can be seen in Colour Plate 16. Height 13.2 cm.*

PLATE 681: *Three Dudson tankard-shaped jugs in redware covered with a black Jackfield-type glaze, c.1880. The right-hand example is decorated with the same process as the redware jug in Plate 680; the other two are enamelled in colours. Unmarked except for painted pattern numbers '4/7101', '4/4346' and '5862' respectively. Heights 14.8 cm, 17.4 cm, and 18.7 cm.*

The final jug represents a large number of mugs and jugs made in varying levels of quality for presentation purposes (Plate 682). The jug itself and the basic decoration are too plain to be included in any other chapter, although the gilt inscription is reasonably well hand-painted. This example dating from 1865 is of good quality, but others can be very poor, particularly those made in the many small china factories which were dotted throughout Longton in the second half of the nineteenth century.

PLATE 682: *Glazed white stoneware jug by G. F. Bowers, monogrammed and dated 1865. The ground is maroon but note the good-quality gilding. Ornate black-printed maker's mark with gilt pattern number '2943'. Height 25.4 cm.* (Courtesy: City Museum & Art Gallery, Stoke-on-Trent)

PLATE 683: *Octagonal earthenware jug covered with a streaky matt green glaze by Wedgwood & Co. Ltd, c.1900–10. Printed unicorn trademark with maker's name and 'MADE IN ENGLAND'. Height 20 cm.*

15.
The Twentieth Century

Towards the end of the nineteenth century a steady decline in standards of day-to-day pottery and china became quite marked. The potters were driven to produce wares in large quantities for the mass market, and both quality and design inevitably suffered. Although most decorative techniques remained in use, few mass-produced wares were of any real merit. One early twentieth-century jug demonstrates this general fall in standards most effectively (Plate 683). It is not surprising that factory-made wares from this period have found little favour with collectors.

This is, of course, a sweeping generalization, and it would be misleading to suggest that no interesting wares were made. One shining light was the movement away from mass-production and back to craftsmanship, clearly seen in the rise to prominence of the Doulton artist-decorated stonewares and similar wares from the Martin Brothers (see Chapter 12). Other potters followed this lead, by no means all restricting themselves to the relatively coarse brown stoneware. Most of these hand-crafted wares are decorative rather than functional, although usable jugs can be found amongst the vases and other ornamental wares.

William Moorcroft began to design wares when working for Macintyre, and subsequently set up his own firm in 1913 when they discontinued their art department. Although he concentrated on ornamental pieces, particularly vases, two hot water jugs are typical of his work with Macintyre (Plates 684–5). These would normally have been part of sets, with matching teapots and basins. Moorcroft's slip-trailing technique involves creating a design by squeezing lines of slip on to the surface of a pot, the resulting areas then being filled with different colours. Earlier examples have a lighter, more intricate character, whereas later wares are more sweeping and dramatic, using a distinctive and darker colour palette. Moorcroft produced some interesting commemorative pieces, including one bulbous jug marking the coronation of King George VI (Plate 686).

Moorcroft was not the only potter to utilize slip-trailing. In the 1870s Mintons realized the potential of artistic wares and set up a pottery studio in London. Although this was relatively short-lived, the firm continued to develop attractive individual designs. Among these are the secessionist wares, introduced in 1902 and named after the Viennese Secession Movement. Most examples are decorative vases, but a

PLATE 684: *Hot-water jug in 'Gesso Faience' by James Macintyre & Co. Ltd, c.1905–1913. This is a typical design by William Moorcroft with raised sprays of flowers and foliage in blue and white on a green ground. A metal swing lid is missing. Printed maker's mark.* (Courtesy: Christie's, South Kensington)

wash jug is shown here (Plate 687).

Neither Moorcroft nor Mintons produced these wares in real quantity, and after the First World War the major manufacturers made something of a comeback. The Doulton factory had already been moving away from brown stoneware and making some good quality finer wares. One excellent example is a rare pub jug (Plate 688) but it is their series ware which is most readily recognized. This featured attractive and brightly coloured printed designs, and judging by the number that have survived, they proved very popular. The jug with a Gallant Fishers subject is just one from a wide range of different series (Plate 689). It shows to good effect the use of an attractive printed design allied to a novel shape.

PLATE 687: *Minton Secessionist wash jug, c.1902-14. This typical design with slip-trailed square flowers supported on sinuous stems is decorated in shades of green, ochre and blue. Printed maker's mark. Height 30.5 cm.* (Courtesy: Christie's, South Kensington)

PLATE 685: *Another Moorcroft-designed Macintyre hot-water jug, c.1907–13. This example has a white ground and is fitted with a 'Dura' metal lid. Printed maker's mark with registration number '508931'. Height 18 cm.* (Courtesy: Sotheby's, Sussex)

PLATE 688: *Rare and fine Royal Doulton jug made for the Barnsley Brewery Company. The white body is covered with coloured transfers and the inscription on the front is accompanied by others for Brown Corbett's Irish Whisky and Edward Young & Co. on the sides. Royal Doulton factory mark. Height 17.3 cm.* (Courtesy: BBR Auctions, Barnsley)

PLATE 686: *King George VI and Queen Elizabeth coronation jug made by William Moorcroft, c.1937. This darker style is typical of the later wares. Impressed factory mark with Moorcroft's signature in blue. Height 16.5 cm.* (Courtesy: Christie's, South Kensington)

PLATE 689: *Attractive and typical series ware jug made by Royal Doulton, c.1910–30. The Gallant Fishers subject includes the inscription 'Of recreation there is none so free as fishing is alone' around the inside rim. Printed maker's mark. Height 17 cm.* (Courtesy: Dreweatt Neate, Newbury)

The Doulton name features amongst the most collected of all twentieth-century factories with world-wide interest in their figures and character jugs, but another useful jug must suffice here (Plate 690). This is made in 'Queensware' with coloured relief-moulded scenes and its desirability is considerably enhanced by the subject matter. Sporting items are always in demand, with golf and cricket commanding the highest premiums.

There was something of a fashion for moulded and coloured wares in the 1930s, another example originating at the Crown Devon pottery of Fieldings (Colour Plate 35). This design is one of many commemoratives made for the unheld coronation of Edward VIII.

The fashion for cheerful, brightly-coloured wares became almost a craze, and widespread demand was met largely by the reintroduction of hand-painted patterns. Early examples can be identified with the Art Deco movement associated with the Paris Exhibition of 1925. Some larger potteries employed artists to design wares which could be hand-painted in quantity, perhaps best typified by the highly collectable designs by Clarice Cliff for Wilkinsons. They included several different jugs, of which the most popular were the Lotus and Isis shapes. Examples feature a range of typical floral, geometric and landscape patterns in the 'Bizarre' and 'Fantasque' series (Plates 691–3). A less common 'Bizarre' jug is also shown (Plate 694). The bright and cheerful effect of these jugs is best seen in colour (Colour Plate 36).

PLATE 691: *Three typical Clarice Cliff Lotus jugs made by Wilkinsons in the 1930s. The example on the right is one of the 'Fantasque' designs with an orange ground and a broad colourful band of fruit overlapping in Cubist manner. Printed maker's marks with Clarice Cliff facsimile signature. Heights around 29 cm.* (Courtesy: Sotheby's, Sussex)

Although Clarice Cliff wares have become particularly collectable, other female designers made names for themselves, including Charlotte Rhead and Susie Cooper. Neither made jugs in significant numbers but Susie Cooper tea and dinner wares sometimes include utilitarian jugs (Plate 695).

PLATE 694: *Attractive but less common jug shape designed by Clarice Cliff for Wilkinsons. Again titled 'Bizarre' the design in brown, orange, yellow, and ochre is known as the Coral Firs pattern. Printed marks. Height 28 cm.* (Courtesy: Dreweatt Neate, Newbury)

PLATE 692: *Clarice Cliff Isis jug, again made in the 1930s. This 'Bizarre' design is known as the Secrets pattern, with red-roofed cottages nestling among meadows along a hilly coastline. Printed maker's mark. Height 24 cm.* (Courtesy: Sotheby's, Sussex)

PLATE 693: *Another Clarice Cliff 'Bizarre' Lotus jug made by Wilkinsons, c.1929–30. This gaudy Blue-W pattern is predominantly painted in orange, blue and yellow. Printed maker's mark with facsimile signature 'Bizarre by Clarice Cliff'. Height 30.5 cm.* (Courtesy: Francis Fine Art Auctioneers, Horsham)

PLATE 695: *Dutch-shape jug made by Grimwades for the Susie Cooper pottery, c.1932. Decorated in red, black, green and grey with pattern number E244, known as 'Tadpoles'. Triangular mark 'A Susie Cooper Production' stamped over the original Grimwades mark. Height 14.5 cm.* (Courtesy: City Museum & Art Gallery, Stoke-on-Trent)

Other Staffordshire factories also produced brightly coloured hand-painted jugs. These are represented here by two factories, Wade, Heath & Co. (Plates 696–7) and Myott, Son & Co. (Plates 698–9). The flamboyant shapes are all quite typical of this exciting period. Two further decorative but anonymous jugs of lesser quality are titled 'Trent' and 'Tudor' (Plates 700–1).

Another factory active in this market for hand-painted wares was the Poole Pottery. Their artists developed a distinctive style using a semi-matt finish in rather softer colours, particularly shades of blue, mauve and purple, on a light background (Colour Plate 37). In practice, the firm experimented with many different techniques, represented here by a simple yet attractive 1920s jug with traditional combed-slip decoration (Plate 702).

The Fife Pottery of Robert Heron & Sons also calls for specific mention. They introduced their brightly painted Wemyss ware, named after Lady Grosvenor of

PLATE 697: *Another jug by Wade, Heath & Co. in a bizarre 'Flaxman Ware' shape, c.1936–9. The design is painted in matt colours of green, brown, blue, grey and orange. Informative printed maker's mark with painted pattern number '179'; also impressed 'STREAMLINE' in a curved panel. Height 19.3 cm.* (Courtesy: City Museum & Art Gallery, Stoke-on-Trent)

PLATE 698: *Elegant earthenware jug by Myott, Son & Co., c.1935. The design of flowers is hand-painted in green, yellow, brown, orange and blue enamels on a beige ground. Printed maker's crown mark with number '9807'. Height 21.4 cm.*

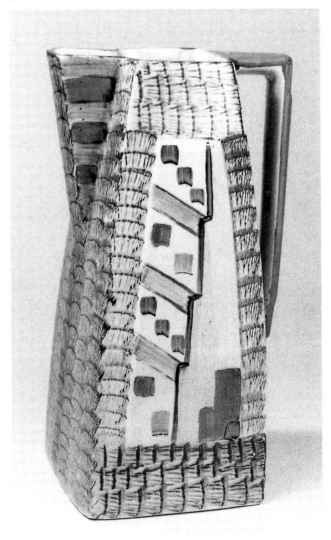

PLATE 696: *Colourful hand-painted jug of a typical shape made by Wade, Heath & Co., c.1934–9. This example with ivory glaze is enamelled in yellow, blue, green, orange and brown. Red-printed lion trademark with indistinct pattern number '3582' painted in green. Height 21.4 cm.* (Courtesy: City Museum & Art Gallery, Stoke-on-Trent)

PLATE 699: *Another distinctive earthenware jug by Myott, Son & Co., c.1935. This design, hand-painted in green, brown, orange and purple enamels on a cream ground, is clearly for a right-hander – the reverse is very sparse. Printed maker's crown mark with pattern number '828' painted in black. Height 16.4 cm.*

PLATE 701: *Another bright earthenware jug titled 'Tudor', c.1935–40, presumably by the same unknown maker as the previous example. The ivory glazed body is hand-painted in yellow, orange, black and green enamels, but also has a silvered rim. Impressed and printed title marks. Height 16.7 cm.*

PLATE 702: *Poole Pottery earthenware jug decorated with combed slip, c.1920–30. The colouring is predominantly white, dark brown and blue. Incised maker's mark. Height 15.5 cm.*

PLATE 700: *Colourful dumpy earthenware jug titled 'Trent' by an unknown maker, c.1935–40. The ivory glazed body is hand-painted in yellow, orange, black and grey enamels. Impressed and printed title marks. Height 16.2 cm.*

Wemyss Castle, during the nineteenth century but it remained in production until the pottery closed in 1930. Even then, the designs were taken on by the Bovey Tracey Pottery Co. who continued to make wares in the same style. Examples span the nineteenth and twentieth centuries, but the globular wash jug shown is very typical (Plate 703). As with many other pieces, it was sold through the important London retailing firm of Thomas Goode & Co.

Although most of the wares discussed above were designed by artists or made using hand-decorating techniques, they were generally put into production in reasonable quantities. The movement away from mass-production also encouraged many smaller potteries and towards the end of the nineteenth century a distinctive style emerged in the West Country slipwares. Utilitarian jugs were made, although it is fair to say that most examples are either purely decorative or produced for the souvenir market which developed alongside the growth of tourism. Examples include jugs from Brannam of Barnstaple (Plate 704) and the Aller Vale Pottery near Torquay (Plate 705).

The same period saw considerable developments in the art pottery movement with individual potters making wares in limited quantities. Although these were normally purely decorative and outside the scope of this volume, three quite useful jugs are shown. One dates from about 1927, made by Michael Cardew at Winchcombe (Plate 706); the others were potted by Paul Barron (Plate 707) and David Leach, son of the famous Bernard Leach (Plate 708). It is encouraging to note the increase in interest in these 'studio' wares, which has developed into a very strong market for today's contemporary ceramics.

No short chapter of this type can hope to do justice to a period which has been amongst the most turbulent in world history. The effect on design and production of everyday articles has been quite dramatic and as collectors and historians develop our knowledge, no doubt we shall be able to look back with some wonder on the age. Larger jugs, with the exception of those made more as decorative objects, are now almost extinct, and although it is difficult to believe, it may be that we shall never again see them made in quantity. It is hoped that this volume, limited though it may be, can serve as a celebration of jugs through the ages, and it is the fervent hope of the author that a final chapter will never need to be written.

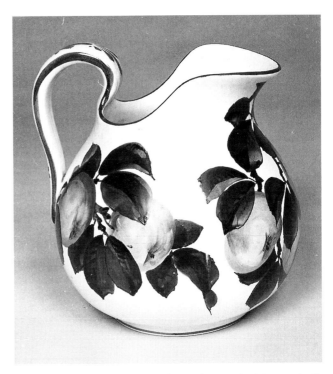

PLATE 703: *Wemyss ware wash jug decorated with a typically colourful design of fruit beneath a green-lined rim. Impressed maker's mark with retailer's mark for Thomas Goode & Co. of London. Height 24.8 cm. (Courtesy: Dreweatt Neate, Newbury)*

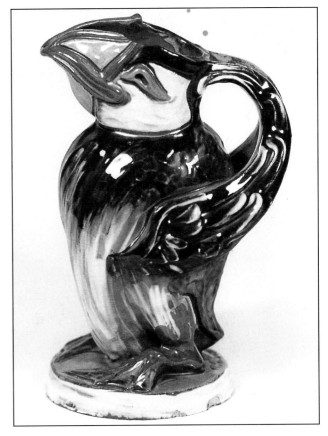

PLATE 704: *Purely decorative Puffin jug made at Brannam's Barnstaple pottery, c.1900. The surface is covered with brown, yellow, green and blue slips. Incised mark with initials 'PT'. Height 16.5 cm.*

PLATE 705: *Two typical Aller Vale jugs, c.1890–1900. The left-hand jug is covered with cream slip, incised and decorated with green and yellow glazes. The other has a brown body covered with yellow slip, incised with a typical motto and with brushed-on green and brown slip designs.*

PLATE 706: *Earthenware jug made at Winchcombe by Michael Cardew, c.1927. The band of painted swirls is in ochre and brown. Impressed Winchcombe Pottery seal mark. Height 23 cm. (Courtesy: Bonhams, Knightsbridge)*

PLATE 707: *Stoneware jug by Paul Barron (1917–83). The brown-glazed body is decorated with vertical light brown wavy lines and a green tinged rim. Impressed initial 'B' seal mark. Height 18 cm. (Courtesy: Bonhams, Knightsbridge)*

PLATE 708: *Simple but attractive earthenware jug by David Leach. The design is glazed in ochre over dark brown slip. Impressed 'DL' initial mark. Height 19.5 cm. (Courtesy: Bonhams, Knightsbridge)*

Bibliography

In compiling any general reference work an extensive bibliography is inevitable. The books listed below are those which are specifically mentioned in the text or which the current author has found most useful in assembling this volume. Many other books on ceramics include some information or illustrations which may well be of interest to jug collectors.

Askey, Derek, *Stoneware Bottles from Bellarmines to Ginger Beers 1500–1949*, Bowman Graphics, Brighton, 1981.

Atterbury, Paul and Batkin, Maureen, *The Dictionary of Minton*, Antique Collectors' Club, Woodbridge, 1990.

Baker, John C., *Sunderland Pottery*, 5th edition, Tyne and Wear County Council, 1984.

Bergesen, Victoria, *Majolica: British, Continental and American Wares 1851–1915*, Barrie & Jenkins, London, 1989.

Bergesen, Victoria, *Bergesen's Price Guide, British Ceramics*, Barrie & Jenkins, London, 1992.

Branyan, Lawrence, French, Neal and Sandon, John, *Worcester Blue and White Porcelain 1751–1790*, 2nd edition, Barrie & Jenkins, London, 1989.

Cameron, Elisabeth, *Encyclopedia of Pottery and Porcelain, the Nineteenth and Twentieth Centuries*, Faber & Faber, London, 1986.

Coysh, A. W. and Henrywood, R. K., *The Dictionary of Blue and White Printed Pottery 1780–1880*, Antique Collectors' Club, Woodbridge, 1982.

Coysh, A. W. and Henrywood, R. K., *The Dictionary of Blue and White Printed Pottery 1780–1880, Volume 2*, Antique Collectors' Club, Woodbridge, 1989.

Cushion, J. P. and Honey, W. B., *Handbook of Pottery and Porcelain Marks*, 4th edition, Faber & Faber, London, 1980.

Cushion, John and Margaret, *A Collector's History of British Porcelain*, Antique Collectors' Club, Woodbridge, 1992.

Drakard, David, *History and Humour in the Reign of George III, 1760–1820*, Jonathan Horne Publications, London, 1992.

Drakard, David, and Holdway, Paul, *Spode Printed Ware*, Longman, London, 1983.

Dudson, Audrey M., *Dudson, A Family of Potters Since 1800*, Dudson Publications, Stoke-on-Trent, 1985.

Edwards, Diana, *Neale Pottery and Porcelain*, Barrie & Jenkins, London, 1987.

Edwards Roussel, Diana, *The Castleford Pottery 1790–1821*, Wakefield Historical Publications, Wakefield, 1982.

Godden, Geoffrey A., *Encyclopaedia of British Pottery and Porcelain Marks*, Barrie & Jenkins, London, 1964.

Godden, Geoffrey A., *British Pottery, An Illustrated Guide*, Barrie & Jenkins, London, 1974.

Godden, Geoffrey A. (editor), *Staffordshire Porcelain*, Granada Publishing, London, 1983.

Godden, Geoffrey A., *Godden's Guide to Mason's China and the Ironstone Wares*, 2nd edition, Antique Collectors' Club, Woodbridge, 1984.

Godden, Geoffrey A., *Eighteenth-century English Porcelain, a Selection from the Godden Reference Collection*, Granada Publishing, London, 1985.

Godden, Geoffrey A., *English China*, Barrie & Jenkins, London, 1985.

Godden, Geoffrey A., *Ridgway Porcelains*, 2nd edition, Antique Collectors' Club, Woodbridge, 1985.

Godden, Geoffrey A., *Encyclopaedia of British Porcelain Manufacturers*, Barrie & Jenkins, London, 1988.

Godden, Geoffrey A., and Gibson, Michael, *Collecting Lustreware*, Barrie & Jenkins, London, 1991.

Haggar, Reginald and Adams, Elizabeth, *Mason Porcelain & Ironstone 1796–1853*, Faber & Faber, London, 1977.

Halfpenny, Pat, *English Earthenware Figures 1740–1840*, Antique Collectors' Club, Woodbridge, 1991.

Hawkins, Jennifer, *The Poole Potteries*, Barrie & Jenkins, London, 1980.

Henrywood, R. K., *Relief-moulded Jugs 1820–1900*, Antique Collectors' Club, Woodbridge, 1984.

Henrywood, R. K., *Bristol Potters 1775–1906*, Redcliffe Press, Bristol, 1992.

Henrywood, R. K., *Jugs*, Shire Publications, Princes Risborough, 1992.

Holgate, David, *New Hall*, Faber & Faber, London, 1987.

Hughes, Gareth and Pugh, Robert, *Llanelly Pottery*, Llanelli Borough Council, Llanelli, 1990.

Hughes, Kathy, *A Collector's Guide to Nineteenth-century Jugs*, Routledge & Kegan Paul, London, 1985.

Hughes, Kathy, *A Collector's Guide to Nineteenth-century Jugs, Volume 2*, Taylor Publishing Company, Dallas, 1991.

Lawrence, Heather, *Yorkshire Pots and Potteries*, David & Charles, Newton Abbot, 1974.

Lewis, Griselda, *A Collector's History of English Pottery*, 4th edition, Antique Collectors' Club, Woodbridge, 1987.

Lewis, John and Griselda, *Pratt Ware, English and Scottish Relief-decorated and Underglaze Coloured Earthenware, 1780–1840*, Antique Collectors' Club, Woodbridge, 1984.

Lockett, Terence A., *Davenport Pottery and Porcelain 1794–1887*, David & Charles, Newton Abbot, 1972.

Lockett, Terence A. and Godden, Geoffrey A., *Davenport China, Earthenware and Glass 1794–1887*, Barrie & Jenkins, London, 1989.

May, John and Jennifer, *Commemorative Pottery 1780–1900*, Heinemann, London, 1972.

Northern Ceramic Society, *Stonewares and Stone Chinas of Northern England to 1851*, Catalogue of the society's exhibition held at the City Museum and Art Gallery, Stoke-on-Trent, 1982.

Northern Ceramic Society, *Creamware and Pearlware*, Catalogue of the society's exhibition held at the City Museum and Art Gallery, Stoke-on-Trent, 1986.

Oswald, A., Hildyard, R. J. C. and Hughes, R. G., *English Brown Stoneware 1670–1900*, Faber & Faber, London, 1982.

Pearson, Kevin, *The Character Jug Collectors Handbook*, 5th edition, Kevin Francis Publishing, London, 1992.

Reilly, Robin, *Wedgwood*, Macmillan, London, 1989.

Reilly, Robin, and Savage, George, *The Dictionary of Wedgwood*, Antique Collectors' Club, Woodbridge, 1980.

Schuler, Vic, *British Toby Jugs*, Kevin Francis Publishing, London, 1986.

Smith, Alan, *The Illustrated Guide to Liverpool Herculaneum Pottery*, Barrie & Jenkins, London, 1970.

Towner, Donald, *Creamware*, Faber & Faber, London, 1978.

Whiter, Leonard, *Spode, A History of the Family, Factory and Wares from 1733 to 1833*, Barrie & Jenkins, London, 1970.

Williams-Wood, Cyril, *English Transfer-printed Pottery and Porcelain, a History of Over-glaze Printing*, Faber & Faber, London, 1981.

Index

Numbers in italic refer to Plates.

INDEX